Race, Nation, Class

V

Race, Nation, Class

Ambiguous Identities

———◆———

ETIENNE BALIBAR
AND
IMMANUEL WALLERSTEIN

*Translation of Etienne Balibar
by Chris Turner*

VERSO

London · New York

First published as *Race, nation, classe: les identités ambiguës*
by Editions La Découverte, Paris 1988
This translation first published by Verso 1991
© Editions La Découverte 1988
English-language edition © Verso 1991
All rights reserved

Verso
UK: 6 Meard Street, London W1V 3HR
USA: 29 West 35th Street, New York, NY 10001–2291

Verso is the imprint of New Left Books

British Library Cataloguing in Publication Data

Balibar, Etienne
    Race, nation, class: ambiguous identities.
    I. Title II. Wallerstein, Immanuel, *1930–*
    305.8

    ISBN 0-86091-327-9
    ISBN 0-86091-542-5 pbk

US Library of Congress Cataloging-in-Publication Data

Balibar, Etienne, 1942–
        [Race, nation, classe. English]
        Race, nation, class: ambiguous identities / Etienne Balibar and
    Immanuel Wallerstein: translation by Chris Turner.
            p.   cm.
        Translation of: Race, nation, classe.
        ISBN 0-86091-327-9. — ISBN 0-86091-542-5 (pbk.)
        1. Racism. 2. Nationalism. 3. Social classes. 4. Social
    conflict. I. Wallerstein, Immanuel Maurice, 1930–   . II. Title.
    HT 1521-B3313   1991
    305.8—dc20

Typeset by Leaper & Gard Ltd, Bristol
Printed and bound in Finland
by Werner Söderström Oy

Contents

Acknowledgements

We would like to thank the colleagues who have been kind enough to contribute papers to the seminar out of which this book arose: Claude Meillassoux, Gérard Noiriel, Jean-Loup Amselle, Pierre Dommergues, Emmanuel Terray, Véronique de Rudder, Michelle Guillon, Isabelle Taboarda-Leonetti, Samir Amin, Robert Fossaert, Eric Hobsbawm, Ernest Gellner, Jean-Marie Vincent, Kostas Vergopoulos, Françoise Duroux, Marcel Drach, Michel Freyssenet. We also thank all the participants in the discussions, whom it is impossible to name, but whose comments were not formulated in vain.

Some chapters of the book have been previously published and are reprinted here with permission. Chapter 2 first appeared in Joan Smith *et al.*, eds, *Racism, Sexism, and the World-System*, Greenwood Press 1988; a section of chapter 3 was published in *M*, no. 18, December 1987–January 1988; chapter 4 was published in *Sociological Forum*, vol. II, no. 2, 1987; chapter 5 in *Review*, vol. XIII no. 3, 1990; chapter 6 in Joan Smith *et al.*, eds, *Households in the World Economy*, Sage 1984; chapter 7 in Immanuel Wallerstein, *The Capitalist World-Economy*, Cambridge University Press 1979; chapter 8 in *Thesis Eleven*, no. 8, 1984; chapter 9 in *New Left Review*, no. 167, 1988; chapter 10 was first delivered at the 'Hannah Arendt Memorial Symposium in Political Philosophy', New School for Social Research, New York, 15–16 April 1987; chapter 11 first appeared in E. Campbell, ed., *Racial Tensions and National Identity*, Vanderbilt University Press 1972; chapter 12 is a revised version of a paper delivered in May 1987 to the seminar 'Gli Estranei – Seminario di studi su razzismo e antirazzismo negli anni '80', organized by Clara Gallini at the Instituto Universario Orientale, Naples; chapter 13 is a revised version of a paper presented at the Maison des Sciences de l'Homme in 1985.

To our friends
Mokhtar Mokhtefi and Elaine Klein

Preface

Etienne Balibar

The essays we bring together in this volume and which together we present to the English reader represent stages in our own personal work for which we each assume responsibility. Circumstances have, however, made them the elements of a dialogue which has grown closer in recent years and which we would now like to share with the reader. It is our contribution to the elucidation of a burning question: *What is the specificity of contemporary racism?* How can it be related to class division within capitalism and to the contradictions of the nation-state? And, conversely, in what respects does the phenomenon of racism lead us to rethink the articulation of nationalism and the class stuggle? Through this question, the book is also our contribution to a much wider discussion, which has been going on for more than a decade now within 'Western Marxism'. We might hope that, as a result of the discussion, 'Western Marxism' will be sufficiently renewed to get abreast of its times once again. It is by no means accidental, of course, that this discussion presents itself as an international one; nor that it combines philosophical reflection with historical synthesis, and an attempt at conceptual recasting with the analysis of political problems that are more than urgent today (particularly in France). Such at least is the conviction we hope our readers will share.

Perhaps I may be allowed to supply some personal background here. When I met Immanuel Wallerstein for the first time in 1981, I already knew the first volume of his work *The Modern World-System* (which appeared in 1974), but I had not yet read the second. I did not know, therefore, that he had credited me in that book with providing a 'self-

1

conscious' theoretical presentation of the 'traditional' Marxist thesis concerning the periodization of modes of production – the thesis which identifies the age of manufacture with a period of transition, and the beginning of the properly capitalist mode with the industrial revolution; as against those writers who, in order to mark the beginnings of modernity, propose situating the break in historical time either around 1500 (with European expansion, the creation of the world market) or around 1650 (with the first 'bourgeois' revolutions and the Scientific Revolution). By the same token, I was also not aware that I was myself going to find his analysis of Dutch hegemony in the seventeenth century of assistance in situating the intervention of Spinoza (with his revolutionary characteristics, in relation not only to the 'medieval' past but also to contemporary tendencies) within the strangely atypical set of struggles between the political and religious parties of the time (with their combination of nationalism and cosmopolitanism, democratism and 'fear of the masses').

Conversely, what Wallerstein did not know was that, from the beginning of the 1970s, following the discussions to which our 'structuralist' reading of *Capital* gave rise, and precisely in order to escape the classical aporias of the 'periodization' of the class struggle, I had recognized the need to situate the analysis of class struggles and their reciprocal effects on the development of capitalism within the context of social formations and not simply of the mode of production considered as an ideal mean or as an invariant system (which is a wholly mechanistic conception of structure). It therefore followed, on the one hand, that a determining role in the configuration of relations of production had to be attributed to *all* the historical aspects of the class struggle (including those which Marx subsumed under the equivocal concept of superstructure). And, on the other hand, the implication was that the question of the reproduction space of the capital–labour (or wage labour) relation had to be posed right at the very heart of the theory, giving full weight to Marx's constant insistence that capitalism implies the extension of accumulation and of the proletarianization of labour-power to the whole world, though, in so doing, one had to go beyond the abstraction of the undifferentiated 'world market'.

Alongside this, the emergence of the specific struggles of immigrant workers in France in the seventies and the difficulty of expressing these politically, together with Althusser's thesis that every social formation is based on the combination of several modes of production, had convinced me that the division of the working class is not a secondary or residual phenomenon, but a structural (though this does not mean invariant) characteristic of present-day capitalist societies, which determines all the perspectives for revolutionary transformation and even for the daily organization of the movement for social change.[1]

Last, from the Maoist critique of 'real socialism' and the history of the 'cultural revolution' (as I perceived it), I had retained not, of course, the demonization of revisionism and the nostalgia for Stalinism, but the insight that the 'socialist mode of production' in reality constitutes an unstable combination of state capitalism and proletarian tendencies towards communism. Precisely by their disparate nature, these various rectifications all tended to substitute a problematic of 'historical capitalism' for the formal antithesis between structure and history; and to identify as a central question of that problematic the variation in the relations of production as these were articulated together in the long transition from non-commodity societies to societies of 'generalized economy'.

Unlike others, I was not exaggeratedly sensitive to the *economism* for which Wallerstein's analyses have frequently been criticized. It is, in fact, important to clarify what we mean by this term. In the tradition of Marxist orthodoxy, economism figures as a determinism of the development of the productive forces: in its way, the Wallersteinian model of the world-economy in fact substituted for that determinism a dialectic of capitalist accumulation and its contradictions. In asking under what historical conditions the cycle or phases of expansion and recession could become established, Wallerstein was not far removed from what seems to me to be Marx's authentic thesis, and an expression of his *critique* of economism: the primacy of the social relations of production over the productive forces, so that the contradictions of capitalism are not contradictions *between* relations of production and productive forces (between, for example, the 'private' character of one and the 'social' character of the other, as the formulation endorsed by Engels has it), but – among other things – 'contradictions of progress'. Moreover, what is called the critique of economism is most often undertaken in the name of a claim that the political sphere and the state are autonomous, either in relation to the sphere of the market economy or in relation to the class struggle itself, which comes down practically to reintroducing the liberal *dualism* (state/civil society, politics/economics) which Marx criticized so tellingly. Now Wallerstein's explanatory model, as I understand it, made it possible both to conceive the overall structure of the system as one of generalized economy and to conceive the processes of state formation and the policies of hegemony and class alliances as forming the texture of that economy. From that point on, the question of why capitalist socialist formations took the form of nations – or, more precisely, the question of what differentiates nations that are individualized around a 'strong' state apparatus and the dependent nations whose unity is impeded both from within and without, and how that difference is transformed with the history of capitalism – ceased to be a blind spot and became a decisive issue.

To tell the truth, it was at this point that queries and objections arose in my mind. I shall mention three of these briefly, leaving it to the reader to decide whether or not they are the product of a 'traditional' conception of historical materialism.

First, I remained convinced that the hegemony of the dominant classes was based, in the last analysis, on their capacity to organize the labour process and, beyond that, the reproduction of labour-power itself in a broad sense which includes both the workers' subsistence and their cultural formation. To put it another way, what is at issue here is the *real subsumption* which Marx, in *Capital*, made the index of the establishment of the capitalist mode of production properly so-called – that is, the point of no return for the process of unlimited accumulation and the valorization of value. If one thinks about it carefully, the idea of this 'real' subsumption (which Marx opposes to merely 'formal' subsumption) goes a long way beyond the integration of the workers into the world of the contract, of money incomes, of law and official politics: it implies a transformation of human individuality, which extends from the education of the labour force to the constitution of a 'dominant ideology' capable of being adopted by the dominated themselves. No doubt Wallerstein would not disagree with such an idea, since he stresses the way in which *all* social classes, all status-groups which form within the framework of the capitalist world-economy are subject to the effects of 'commodification' and the 'system of states'. One may, however, ask whether, to describe the conflicts and developments which result from these, it is sufficient, as he does, to draw up the table of the historical actors, their interests and their strategies of alliance or confrontation. *The very identity of the actors depends upon the process of formation and maintenance of hegemony.* Thus the modern bourgeoisie formed itself into a class which managed the proletariat, after having been a class which managed the peasantry: it had to acquire political skills and a 'self-consciousness' which anticipated the way that resistance to it would be expressed and which transformed itself with the nature of that resistance.

The *universalism* of the dominant ideology is therefore rooted at a much deeper level than the world expansion of capital and even than the need to procure common rules of action for all those who manage that expansion.[2] It is rooted in the need to construct, in spite of the antagonism between them, an ideological 'world' shared by exploiters and exploited alike. The egalitarianism (whether democratic or otherwise) of modern politics is a good illustration of this process. This means both that all class domination has to be formulated in the language of

universality, and that there are in history a great number of univer-
salities, which are mutually incompatible. Each of them – and this is also
the case with dominant ideologies in the present period – is shot through
with the specific tension of a particular form of exploitation, and it is not
by any means certain that a single hegemony can simultaneously
encompass all the relations of domination that exist within the framework of the capitalist world-economy. In plain language, I am saying
that I doubt whether a 'world bourgeoisie' exists. Or, to put it more
precisely, I entirely acknowledge that the extension of the process of
accumulation to the world scale implies the constitution of a 'world-wide
class of capitalists', among whom incessant competition is the law (and,
paradox for paradox, I see the need to include in that capitalist class
both those at the helm of 'free enterprise' and those who manage
'socialist' state protectionism), but I do not, for all that, believe that class
to be a *world bourgeoisie* in the sense of a class organized in institutions,
which is the only kind of class that is historically concrete.

To this question, I imagine Wallerstein would immediately retort that
there is indeed an institution which the world bourgeoisie shares and
which tends to confer concrete existence upon it, above and beyond its
internal conflicts (even when these take the violent form of military
conflicts) and particularly above and beyond the quite different conditions of its hegemony over the dominated populations! That institution
is the *system of states* itself, the vitality of which has become particularly
evident since, in the wake of revolutions and counter-revolutions,
colonizations and decolonizations, the form of the nation-state has been
formally extended to the whole of humanity. I have myself argued for
many years that every bourgeoisie is a 'state bourgeoisie', even where
capitalism is not organized as a planned state capitalism, and I believe
that we would agree on this point. One of the most pertinent questions
which Wallerstein seems to me to have raised is that of why the world-
economy was unable to transform itself (in spite of various attempts to
do so, from the sixteenth century to the twentieth) into a politically
unified world-*empire*, why, in the world-economy, the political institution has taken the form of an 'interstate system'. No a priori answer
can be given to this question: we have precisely to reconstruct the
history of the world-economy, and particularly that of the conflicts of
interest, the 'monopoly' phenomena and the unequal developments of
power which have repeatedly manifested themselves at its 'core' – which
is in fact today less and less localized in a single geographical area – as
well as the history of the *uneven resistances* of its 'periphery'.

But precisely this answer (if it is correct) leads me to reformulate my
objection. At the end of *The Modern World-System* (vol. I), Wallerstein
proposed a criterion for identifying relatively autonomous 'social

systems': the criterion of the *internal autonomy* of their development (or of their dynamic). He drew a radical conclusion from this: most of the historical units to which we generally apply the label 'social systems' (from 'tribes' to nation-states) are not in reality social systems but merely dependent units; the only systems properly so-called which history has known have been, on the one hand, subsistence communities and, on the other, the 'worlds' (the world-empires and the world-economies). Reformulated in Marxist terminology, this thesis would lead us to think that the only social formation in the true sense in the world today is the world-economy itself, because it is the largest unit within which historical processes become interdependent. In other words, the world-economy would not only be an economic unit and a system of states, but also a social unit. In consequence the dialectic of its development would itself be a *global* dialectic or at least one characterized by the primacy of global constraints over *local* relations of force.

It is beyond doubt that this account has the merit of synthetically explaining the phenomena of the globalization of politics and ideology which we have seen occurring over several decades and which appear to us to be the outcome of a cumulative process extending over many centuries. It is particularly strikingly exemplified in periods of crisis. It provides – as we shall see in the essays which follow – a powerful instrument for interpreting the ubiquitous *nationalism* and *racism* of the modern world, while avoiding confusing them with other phenomena of 'xenophobia' or 'intolerance' seen in the past: the one (nationalism) as a reaction to domination by states of the core, the other (racism) as an institutionalization of the hierarchies involved in the world-wide division of labour. And yet I wonder whether, in this form, Wallerstein's thesis does not impose on the muultiplicity of social conflicts a formal – or at least unilateral – uniformity and globalism. It seems to me that what characterizes these conflicts is not only transnationalization, but the decisive role that is increasingly played in them by localized social relations or local forms of social conflict (whether these be economic, religious or politico-cultural), the 'sum' of which is not immediately totalizable. In other words, taking in my turn as my criterion not the extreme outer limit within which the regulation of a system takes place, but the specificity of social movements and the conflicts which arise within it (or, if one prefers, the specific form in which the global contradictions are reflected in it), I wonder whether the *social units* of the contemporary world do not have to be distinguished from its *economic unity*. After all, why should the two coincide? By the same token, I would suggest that the overall movement of the world-economy is the random *result* of the movement of its social units rather than its cause. But I do acknowledge that it is difficult to identify the social units in question in any simple way, since they do not coincide purely and simply with national units and may in part overlap (why would a social unit be closed and, *a fortiori*, autarkic?).[3]

Which brings me to a third question. The power of Wallerstein's model, generalizing and concretizing as it does Marx's initial insights into the 'law of population' implied in the endless accumulation of capital, is that it shows this accumulation has unceasingly imposed (both by force and by law) a redistribution of populations into the socio-occupational categories of its 'division of labour' either by coming to terms with their resistance or by breaking it, indeed by using their strategies of subsistence and by playing off their interests against one another. The basis of capitalist social formations is a division of labour (in the broad sense, including the various 'functions' needed for the production of capital), or, rather, the basis of social transformations is the transformation of the division of labour. But is it not cutting a few corners to base the whole of what Althusser not so long ago termed the *society effect* on the division of labour? In other words, can we take the view (as Marx did in certain 'philosophical' texts) that societies or social formations are kept 'alive' and form relatively durable units simply by virtue of the fact that they organize production and exchange in terms of certain historical relations?

Do not misunderstand me here: the point is not that we should rerun the conflict between materialism and idealism and suggest that the economic unity of societies has to be supplemented or replaced by a symbolic unity, whose definition we would seek either in the sphere of law or religion or the prohibition of incest and so on. The point is rather to ask whether Marxists were not by chance victims of a gigantic illusion regarding the meaning of their own analyses, which are, in large part, inherited from liberal economic ideology (and its implicit anthropology). The *capitalist* division of labour has nothing to do with a complementarity of tasks, individuals and social groups: it leads rather, as Wallerstein himself forcefully reiterates, to the polarization of social formations into antagonistic classes whose interests are decreasingly 'common' ones. How is the unity (even the conflictual unity) of a society to be based on such a division? Perhaps we should then invert our interpretation of the Marxist thesis. Instead of representing the capitalist division of labour to ourselves as what founds or institutes human societies as relatively stable 'collectivities', should we not conceive this as what *destroys* them? Or rather as what *would destroy* them by lending their internal inequalities the form of irreconcilable antagonisms, *if* other social practices, which are equally material, but irreducible to the behaviour of *homo œconomicus* – for example the practice of linguistic communication and sexuality, or technique and knowledge – did not set

limits to the imperialism of the relation of production and transform it
from within?

If this is so, the history of social formations would be not so much a
history of non-commodity communities making the transition to market
society or a society of generalized exchange (including the exchange of
human labour-power) – the liberal or sociological representation which
has been preserved in Marxism – as a history of the *reactions* of the
complex of 'non-economic' social relations, which are the binding agent
of a historical collectivity of individuals, to the de-structuring with which
the expansion of the value form threatens them. It is these reactions
which confer upon social history an aspect that is irreducible to the
simple 'logic' of the extended reproduction of capital or even to a
'strategic game' among actors defined by the division of labour and the
system of states. It is these reactions also which underlie the intrinsically
ambiguous ideological and institutional productions, which are the true
substance of politics (for example, the ideology of human rights, and
also racism, nationalism, sexism and their revolutionary antitheses).
Finally, it is these too which account for the ambivalent effects of class
struggles to the extent that, seeking to effect the 'negation of the
negation' – that is, to *destroy the mechanism which is tending to destroy*
the conditions of social existence – they also aim, in utopian fashion, to
restore a lost unity and thus offer themselves for 'recuperation' by
various forces of domination.

Rather than engaging in a discussion at this level of abstraction, it
seemed to us from the outset that it was better to redeploy the theoretical tools at our disposal in the analysis, to be undertaken together, of
a crucial question raised by the present situation – a question of
sufficient difficulty to enable the encounter between our two positions to
progress. This project materialized in a seminar which we organized over
three years (1985–87) at the Maison des Sciences de l'Homme in Paris.
The seminar was devoted successively to the themes 'Racism and
Ethnicity', 'Nation and Nationalism' and 'Classes'. The texts which
follow are not literal transcripts of our contributions, but rework the
original substance of these seminars, supplementing them on several
points. Some of these texts have been presented or published in other
places (see pp. x–xi for sources). We have rearranged them in such
a way as to bring out the points of conflict and convergence. We do
not claim absolute coherence or exhaustiveness for this collection, which
is designed rather to open up questions, to explore some paths of
investigation. It is much too early to draw any conclusions. We do,
however, hope that readers will find here something to fuel their
thinking and criticism.

In Part I, 'Universal Racism', we attempt to sketch out an alternative problematic to the ideology of 'progress' which was imposed by liberalism and has largely been taken over (we shall see further on in what conditions) by the Marxist philosophy of history. We observe that, in traditional or new forms (the derivation of which is, however, recognizable), *racism is not receding, but progressing* in the contemporary world. There is uneven development and there are critical phases in this phenomenon, the manifestations of which we should be careful not to confuse, but it can only be explained in the last analysis by structural causes. To the extent that what is in play here – whether in academic theories, institutional or popular racism – is the categorization of humanity into artificially isolated types, there must be a violently conflictual split at the level of social relations themselves. We are not therefore dealing with a mere 'prejudice'. Moreover, it has to be the case that, above and beyond historical transformations as decisive as decolonization, this split is reproduced within the world-wide framework created by capitalism. Thus we are dealing neither with a relic nor an archaism. Does it not, however, run against the logic of generalized economy and individualist rights? In no way. We both believe that the universalism of bourgeois ideology (and therefore also its humanism) is not incompatible with the system of hierarchies and exclusions which, above all, takes the form of racism and sexism. Just as racism and sexism are part of the same system.

As regards the detail of the analysis, we do, however, diverge on several points. Wallerstein sees universalism as deriving from the very form of the market (the universality of the accumulation process), racism from the splitting of the labour force between core and periphery, and sexism from the opposition between male 'work' and the female 'non-work' performed in the household, which he sees as a basic institution of historical capitalism. For my own part, I think the specific articulation of racism is within nationalism, and I believe I am able to demonstrate that universality is paradoxically present in racism itself. The time dimension here becomes decisive: the whole question is opened up of how the memory of past exclusions is transferred into the exclusions of the present, or how the internationalization of population movements and the change in the political role of nation-states can lead into a neo-racism, or even a 'post-racism'.

In Part II, 'The Historical Nation', we attempt to revive discussion of the categories of 'people' and 'nation'. We have rather different methods: I proceed diachronically, seeking out the line of development of the nation form; Wallerstein, in synchronic fashion, examines the functional place which the national superstructure occupies among other political institutions in the world-economy. As a result, we bring the same differences to our articulation of the class struggle and the national formation. To be extremely schematic, one might say that my position consists in inscribing historical class struggles in the nation form (though they represent its antithesis), whereas Wallerstein's position inscribes the nation, with other forms, in the field of the class struggle (even though classes only ever become classes 'for themselves' [*für sich*] in exceptional circumstances – a point we shall return to later).

It is here, no doubt, that the meaning of the concept, 'social formation', comes into play. Wallerstein suggests we should distinguish three great historical modes of the construction of the 'people': *race, nation* and *ethnicity*, which relate to different structures of the world-economy; he stresses the historical break between the 'bourgeois' state (the nation-state) and earlier forms of the state (in fact, in his view, the very term state is ambiguous). For my own part, seeking to characterize the transition from the 'pre-national' to the 'national' state, I attach great importance to another of his ideas (not taken up by him here), namely that of their *plurality of political forms* during the constitutive period of the world-economy. I pose the problem of the constitution of the people (what I call *fictive ethnicity*) as a problem of internal hegemony and I attempt to analyse the role played in its production by the institutions which variously give body to the language community and the race community. As a result of these differences, it seems to me that Wallerstein is better at explaining the ethnicization of *minorities*, whereas I am better at explaining the ethnicization of *majorities*; perhaps he is too 'American' and I too 'French' ... What is certain, however, is that it appears equally essential to us to think 'nation' and 'people' as historical constructs, by means of which *current* institutions and antagonisms can be *projected into the past* to confer a relative stability on the communities on which the sense of individual 'identity' depends.

In Part III, 'Classes: Polarization and Overdetermination', we ask what radical transformations should be made to the schemas of Marxist orthodoxy (that is to say, in short, to the evolutionism of the 'mode of production' in its different variants), in order to be able, following up Marx's most original indications, actually to analyse capitalism as historical system (or structure). It would be wearisome to summarize our propositions in advance. Hostile readers will be able to enjoy counting up the contradictions between our 'reconstructions'. We live up to the law that two 'Marxists', whoever they may be, always prove incapable of according the same meaning to the same concepts ... But let us not jump to the conclusion that this is a mere scholastic game. On rereading this section, what actually strikes me as most significant is the extent to which, given that we start out from such different premises, we agree in our ultimate conclusions.

What is at issue, quite obviously, is the articulation of the 'economic' and the 'political' aspects of the class struggle. Wallerstein is faithful to the problematic of the 'class *an sich*' and the 'class *für sich*' (which I reject) but he combines this with theses which are, to say the least, provocative regarding the main aspect of proletarianization (which is *not*, in his view, the generalization of wage labour). According to his argument, payment of a wage is a development which takes place *in spite of* the immediate interest of the capitalists, as an effect of two things: crises of realization and workers' struggles against 'peripheral' super-exploitation (that of part-time wage labour). My objection to this is that his reasoning here assumes that all exploitation is 'extensive', that there is not, in other words, a further form of super-exploitation associated with the intensification of wage labour that is subjected to technological revolutions (what Marx calls 'real subsumption', the production of 'relative surplus-value'). But these divergences in analysis – which might be seen as reflecting a 'peripheral' by contrast with a 'core' point of view – remain subordinate to three common ideas:

1. Marx's thesis concerning the polarization of classes in capitalism is not an unfortunate error, but the *strong point* of his theory. However, it has to be carefully distinguished from the ideological representation of a 'simplification of class relations' with the development of capitalism, an idea bound up with historical catastrophism.

2. There is no 'ideal type' of classes (proletariat and bourgeoisie) but there are *processes* of proletarianization and *embourgeoisement*,[4] each of which involves its own internal conflicts (what I shall, for my part, following Althusser, term the 'overdetermination' of the antagonism): in this way we can see how the history of the capitalist *economy* depends on *political* struggles within the national and transnational space.

3. The 'bourgeoisie' cannot be defined by mere accumulation of profit (or by productive investment): this is a necessary, but not a suffi-cient condition. The reader will find here Wallerstein's argument concerning the bourgeoisie's quest for monopoly positions and the transformation of profit into rents, guaranteed by the state in a variety of historical modalities. This is a point to which it will certainly be neces-sary to return. The historicization (and therefore dialecticization) of the concept of classes in 'Marxist sociology' is only just beginning (which amounts to saying that there is still work to do to dismantle the ideology which has set itself up as Marxist sociology). Here again, we are reacting to our national traditions: contrary to a prejudice firmly held in France, I am intent upon demonstrating that the bourgeois/capitalist is not a parasite; for his part Wallerstein, coming from the country where the myth of the 'manager' was created, is keen to show that the bourgeois is not the opposite of the aristocrat (neither in the past nor today).

For different reasons, I totally agree that, in present-day capitalism, generalized formal education has become not only 'reproductive', but *productive* of class differences. It is merely that, being less 'optimistic' than he is, I do not believe that this 'meritocratic' mechanism is politically *more fragile* than the historical mechanisms for acquiring privileged social status that preceded it. This has to do, in my view, with the fact that schooling – at least in the 'developed' countries – is constituted both as a means for the selection of managerial staff and as an ideological apparatus well suited to naturalizing social divisions 'technically' and 'scientifically', in particular the division between manual and intellectual labour, or between the management and the performance of labour, in the successive forms those divisions have assumed. Now this naturalization, which, as we shall see, is by no means unrelated to racism, is no less effective than other historical legitimations of privilege.

Which leads us directly to our last point, summed up in the phrase 'Displacements of Social Conflict?'. The object of this fourth section is to return to the question raised at the beginning (that of racism or more generally of 'community' status and identity), referring to the determinations discussed above and preparing the ground for practical conclusions – though these are still quite some way off. We are also concerned here to evaluate the degree to which we have moved away from some classic themes in sociology and history. Naturally, the differences in approach and the more or less important divergences which appeared earlier remain; there is no question therefore of bringing things to a conclusion. If I wanted to press a point, I would say that this time it is Wallerstein who is much less optimistic than I, since he sees 'group' consciousness as necessarily winning out over 'class' consciousness or at least as constituting the necessary form of its historical realization. It is true that, at the (asymptotic) limit, the two terms come together again, in his view, in the transnationalization of inequalities and conflicts. For my part, I do not believe that racism is the expression of class structure; rather, it is a typical form of political alienation inherent in class struggles in the field of nationalism, in particularly ambivalent forms (racialization of the proletariat, workerism and 'interclass' consensus in the present crisis). It is true that my reasoning is based essentially on the example of the situation and history of France, where the question of the renewal of internationalist practices and ideologies today hangs uncertainly in the balance. It is true also that, *in practice*, the 'proletarian nations' of the Third World or, more exactly, their pauperized masses, and the 'new proletarians' of Western Europe and elsewhere – in their diversity – have a single enemy: institutional racism and its extensions – or anticipations – in mass politics. And they have the same stumbling block to overcome: the confusion of ethnic particularism or politico-religious universalism with ideologies that are liber-atory *in themselves.* This is probably the essential point, the one to which more thought should be devoted and on which more research should be carried out with those concerned, outside university circles. Having the same enemy does not, however, imply either having the same immediate interests or the same form of consciousness or, *a fortiori,* a totalization of the various struggles. Such a totalization is in fact only a tendency and there are structural obstacles in its way. For it to prevail, favourable conjunctures will be needed – and political practices. This is why, in the course of this book, I have maintained, particularly, that the (re-)constitution on new bases (and in new words perhaps) of a class ideology, capable of counteracting today's (and tomorrow's) galloping nationalism, has as a pre-condition – which already determines its content – an effective anti-racism.

Notes

1. I must single out here, from among many influences, the crucial part played by the research of Yves Duroux, Claude Meillassoux and Suzanne de Brunhoff on the repro-duction of labour-power and the 'wage form' in shaping these reflections.
2. As suggested by Wallerstein, most notably in *Historical Capitalism*, Verso, London 1983, pp. 80 *et seq.*
3. I recognize also that this point of view casts doubt upon the perspective of a 'convergence' between 'antisystemic movements'. (Wallerstein groups under 'anti-systemic movements' not only the socialist movements of the working class and national liberation movements, but also women's struggle against sexism and the struggles of the oppressed minorities, who are all potential participants in a 'world family of antisystemic movements', *Historical Capitalism*, p. 109.) The point is that these movements seem to me to be ultimately 'non-contemporaneous' and sometimes mutually incompatible, being bound up with *universal* but *distinct* contradictions, with social conflicts that are unequally decisive in different 'social formations'. I see their condensation into a single bloc not as a long-term tendency, but as a conjunctural coming together, the duration of which depends on political innovations. This is true, first and foremost, of the 'convergence' between feminism and the class struggle: it would be interesting to inquire why hardly any 'conscious' feminist movements have developed within social formations in which there is not also an organized class struggle, even though the two movements have never managed to combine. Does this have to do with the division of labour? Or with the political form of struggles? Or with the unconscious of 'class consciousness'?
4. I prefer to use the French term *embourgeoisement* rather than 'bourgeoisification' which Wallerstein uses, in spite of the possible ambiguity of the term. (And yet is there indeed any ambiguity? Just as soldiers are recruited from the civilian population, so bourgeois, down to the *n*th generation, have been recruited from the non-bourgeois.)

PART I

Universal Racism

1

Is There a 'Neo-Racism'?

Etienne Balibar

To what extent is it correct so speak of a neo-racism? The question is forced upon us by current events in forms which differ to some degree from one country to another, but which suggest the existence of a transnational phenomenon. The question may, however, be understood in two senses. On the one hand, are we seeing a new historical upsurge of racist movements and policies which might be explained by a crisis conjuncture or by other causes? On the other hand, in its themes and its social significance, is what we are seeing only a *new* racism, irreducible to earlier 'models', or is it a mere tactical adaptation? I shall concern myself here primarily with this second aspect of the question.[1]

First of all, we have to make the following observation. The neo-racism hypothesis, at least so far as France is concerned, has been formulated essentially on the basis of an internal critique of theories, of discourses tending to legitimate policies of exclusion in terms of anthropology or the philosophy of history. Little has been done on finding the connection between the newness of the doctrines and the novelty of the political situations and social transformations which have given them a purchase. I shall argue in a moment that the theoretical dimension of racism today, as in the past, is historically essential, but that it is neither autonomous nor primary. Racism – a true 'total social phenomenon' – inscribes itself in practices (forms of violence, contempt, intolerance, humiliation and exploitation), in discourses and representations which are so many intellectual elaborations of the phantasm of prophylaxis or segregation (the need to purify the social body, to preserve 'one's own' or 'our' identity from all forms of mixing, interbreeding or invasion) and which are articulated around stigmata of otherness (name, skin colour, religious practices). It therefore organizes affects (the psychological study of these has concentrated upon describing their obsessive character and also their 'irrational' ambivalence) by conferring upon them a stereotyped form, as regards both their 'objects' and their 'subjects'. It is this combination of practices, discourses and representations in a network of affective stereotypes which enables us to give an account of the formation of a racist community (or a community of racists, among whom there exist bonds of 'imitation' over a distance) and also of the way in which, as a mirror image, individuals and collectivities that are prey to racism (its 'objects') find themselves constrained to see themselves as a community.

But however absolute that constraint may be, it obviously can never be cancelled out as constraint *for its victims*: it can neither be interiorized without conflict (see the works of Memmi) nor can it remove the contradiction which sees an identity as community ascribed to collectivities which are simultaneously denied the right to define themselves (see the writings of Frantz Fanon), nor, most importantly, can it reduce the permanent excess of actual violence and acts over discourses, theories and rationalizations. From the point of view of its victims, there is, then, an essential dissymmetry within the racist complex, which confers upon its acts and 'actings out' undeniable primacy over its doctrines, naturally including within the category of actions not only physical violence and discrimination, but words themselves, the violence of words in so far as they are acts of contempt and aggression. Which leads us, in a first phase, to regard shifts in doctrine and language as relatively incidental matters: should we attach so much importance to justifications which continue to retain the same structure (that of a denial of rights) while moving from the language of religion into that of science, or from the language of biology into the discourses of culture or history, when in practice these justifications simply lead to the same old acts?

This is a fair point, even a vitally important one, but it does not solve all the problems. For the destruction of the racist complex presupposes not only the revolt of its victims, but the transformation of the racists themselves and, consequently, *the internal decomposition of the community created by racism*. In this respect, the situation is entirely analogous, as has often been said over the last twenty years or so, with that of sexism, the overcoming of which presupposes both the revolt of women and the break-up of the community of 'males'. Now, racist theories are indispensable in the formation of the racist community. There is in fact no racism without theory (or theories). It would be quite futile to inquire whether racist theories have emanated chiefly from the elites or the masses, from the dominant or the dominated classes. It is, however, quite clear that they are 'rationalized' by intellectuals. And it is of the utmost importance that we enquire into the function fulfilled by the theory-building of academic racism (the prototype of which is the evolutionist anthropology of 'biological' races developed at the end of the nineteenth century) in the crystallization of the community which forms around the signifier, 'race'.

This function does not, it seems to me, reside solely in the general organizing capacity of intellectual rationalizations (what Gramsci called their 'organicity' and Auguste Comte their 'spiritual power') nor in the fact that the theories of academic racism elaborate an image of community, of original identity in which individuals of all social classes may recognize themselves. It resides, rather, in the fact that the theories of academic racism mimic scientific discursivity by basing themselves upon visible 'evidence' (whence the essential importance of the stigmata of race and in particular of bodily stigmata), or, more exactly, they mimic the way in which scientific discursivity articulates 'visible facts' to 'hidden causes' and thus connect up with a spontaneous process of theorization inherent in the racism of the masses.[2] I shall therefore venture the idea that the racist complex inextricably combines a crucial function of *misrecognition* (without which the violence would not be tolerable to the very people engaging in it) and a 'will to know', a violent *desire for* immediate *knowledge* of social relations. These are functions which are mutually sustaining since, both for individuals and for social groups, their own collective violence is a distressing enigma and they require an urgent explanation for it. This indeed is what makes the intellectual posture of the ideologues of racism so singular, however sophisticated their theories may seem. Unlike for example theologians, who must maintain a distance (though not an absolute break, unless they lapse into 'gnosticism') between esoteric speculation and a doctrine designed for popular consumption, historically effective racist ideologues have always developed 'democratic' doctrines which are immediately intelligible to the masses and apparently suited from the outset to their supposed low level of intelligence, even when elaborating elitist themes. In other words, they have produced doctrines capable of providing immediate interpretative keys not only to what individuals are *experiencing* but to what they *are* in the social world (in this respect, they have affinities with astrology, characterology and so on), even when these keys take the form of the revelation of a 'secret' of the human condition (that is, when they include a *secrecy effect* essential to their imaginary efficacy: this is a point which has been well illustrated by Léon Poliakov).[3]

This is also, we must note, what makes it difficult to *criticize* the content and, most importantly, the influence of academic racism. In the very construction of its theories, there lies the presupposition that the 'knowledge' sought and desired by the masses is an elementary knowledge which simply justifies them in their spontaneous feelings or brings them back to the truth of their instincts. Bebel, as is well known, called anti-Semitism the 'socialism of fools' and Nietzsche regarded it more or less as the politics of the feeble-minded (though this in no way prevented him from taking over a large part of racial mythology himself). Can we ourselves, when we characterize racist doctrines as strictly demagogic theoretical elaborations, whose efficacity derives from the advance response they provide for the masses' desire for knowledge, escape this same ambiguous position? The category of the 'masses' (or the 'popular') is not itself neutral, but communicates directly with the logic of a naturalization and racization of the social. To begin to dispel this ambiguity, it is no doubt insufficient merely to examine the way the racist 'myth' gains its hold upon the masses; we also have to ask why other sociological theories, developed within the framework of a division between 'intellectual' and 'manual' activities (in the broad sense), are unable to fuse so easily with this desire to know. Racist myths (the 'Aryan myth', the myth of heredity) are myths not only by virtue of their pseudo-scientific content, but in so far as they are forms of imaginary transcendence of the gulf separating intellectuality from the masses, forms indissociable from that implicit fatalism which imprisons the masses in an allegedly natural infantilism.

We can now turn our attention to 'neo-racism'. What seems to pose a problem here is not the *fact* of racism, as I have already pointed out – practice being a fairly sure criterion (if we do not allow ourselves to be deceived by the denials of racism which we meet among large sections of the political class in particular, which only thereby betrays the complacency and blindness of that group) – but determining to what extent the relative novelty of the language is expressing a *new* and lasting articulation of social practices and collective representations, academic doctrines and political movements. In short, to use Gramscian language, we have to determine whether something like a hegemony is developing here.

The functioning of the category of *immigration* as a substitute for the notion of race and a solvent of 'class consciousness' provides us with a first clue. Quite clearly, we are not simply dealing with a camouflaging operation, made necessary by the disrepute into which the term 'race' and its derivatives has fallen, nor solely with a consequence of the transformations of French society. Collectivities of immigrant workers have for many years suffered discrimination and xenophobic violence in which racist stereotyping has played an essential role. The interwar period, another crisis era, saw the unleashing of campaigns in France against 'foreigners', Jewish or otherwise, campaigns which extended beyond the activities of the fascist movements and which found their logical culmination in the Vichy regime's contribution to the Hitlerian enterprise. Why did we not at that period see the 'sociological' signifier definitively replace the 'biological' one as the key representation of hatred and fear of the other? Apart from the force of strictly French traditions of anthropological myth, this was probably due, on the one hand, to the institutional and ideological break which then existed between the perception of immigration (essentially European) and colonial experience (on the one side, France 'was being invaded', on the other it 'was dominant') and, on the other hand, because of the absence of a new model of articulation between states, peoples and cultures on a world scale.[4] The two reasons are indeed linked. The new racism is a racism of the era of 'decolonization', of the reversal of population movements between the old colonies and the old metropolises, and the division of humanity within a single political space. Ideologically, current racism, which in France centres upon the immigration complex, fits into a framework of 'racism without races' which is already widely developed in other countries, particularly the Anglo-Saxon ones. It is a racism whose dominant theme is not biological heredity but the insurmountability of cultural differences, a racism which, at first sight, does not postulate the superiority of certain groups or peoples in relation to others but 'only' the harmfulness of abolishing frontiers, the incompatibility of life-styles and traditions; in short, it is what P. A. Taguieff has rightly called a *differentialist racism*.[5]

To emphasize the importance of the question, we must first of all bring out the political consequences of this change. The first is a destabilization of the defences of traditional anti-racism in so far as its argumentation finds itself attacked from the rear, if not indeed turned against itself (what Taguieff excellently terms the '*turn-about effect*' of differentialist racism). It is granted from the outset that races do not constitute isolable biological units and that in reality there are no 'human races'. It may also be admitted that the behaviour of individuals and their 'aptitudes' cannot be explained in terms of their blood or even their genes, but are the result of their belonging to historical 'cultures'. Now anthropological culturalism, which is entirely orientated towards the recognition of the diversity and equality of cultures – with only the polyphonic ensemble constituting human civilization – and also their transhistorical *permanence*, had provided the humanist and cosmopolitan anti-racism of the post-war period with most of its arguments. Its value had been confirmed by the contribution it made to the struggle against the hegemony of certain standardizing imperialisms and against the elimination of minority or dominated civilizations – 'ethnocide'. Differentialist racism takes this argumentation at its word. One of the great figures in anthropology, Claude Lévi-Strauss, who not so long ago distinguished himself by demonstrating that all civilizations are equally complex and necessary for the progression of human thought, now in 'Race and Culture' finds himself enrolled, whether he likes it or not, in the service of the idea that the 'mixing of cultures' and the suppression of 'cultural distances' would correspond to the intellectual death of humanity and would perhaps even endanger the control mechanisms that ensure its biological survival.[6] And this 'demonstration' is immediately related to the 'spontaneous' tendency of human groups (in practice national groups, though the anthropological significance of the political category of nation is obviously rather dubious) to preserve their traditions, and thus their identity. What we see here is that biological or genetic naturalism is not the only means of naturalizing human behaviour and social affinities. At the cost of abandoning the hierarchical model (though the abandonment is more apparent than real, as we shall see), *culture can also function like a nature,* and it can in particular function as a way of locking individuals and groups a priori into a genealogy, into a determination that is immutable and intangible in origin.

But this first turn-about effect gives rise to a second, which turns matters about even more and is, for that, all the more effective: if insurmountable cultural difference is our true 'natural milieu', the atmosphere indispensable to us if we are to breathe the air of history, then the abolition of that difference will necessarily give rise to defensive reactions, 'interethnic' conflicts and a general rise in aggressiveness. Such reactions, we are told, are 'natural', but they are also dangerous. By an astonishing volte-face, we here see the differentialist doctrines themselves proposing *to explain racism* (and to ward it off).

In fact, what we see is a general displacement of the problematic. We now move from the theory of races or the struggle between the races in human history, whether based on biological or psychological principles, to a theory of 'race relations' within society, *which naturalizes not racial belonging but racist conduct.* From the logical point of view, differentialist racism is a meta-racism, or what we might call a 'second-position' racism, which presents itelf as having drawn the lessons from the conflict between racism and anti-racism, as a politically operational theory of the causes of social aggression. If you want to avoid racism, you have to avoid that 'abstract' anti-racism which fails to grasp the psychological and sociological laws of human population movements; you have to respect the 'tolerance thresholds', maintain 'cultural distances' or, in other words, in accordance with the postulate that individuals are the exclusive heirs and bearers of a single culture, segregate collectivities (the best barrier in this regard still being national frontiers). And here we leave the realm of speculation to enter directly upon political terrain and the interpretation of everyday experience. Naturally, 'abstract' is not an epistemological category, but a value judgement which is the more eagerly applied when the practices to which it corresponds are the more concrete or effective: programmes of urban renewal, anti-discrimination struggles, including even positive discrimination in schooling and jobs (what the American New Right calls 'reverse discrimination'; in France too we are more and more often hearing 'reasonable' figures who have no connection with any extremist movements explaining that 'it is anti-racism which creates racism' by its agitation and its manner of 'provoking' the mass of the citizenry's national sentiments).[7]

It is not by chance that the theories of differentialist racism (which from now on will tend to present itself as the *true anti-racism* and therefore the true humanism) here connect easily with 'crowd psychology', which is enjoying something of a revival, as a general explanation of irrational movements, aggression and collective violence, and, particularly, of xenophobia. We can see here the double game mentioned above operating fully: the masses are presented with an explanation of their own 'spontaneity' and at the same time they are implicitly disparaged as a 'primitive' crowd. The neo-racist ideologues are not mystical heredity theorists, but 'realist' technicians of social psychology ...

In presenting the turn-about effects of neo-racism in this way, I am doubtless simplifying its genesis and the complexity of its internal variations, but I want to bring out what is strategically at stake in its development. Ideally one would wish to elaborate further on certain aspects and add certain correctives, but these can only be sketched out rudimentarily in what follows.

The idea of a 'racism without race' is not as revolutionary as one might imagine. Without going into the fluctuations in the meaning of the word 'race', whose historiosophical usage in fact predates any reinscription of 'genealogy' into 'genetics', we must take on board a number of major historical facts, however troublesome these may be (for a certain anti-racist vulgate, and also for the turn-abouts forced upon it by neo-racism).

A racism which does not have the pseudo-biological concept of race as its main driving force has always existed, and it has existed at exactly this level of secondary theoretical elaborations. Its prototype is anti-Semitism. Modern anti-Semitism – the form which begins to crystallize in the Europe of the Enlightenment, if not indeed from the period in which the Spain of the *Reconquista* and the Inquisition gave a statist, nationalistic inflexion to theological anti-Judaism – is *already* a 'culturalist' racism. Admittedly, bodily stigmata play a great role in its phantasmatics, but they do so more as signs of a deep psychology, as signs of a spiritual inheritance rather than a biological heredity.[8] These signs are, so to speak, the more revealing for being the less visible and the Jew is more 'truly' a Jew the more indiscernible he is. His essence is that of a cultural tradition, a ferment of moral disintegration. Anti-Semitism is supremely 'differentialist' and in many respects the whole of current differentialist racism may be considered, from the formal point of view, *as a generalized anti-Semitism.* This consideration is particularly important for the interpretation of contemporary Arabophobia, especially in France, since it carries with it an image of Islam as a 'conception of the world' which is incompatible with Europeanness and an enterprise of universal ideological domination, and therefore a systematic confusion of 'Arabness' and 'Islamicism'.

This leads us to direct our attention towards a historical fact that is even more difficult to admit and yet crucial, taking into consideration the French national form of racist traditions. There is, no doubt, a specifically French branch of the doctrines of Aryanism, anthropometry and biological geneticism, but the true 'French ideology' is not to be found in these: it lies rather in the idea that the culture of the 'land of the Rights of Man' has been entrusted with a universal mission to educate the human race. There corresponds to this mission a practice of assimilating dominated populations and a consequent need to differentiate and rank individuals or groups in terms of their greater or lesser aptitude for – or resistance to – assimilation. It was this simultaneously subtle and crushing form of exclusion/inclusion which was deployed in the process of colonization and the strictly French (or 'democratic') variant of the 'White man's burden'. I return in later chapters to the paradoxes of universalism and particularism in the functioning of racist ideologies or in the racist aspects of the functioning of ideologies.[9]

Conversely, it is not difficult to see that, in neo-racist doctrines, the suppression of the theme of hierarchy is more apparent than real. In fact, the idea of hierarchy, which these theorists may actually go so far as loudly to denounce as absurd, is reconstituted, on the one hand, in the practical application of the doctrine (it does not therefore need to be stated explicitly), and, on the other, in the very type of criteria applied in thinking the difference between cultures (and one can again see the logical resources of the 'second position' of meta-racism in action).

Prophylactic action against racial mixing in fact occurs in places where the established culture is that of the state, the dominant classes and, at least officially, the 'national' masses, whose style of life and thinking is legitimated by the system of institutions; it therefore functions as a undirectional block on expression and social advancement. No theoretical discourse on the dignity of all cultures will really compensate for the fact that, for a 'Black' in Britain or a '*Beur*' in France, the assimilation demanded of them before they can become 'integrated' into the society in which they already live (and which will always be suspected of being superficial, imperfect or simulated) is presented as progress, as an emancipation, a conceding of rights. And behind this situation lie barely reworked variants of the idea that the historical cultures of humanity can be divided into two main groups, the one assumed to be universalistic and progressive, the other supposed irremediably particularistic and primitive. It is not by chance that we encounter a paradox here: a 'logically coherent' differential racism would be uniformly conservative, arguing for the fixity of *all* cultures. It is in fact conservative, since, on the pretext of protecting European culture and the European way of life from 'Third Worldization', it utopianly closes off any path towards real development. But it immediately reintroduces the old distinction between 'closed' and 'open', 'static' and 'enterprising', 'cold' and 'hot', 'gregarious' and 'individualistic' societies – a distinction which, in its turn, brings into play all the ambiguity of the notion of culture (this is particularly the case in French!).

The difference between cultures, considered as separate entities or separate symbolic structures (that is, 'culture' in the sense of *Kultur*), refers on to cultural inequality within the 'European' space itself or, more precisely, to 'culture' (in the sense of *Bildung*, with its distinction between the academic and the popular, technical knowledge and folklore and so on) as a structure of inequalities tendentially reproduced in an industrialized, formally educated society that is increasingly internationalized and open to the world. The 'different' cultures are those which constitute obstacles, or which are established as obstacles (by schools or the norms of international communication) to the acquisition of culture. And, conversely, the 'cultural handicaps' of the dominated classes are presented as practical equivalents of alien status, or as ways of life particularly exposed to the destructive effects of mixing (that is, to the effects of the material conditions in which this 'mixing' occurs).[10] This latent presence of the hierarchic theme today finds its chief expression in the priority accorded to the individualistic model (just as, in the previous period, openly inegalitarian racism, in order to postulate an essential fixity of racial types, had to presuppose a differentialist anthropology, whether based on genetics or on *Völkerpsychologie*): the cultures supposed implicitly superior are those which appreciate and promote 'individual' enterprise, social and political individualism, as against those which inhibit these things. These are said to be the cultures whose 'spirit of community' is constituted by individualism.

In this way, we see how the *return of the biological theme* is permitted and with it the elaboration of new variants of the biological 'myth' within the framework of a cultural racism. There are, as we know, different national situations where these matters are concerned. The ethological and sociobiological theoretical models (which are themselves in part competitors) are more influential in the Anglo-Saxon countries, where they continue the traditions of Social Darwinism and eugenics while directly coinciding at points with the political objectives of an aggressive neo-liberalism.[11] Even these tendentially biologistic ideologies, however, depend fundamentally upon the 'differentialist revolution'. What they aim to explain is not the constitution of races, but the vital importance of cultural closures and traditions for the accumulation of individual aptitudes, and, most importantly, the 'natural' bases of xenophobia and social aggression. Aggression is a fictive essence which is invoked by all forms of neo-racism, and which makes it possible in this instance to displace biologism one degree: there are of course no 'races', there are only populations and cultures, but there are biological (and biophysical) causes and effects of culture, and biological reactions to cultural difference (which could he said to constitute something like the indelible trace of the 'animality' of man, still bound as ever to his extended 'family' and his 'territory'). Conversely, where pure culturalism seems dominant (as in France), we are seeing a progressive drift towards the elaboration of discourses on biology and on culture as the external regulation of 'living organisms', their reproduction, performance and health. Michel Foucault, among others, foresaw this.[12]

It may well be that the current variants of neo-racism are merely a transitional ideological formation, which is destined to develop towards discourses and social technologies in which the aspect of the historical recounting of genealogical myths (the play of substitutions between race, people, culture and nation) will give way, to a greater or lesser degree, to the aspect of psychological assessment of intellectual aptitudes and dispositions to 'normal' social life (or, conversely, to criminality and deviance), and to 'optimal' reproduction (as much from the affective as the sanitary or eugenic point of view), aptitudes and dispositions which a battery of cognitive, sociopsychological and statistical sciences would then undertake to measure, select and monitor, striking a balance between hereditary and environmental factors ... In other words, that ideological formation would develop towards a 'post-racism'. I am all the more inclined to believe this since the internationalization of social relations and of population movements within the framework of a system of nation-states will increasingly lead to a rethinking of the notion of frontier and to a redistributing of its modes of application; this will accord it a function of social prophylaxis and tie it in to more individualized statutes, while technological transformations will assign educational inequalities and intellectual hierarchies an increasingly important role in the class struggle within the perspective of a generalized techno-political selection of individuals. In the era of nation-enterprises, the true 'mass era' is perhaps upon us.

Notes

1. It was only after writing this article that Pierre-André Taguieff's book, *La Force du préjugé. Essai sur le racisme et ses doubles* (La Découverte, Paris, 1988), became known to me. In that book he considerably develops, completes and nuances the analyses to which I have referred above, and I hope, in the near future, to be able to devote to it the discussion it deserves.

2. Colette Guillaumin has provided an excellent explanation of this point, which is, in my opinion, fundamental: 'The activity of categorization is *also* a *knowledge activity. ...* Hence no doubt the ambiguity of the struggle against stereotypes and the surprises it holds in store for us. Categorization is pregnant with knowledge as it is with oppression.' (*L'Idéologie raciste. Genèse et langage actuel*, Mouton, Paris/The Hague 1972, pp. 183 *et seq.*)

3. L. Poliakov, *The Aryan Myth: A History of Racist and Nationalist Ideas in Europe*, transl. E. Howard, Sussex University Press, Brighton 1974; *La Causalité diabolique: essais sur l'origine des persécutions*, Calmann-Lévy, Paris 1980.

4. Compare the way in which, in the United States, the 'Black problem' remained separate from the 'ethnic problem' posed by the successive waves of European immigration and their reception, until, in the 1950s and 60s, a new 'paradigm of ethnicity' led to the latter being projected on to the former (cf. Michael Omi and Howard Winant, *Racial Formation in the United States*, Routledge & Kegan Paul, London, 1986).

5. See in particular his 'Les Présuppositions définitionnelles d'un indéfinissable: le racisme', *Mots*, no. 8, 1984; 'L'Identité nationale saisie par les logiques de racisation. Aspects, figures et problèmes du racisme différentialiste', *Mots*, no. 12, 1986; 'L'Identité française au miroir du racisme différentialiste', *Espaces 89, L'identité française*, Editions Tierce, Paris 1985. The idea is already present in the studies by Colette Guillaumin. See also Véronique de Rudder, 'L'Obstacle culturel: la différence et la distance', *L'Homme et la société*, January 1986. Compare, for the Anglo-Saxon world, Martin Barker, *The New Racism: Conservatives and the Ideology of the Tribe*, Junction Books, London 1981.

6. This was a lecture written in 1971 for UNESCO, reprinted in *The View from Afar*, transl. J. Neugroschel and P. Hoss, Basic Books, New York 1985; Cf. the critique by M. O'Callaghan and C. Guillaumin, 'Race et race ... la mode 'naturelle' en sciences humaines', *L'Homme et la société*, nos 31–2, 1974. From a quite different point of view, Lévi-Strauss is today attacked as a proponent of 'anti-humanism' and 'relativism' (cf. T. Todorov, 'Lévi-Strauss entre universalisme et relativisme', *Le Débat*, no. 42, 1986; A. Finkielkraut, *La Défaite de la pensée*, Gallimard, Paris 1987). Not only is the discussion on this point not closed; it has hardly begun. For my own part, I would argue not that the doctrine of Lévi-Strauss 'is racist', but that the racist theories of the nineteenth and twentieth centuries have been constructed within the conceptual field of humanism; it is therefore impossible to distinguish between them on the basis suggested above (see my 'Racism and Nationalism', this volume, pp. 37–67).

7. In Anglo-Saxon countries, these themes are widely treated by 'human ethology' and 'sociobiology'. In France, they are given a directly culturalist basis. An anthology of these ideas, running from the theorists of the New Right to more sober academics, is to be found in A. Béjin and J. Freund, eds, *Racismes, antiracismes*, Méridiens-Klincksieck, Paris 1986. It is useful to know that this work was simultaneously vulgarized in a mass-circulation popular publication, *J'ai tout compris*, no. 3, 1987 ('Dossier choc: *Immigrés: demain la haine*' edited by Guillame Faye).

8. Ruth Benedict, among others, pointed this out in respect of H. S. Chamberlain: 'Chamberlain, however, did not distinguish Semites by physical traits or by genealogy; Jews, as he knew, cannot be accurately separated from the rest of the population in modern Europe by tabulated anthropomorphic measurements. But they were enemies because they had special ways of thinking and acting. "One can very soon become a Jew ..." etc.' (*Race and Racism*, Routledge & Kegan Paul, London 1983 edn, pp. 132 *et seq.*). In her view, it was at once a sign of Chamberlain's 'frankness' and his 'self-contradiction'. This self-contradiction became the rule, but in fact it is not a self-contradiction at all. In anti-Semitism, the theme of the inferiority of the Jew is, as we know, much less important than that of his irreducible otherness. Chamberlain even indulges at times in referring to the 'superiority' of the Jews, in matters of intellect, commerce or sense of community, making them all the more 'dangerous'. And the Nazi enterprise frequently admits that it is an enterprise of *reduction* of the Jews to 'subhuman status' rather than a consequence of any *de facto* subhumanity: this is indeed why its object cannot remain mere slavery, but must become extermination.

9. See this volume, chapter 3, 'Racism and Nationalism'.

10. It is obviously this subsumption of the 'sociological' difference between cultures beneath the institutional hierarchy of Culture, the decisive agency of social classification and its naturalization, that accounts for the keenness of the 'radical strife' and resentment that surrounds the presence of immigrants in schools, which is much greater than that generated by the mere fact of living in close proximity. Cf. S. Boulot and D. Boyson-Fradet, 'L'Echec scolaire des enfants de travailleurs immigrés', *Les Temps modernes*, special number: 'L'Immigration maghrébine en France', 1984.

11. Cf. Barker, *The New Racism*.

12. Michel Foucault, *The History of Sexuality*, vol. 1, *An Introduction*, transl. Robert Jurley, Peregrine, London 1978.

2

The Ideological Tensions of Capitalism: Universalism versus Racism and Sexism

Immanuel Wallerstein

The modern world, we have long been told, is the first to reach beyond the bounds of narrow, local loyalties and to proclaim the universal brotherhood of man. Or so we were told up to the 1970s. Since that time, we have been made conscious that the very terminology of universalist doctrine, as for example the phrase 'the brotherhood of man', belies itself, since this phrase is masculine in gender, thereby implicitly excluding or relegating to a secondary sphere all who are female. It would be easy to multiply linguistic examples, all of which reveal an underlying tension between the continuing ideological legitimation of universalism in the modern world and the continuing reality (both material and ideological) of racism and sexism in this same world. It is this tension, or more precisely this contradiction, that I wish to discuss. For contradictions not only provide the dynamic force of historical systems; they also reveal their essential features.

It is one thing to ask whence universalist doctrine, and how widely it is shared; or to ask why racism and sexism exist and persist. It is quite another to inquire into the origins of the pairing of the two ideologies, indeed what one might argue has been the symbiotic relationship of these presumed opposites. We start with a seeming paradox. The major challenge to racism and sexism has been universalist beliefs; and the major challenge to universalism has been racist and sexist beliefs. We assume that the proponents of each set of beliefs are persons in opposite camps. Only occasionally do we allow ourselves to notice that the enemy, as Pogo put it, is us; that most of us (perhaps all of us) find it perfectly possible to pursue both doctrines simultaneously. This is to be deplored no doubt; but it is also to be explained, and by more than the simple assertion of hypocrisy. For this paradox (or this hypocrisy) is enduring, widespread and structural. It is no passing human failing.

In previous historical systems it was easier to be consistent. However much these previous systems varied in their structures and in their premisses, they all had no hesitation in making some kind of moral and political distinction between the insider and the outsider, in which both the belief and the higher moral qualities of the insider and the sense of obligation by insiders to each other took precedence over any abstract concepts about the human species, if such abstractions were asserted at all. Even the three monotheistic world religions – Judaism, Christianity and Islam – made such distinctions between insiders and outsiders despite their hypothetical commitment to a single God presiding over a singular human species.

This essay discusses first the origins of modern universalist doctrines, then the sources of modern racism and sexism, and finally the realities of the combination of the two ideologies, both in terms of what gave rise to it and what has been its consequences.

There are two main ways of explaining the origins of universalism as an ideology of our present historical system. One is to see universalism as the culmination of an older intellectual tradition. The other is to see it as an ideology particularly appropriate to a capitalist world-economy. The two modes of explanation do not necessarily contradict each other. The argument that it is the outcome or the culmination of a long tradition has to do precisely with the trio of monotheistic religions. The crucial moral leap, it has been argued, occurred when humans (or some humans) ceased to believe in a tribal god and recognized the unicity of God and therefore implicitly the unicity of humanity. To be sure, the argument continues, the three monotheistic religions pursued the logic of their position only part-way. Judaism carved out a special position for the people chosen of God and was reluctant to encourge membership by adoption. Christianity and Islam both lifted the barriers to entry into the group of the chosen, and indeed went in the other direction with proselytization. But both Christianity and Islam normally required an affirmative act of allegiance (which one could make as a formerly non-believing adult by formal conversion) in order to gain full access to the kingdom of God. Modern Enlightenment thought, it is said, simply took this monotheistic logic one step further, deriving moral equality and human rights from human nature itself, a characteristic with which we are all born and as a result of which our rights become entitlements rather than earned privileges.

This is not an incorrect history of ideas. We have several important politico-moral documents of the late eighteenth century that reflect this

Enlightenment ideology, documents that were given widespread credence and adherence as a result of major political upheavals (the French Revolution, the decolonization of the Americas and so on). Furthermore, we can carry the ideological history forward. There were many *de facto* omissions in these ideological documents of the eighteenth century – and most notably those of non-Whites and women. But as time went on, these omissions and others have been rectified by explicitly including these groups under the rubric of universalist doctrine. Today even those social movements whose *raison d'être* is the implementation of racist or sexist policies tend to pay at least lip service to the ideology of universalism, thereby seeming to consider it somehow shameful to assert overtly what they very clearly believe and think should govern political priorities. It is not hard therefore to derive from the history of ideas a sort of secular upward curve of the acceptance of universalist ideology and, based on that curve, to make a claim about the existence of a sort of inevitable world-historical process at work.

The claim, however, that since universalism has only been seriously pursued as a political doctrine in the modern world its origins must be sought in the particular socioeconomic framework of this world also seems very strong. The capitalist world-economy is a system built on the endless accumulation of capital. One of the prime mechanisms that makes this possible is the commodification of everything. These commodities flow in a world market in the form of goods, of capital and of labour-power. Presumably, the freer the flow, the greater the degree of commodification. Consequently, anything that restrains the flow is hypothetically counter-indicated.

Anything that prevents goods, capital or labour-power from being a marketable commodity serves to restrain such flows. Anything that uses as criteria for evaluating goods, capital or labour-power something other than their market value and then gives these other valuations priority makes the item to that extent non-marketable, or at least less marketable. Hence, by a sort of impeccable logic, particularisms of any kind whatsoever are said to be incompatible with the logic of a capitalist system, or at least an obstacle to its optimal operation. It would follow then that within a capitalist system it is imperative to assert and carry out a universalist ideology as an essential element in the endless pursuit of the accumulation of capital. Thus it is that we talk of capitalist social relations as being a 'universal solvent', working to reduce everything to a homogeneous commodity form denoted by a single measure of money.

This is said to have two principal consequences. It is said to permit the greatest possible efficiency in the production of goods. Specifically, in terms of labour-power, if we have a 'career open to talents' (one of the slogans born out of the French Revolution), we are likely to place the most competent persons in the occupation roles most suitable for them in the world division of labour. And we have indeed developed whole institutional mechanisms – the state school system, the civil service, anti-nepotism rules – that are designed to establish what today we call a 'meritocratic' system.

Furthermore, it is said, not only is meritocracy economically efficient but it is also politically stabilizing. To the extent that there are inequalities in the distribution of reward in historical capitalism (as in prior historical systems), resentment of those who receive greater rewards by those who receive fewer is less intense, it is argued, because its justification is offered on the basis of merit and not on the basis of tradition. That is, it is thought that privilege earned by merit is somehow more acceptable, morally and politically, to most people than privilege earned by inheritance.

This is dubious political sociology. The exact opposite is true in fact. While privilege earned by inheritance has long been at least marginally acceptable to the oppressed on the basis of mystical or fatalistic beliefs in an eternal order, which belief at least offers them the comfort of certainty, privilege earned because one is possibly smarter and certainly better educated than someone else is extremely difficult to swallow, except by the few who are basically scrambling up the ladder. Nobody who is not a yuppie loves or admires a yuppie. Princes at least may seem to be kindly father figures. A yuppie is nothing but an overprivileged sibling. The meritocratic system is politically one of the least stable systems. And it is precisely because of this political fragility that racism and sexism enter the picture.

The presumed upward curve of universalist ideology has long been thought theoretically to be matched by a downward curve of the degree of inequality generated by race or gender, both as ideology and as fact. This, however, has simply not been the case empirically. We could even perhaps make the inverse argument that the curves of race and gender inequalities have actually been going up in the modern world, or at least have not been going down – certainly in fact, possibly even as ideology. To see why this might be so, we should look at what the ideologies of racism and sexism actually assert.

Racism is not simply a matter of having an attitude of disdain for or fear of someone of another group as defined by genetic criteria (such as skin colour) or by social criteria (religious affiliation, cultural patterns, linguistic preference and so on). Racism normally includes such disdain and fear, but it is far more than that. Disdain and fear are quite secondary to what defines the practice of racism in the capitalist world-economy. Indeed, it could even be argued that disdain and fear of the other (xenophobia) is an aspect of racism that entails a contradiction.

Xenophobia in all prior historical systems had one primary behavioural consequence: the ejection of the 'barbarian' from the physical locus of the community, the society, the in-group – death being the extreme version of ejection. Whenever we physically eject the other, we gain the 'purity' of environment that we are presumably seeking, but we inevitably lose something at the same time. We lose the labour-power of the person ejected and therefore that person's contribution to the creation of a surplus that we might be able to appropriate on a recurring basis. This represents a loss for any historical system, but it is a particularly serious one in the case of a system whose whole structure and logic are built around the endless accumulation of capital.

A capitalist system that is expanding (which is half the time) needs all the labour-power it can find, since this labour is producing the goods through which more capital is produced, realized and accumulated. Ejection out of the system is pointless. But if one wants to maximize the accumulation of capital, it is necessary simultaneously to minimize the costs of production (hence the costs of labour-power) and minimize the costs of political disruption (hence minimize – not eliminate, because one cannot eliminate – the protests of the labour force). Racism is the magic formula that reconciles these objectives.

Let us look at one of the earliest and most famous discussions about racism as an ideology. When Europeans came to the New World, they encountered peoples whom they slaughtered in large numbers – either directly by the sword or indirectly by disease. A Spanish friar, Bartolomé de Las Casas, took up their cause, arguing that Indians had souls which needed to be saved. Let us pursue the implications of the Las Casas argument which won the formal assent of the church, and eventually of the states. Since Indians had souls, they were human beings, and the rules of natural law applied to them. Therefore, one was not morally permitted to slaughter them indiscriminately (eject them from the domain). One was obliged instead to seek to save their souls (convert them to the universalist value of Christianity). Since they would then be alive and presumably en route to conversion, they could be integrated into the work force – at the level of their skills, of course, which translated into meaning at the bottom level of the occupational and reward hierarchy.

Racism operationally has taken the form of what might be called the 'ethnicization' of the work force, by whch I mean that at all times there has existed an occupational-reward hierarchy that has tended to be correlated with some so-called social criteria. But while the pattern of ethnicization has been constant, the details have varied from place to place and time to time, according to what part of the human genetic and social pools were located in a particular time and place and what the hierarchical needs of the economy were at that time and place.

That is to say, racism has always combined claims based on continuity with the past (genetic and/or social) with a present-orientated flexibility in defining the exact boundaries of these reified entities we call races or ethno-national-religious groupings. The flexibility of claiming a link with the boundaries of the past combined with the constant redrawing of these boundaries in the present takes the form of the creation and constant re-creation of racial and/or ethno-national-religious groups or communities. They are always there and always ranked hierarchically, but they are not always exactly the same. Some groups can be mobile in the ranking system; some groups can disappear or combine with others; while still others break apart and new ones are born. But there are always some who are 'niggers'. If there are no Blacks or too few to play the role, one can invent 'White niggers'.

This kind of system – racism constant in form and in venom, but somewhat flexible in boundary lines – does three things extremely well. It allows one to expand or contract the numbers available in any particular space–time zone for the lowest paid, least rewarding economic roles, according to current needs. It gives rise to and constantly re-creates social communities that actually socialize children into playing the appropriate roles (although, of course, they also socialize them into forms of resistance). And it provides a non-meritocratic basis to justify inequality. This last point is worth underlining. It is precisely because racism is anti-universalistic in doctrine that it helps to maintain capitalism as a system. It allows a far lower reward to a major segment of the work force than could ever be justified on the basis of merit.

But if capitalism as a system begets racism, does it need to beget sexism as well? Yes, because the two are in fact intimately linked. The ethnicization of the work force exists in order to permit very low wages for whole segments of the labour force. Such low wages are in fact only possible because the wage earners are located in household structures for which lifetime wage-income provides only a relatively small proportion of total household income. Such households require the extensive input of labour into so-called subsistence and petty market activities – in part by the adult male to be sure, but in much larger part by the adult female, plus the young and the aged of both sexes.

In such a system, this labour input in non-wage work 'compensates' the lowness of the wage-income and therefore in fact represents an indirect subsidy to the employers of the wage labourers in these households. Sexism permits us not to think about it. Sexism is not just the enforcement of different, or even less appreciated, work roles for women, no more than racism is just xenophobia. As racism is meant to keep people inside the work system, not eject them from it, so sexism intends the same.

The way we induce women – and the young and the aged – to work to create surplus-value for the owners of capital, who do not even pay them a little bit, is by proclaiming that their work is really non-work. We invent the 'housewife' and assert she is not 'working', merely 'keeping house'. Thus, when governments calculate the percentage of the so-called active labour foce who are employed, 'housewives' are neither in the numerator nor in the denominator of the calculation. And with sexism goes automatically ageism. As we pretend that the housewife's work is not creating surplus-value, so we pretend that the multiple work inputs of the non-waged young and aged do not do so either.

None of this reflects working reality. But it does all add up to an ideology which is extremely powerful, and which all fits together. The combination of universalism-meritocracy serving as the basis by which the cadres or middle strata can legitimate the system and racism-sexism serving to structure the majority of the work force works very well. But only to a point, and that for a simple reason – the two ideological patterns of the capitalist world-economy stand in open contradiction to each other. This delicately poised combination threatens always to get out of hand, as various groups start to push the logic of universalism on the one hand and of racism-sexism on the other too far.

We know what happens when racism-sexism goes too far. Racists may try to eject the out-group totally – swiftly, as in the case of the Nazi slaughter of the Jews; less swiftly, as in the pursuit of total apartheid. Taken to this extreme, these doctrines are irrational and, because they are irrational, they are resisted. They are resisted, of course, by the victims, but they are also resisted by powerful economic forces who object not to the racism but to the fact that its primary objective – an ethnicized but productive work force – has been forgotten.

We can also imagine what happens when universalism goes too far. Some people may seek to implement a truly egalitarian allocation of work roles and work rewards in which race (or its equivalent) and gender genuinely play no part. Unlike taking racism too far, there is no swift way one can take universalism too far, for one has to eliminate not merely the legal and institutional barriers to universalism but the internalized patterns of ethnicization, and this inevitably requires at the very least a generation. So it is rather easy to resist universalism's going too far. In the name of universalism itself, one merely has to denounce the so-called reverse racism wherever steps are taken to dismantle the institutionalized apparatus of racism and sexism.

What we see therefore is a system that operates by a tense link between the right dosage of universalism and racism-sexism. There are always efforts to push one side or the other of this equation 'too far'. The result is a sort of zigzag pattern. This could go on forever, except for one problem. Over time, the zigs and zags are getting bigger, not smaller. The thrust towards universalism is getting stronger. So is the thrust towards racism and sexism. The stakes go up. This is for two reasons.

On the one hand, there is the informational impact of the accumulation of historical experience by all participants. On the other hand, there are the secular trends of the system itself. For the zigzag of universalism and racism-sexism is not the only zigzag in the system. There is also the zigzag of economic expansion and contraction, for example, with which the ideological zigzag of universalism and racism-sexism is partially correlated. The economic zigzag is also getting sharper. Why that is so is another story. Yet as the general contradictions of the modern world-system force the system into a long structural crisis, the most acute ideological-institutional locus of the search for a successor system is in fact located in the sharpening tension, the increased zigs and zags, between universalism and racism-sexism. It is not a question of which half of this antinomy will in some sense win out, since they are intimately and conceptually tied to each other. It is a question of whether and how we shall invent new systems that will utilize neither the ideology of universalism nor the ideology of racism-sexism. That is our task, and it is not an easy one.

3

Racism and Nationalism

Etienne Balibar

Racist organizations most often refuse to be designated as such, laying claim instead to the title of *nationalist* and claiming that the two notions cannot be equated. Is this merely a tactical ploy or the symptom of a fear of words inherent in the racist attitude? In fact the discourses of race and nation are never very far apart, if only in the form of disavowal: thus the presence of 'immigrants' on French soil is referred to as the cause of an 'anti-French racism'. The oscillation of the vocabulary itself suggests to us then that, at least in already constituted national states, the organization of nationalism into individual political movements inevitably has racism underlying it.

At least one section of historians has used this to argue that racism – as theoretical discourse and as mass phenonemon – develops 'within the field of nationalism', which is ubiquitous in the modern era.[1] In this view, nationalism would be, if not the sole cause of racism, then at least the determining condition of its production. Or, it is also argued, the 'economic' explanations (in terms of the effects of crises) or 'psychological' explanations (in terms of the ambivalence of the sense of personal identity and collective belonging) are pertinent in that they cast light upon presuppositions or subsidiary effects of nationalism.

Such a thesis confirms, without doubt, that racism has nothing to do with the existence of objective biological 'races'.[2] It shows that racism is a historical – or cultural – product, while avoiding the equivocal position of 'culturalist' explanations which, from another angle, also tend to make racism into a sort of invariant of human nature. It has the advantage of breaking the circle which traces the psychology of racism back to explanations which are themselves purely psychological. Lastly, it performs a critical function in relation to the euphemistic strategies of other historians who are very careful to place racism *outside* the field of nationalism as such, as if it were possible to define the latter without including the racist movements in it, and therefore without going back to the social relations which give rise to such movements and are indissociable from contemporary nationalism (in particular, imperialism).[3] However, this accumulation of good reasons does not necessarily imply that racism is an inevitable consequence of nationalism, nor, *a fortiori*, that without the existence of an overt or latent racism, nationalism would itself be historically impossible.[4] These categories and the connections between them continue to be rather hazy. We should not be afraid to investigate at some length why no form of conceptual 'purism' will work here.

The Presence of the Past

From what models have we, living as we do at the end of the twentieth century, formed our conception of racism, which is enshrined in quasi-official definitions? In part from Nazi anti-Semitism, from the segregation of Blacks in the USA (perceived as a long sequel to slavery) and, lastly, from the 'imperialist' racism of colonial conquest, wars and domination. Theoretical thinking on these models (which is connected with policies of defence of democracy, assertion of human and civil rights, and national liberation) has produced a series of distinctions. In spite of their abstract nature, it is not unhelpful to begin by reviewing these, since they indicate the directions in which the search for causes is to be undertaken, if we are to follow the more or less accepted idea that the suppression of effects depends precisely upon the suppression of their causes.

The first distinction we encounter is that between *theoretical* (or doctrinal) racism and *spontaneous* racism (or racist 'prejudice'), considered at times as a phenomenon of collective psychology and at others as a more or less 'conscious' structure of the individual personality. I shall return to this point.

From a more historical point of view, the singularity of anti-Semitism by comparison with colonial racism, or, in the USA, the need to interpret the racial oppression of the Blacks differently from the discrimination to which immigration 'ethnic groups' are subjected, leads to the distinction being made – in more or less ideal terms – between an *internal* racism (directed against a population regarded as 'a minority' within the national space) and an *external* racism (considered as an extreme form of xenophobia). This, we should note, assumes that we take the national frontier as a prior criterion, and therefore run the risk of this approach being inappropriate to post-colonial or quasi-colonial situations (such as the North American domination of Latin America), in which the notion of frontier is even more equivocal than it is elsewhere.

Ever since the analysis of racist discourse began to apply phenomenological and semantic methods of analysis, it has seemed useful to characterize certain racist postures as *auto-referential* (those in which the bearers of the prejudice, exercising physical or symbolic violence, designate themselves as representatives of a superior race) in opposition to a *hetero-referential* or 'hetero-phobic' racism (in which it is, by contrast, the victims of racism, or, more precisely, of the process of racialization, who are assigned to an inferior or evil race). This poses not only the question of how the race myth forms, but also the question of whether racism is indissociable from it.

Political analysis, whether directed towards current phenomena or seeking to reconstitute the genesis of past phenomena, strives to evaluate the respective contributions of institutional and sociological racisms, a distinction which roughly overlaps that between theoretical racism and spontaneous racism (it is in fact difficult to imagine or name historical institutions which have pursued a goal of racial segregation, without some form of doctrinal justification), but does not purely and simply coincide with it, both because these justifications may be drawn from theoretical ideologies other than a racial mythology, and because the notion of sociological racism contains a dynamic, conjunctural, dimension which goes beyond the psychology of prejudices by calling to our attention the problem posed by collective movements of a racist character. The alternative between institutional and sociologial racism warns us not to dismiss as negligible the differences which separate the presence of racism *within the state* from an (official) state racism. It also suggests that it is important to investigate the vulnerability to racism of certain social classes and the forms they give to it in a given conjuncture. Deep down, it is, however, a mystificatory alternative which principally translates two different strategies, the one of projection, the other of disavowal. Every historical racism is *both* institutional and sociological.

Lastly, confronting the questions of Nazism and colonial racisms (or segregation in the United States) has broadly speaking forced upon us the distinction between a racism of *extermination* or elimination (an 'exclusive' racism) and a racism of *oppression* or exploitation (an 'inclusive' racism), the one aiming to purify the social body of the stain or danger the inferior races may represent, the other seeking, by contrast, to hierarchize and partition society. But it immediately emerges

that, even in extreme cases, neither of these forms ever exists in the pure
state: thus Nazism combined extermination and deportation, 'the final
solution' and slavery, and colonial imperialisms have practised both
forced labour, the establishment of caste regimes, ethnic segregation and
'genocides' or the systematic massacre of populations.

In fact, these distinctions do not so much serve to classify types of
behaviour or ideally pure structures as to identify historical trajectories.
Their relative pertinence leads us both to the common-sense conclusion
that there is not merely a *single* invariant racism but a number of *racisms*, forming a broad, open spectrum of situations, and to a caveat that
may be intellectually and politically indispensable: a determinate racist
configuration has no fixed frontiers; it is a stage in a development which
its own latent potentialities, as well as historical circumstances and the
relations of force within the social formation, will shunt around within
the spectrum of possible racisms. It would, in the end, be difficult to find
contemporary societies from which racism is absent (especially if one is
not content merely to note that its public expressions are inhibited by
the dominant culture or that violent 'acting out' is, to a greater or lesser
degree, curbed by the legal apparatus). Nevertheless, we should not
conclude that we all live in equally 'racist societies', though this pru-
dence must not in its turn become an alibi. And it is at this point that it
becomes clearly necessary to pass beyond mere typologies. Rather than
a single type or a juxtaposition of particular cases to be classified in
formal categories, racism is itself a singular history, though admittedly
not a linear one (with its sharp changes of direction, its subterranean
phases and its explosions), connecting together the conjunctures of
modern humanity and being, in its turn, affected by them. That is why
the figures of Nazi anti-Semitism and colonial anti-racism or indeed of
slavery cannot simply be evoked as models against which to measure the
purity and seriousness of such and such a 'racist upsurge' nor even as
periods or events which mark out the place of racism in history, but they
must be considered as ever active formations, part conscious and part
unconscious, which contribute to structuring behaviour and movements
emerging out of present conditions. Let us emphasize here the paradig-
matic fact that South African apartheid intimately intermixes the traces
of the three formations which we have mentioned (Nazism, colonization,
slavery).

It is, moreover, well known that the defeat of Nazism and the
revelation of the policy of extermination that had been carried out in the
concentration camps not only created an awareness which became part
of what is called universal culture in the contemporary world (though
the consciousness thereby acquired is unequal, uncertain of its content
and its implications and, all in all, distinct from actual knowledge), but it

also led to a prohibition, half juridical and half ethical, which, as with any prohibition, has ambivalent consequences: ranging from the necessity for contemporary racist discourse to avoid the typical statements of Nazism ('slips' excepted) to the possibility of presenting itself, in relation to Nazism, as the *other* of racism, or from the displacement of hatred on to 'objects' other than the Jews to compulsive fascination for the lost secrets of Hitlerianism. I shall maintain seriously (and all the more seriously in that the phenomenon seems to me by no means marginal) that in its very poverty, the imitation of the Nazis among groups of young skinheads in the third generation after the 'Apocalypse' represents one of the forms of collective memory within current racism or, if you prefer, one of the ways in which collective memory contributes to drawing the parameters of present racism – which also means we cannot hope to eliminate it either by simple repression or by mere preaching.

Doubtless no historical experience has, in itself, the power to re-activate itself, and, in order to interpret the way racism fluctuated in the 1980s between lip-service paid to anti-Nazism, eloquent silences and the reproduction of myths, one must take account of the groups against whom it is aimed and their own actions and reactions. For racism is a social relation, not the mere ravings of racist subjects.[5] The fact remains that the present is bound to the singular imprint of the past. Thus when we come to ask in what sense the fixation of racial hatreds upon immigrants from the Maghreb reproduces certain classic features of anti-Semitism, we should not only point to an analogy between the situations of Jewish minorities in Europe at the turn of the twentieth century and 'Arabo-Islamic' minorities in present-day France, nor simply refer these hatreds to the abstract model of an 'internal racism' in which a society projects its frustrations and anxieties (or rather those of the individuals who make it up) on to a part of itself; rather we need also to inquire into the unique drift of anti-Semitism out beyond 'Jewish identity', starting out from the repetition of its themes within what is very much a French tradition and from the fresh impulsion given to it by Hitler.

We shall have to do the same, also, for the imprint of colonial racism. It is none too difficult to discover its ubiquitous effects. First, because not all direct French colonization has disappeared (some 'territories' and their semi-citizen status 'natives' have been through a process of de-colonization). Second, because neo-colonialism is a solid reality which we cannot simply ignore. Last, and most importantly of all, because the privileged 'objects' of present-day racism – the workers and their families who come from the former French colonies – appear as the result of colonization and decolonization and thus succeed in concentrating upon themselves both the continuation of imperial scorn and the resentment that is felt by the citizens of a fallen power, if not indeed a vague phantasmatic longing for revenge. These continuities do not, however, suffice to characterize the situation. They are mediated (as Sartre would have said) or overdetermined (as Althusser would put it) by the reflection within the national space (differently, depending upon the social group or the ideological position) of more far-reaching historical events and tendencies. Here again, though in a mode that is wholly dissimilar to Nazism, a break has taken place. Or, more precisely, an interminable sedimentation and a relatively rapid, but profoundly ambiguous, break.

It might at first sight seem that colonial racism constitutes the prime example of an 'external racism' – an extreme variant of xenophobia combining fear and scorn – perpetuated by the awareness the colonizers have always had, in spite of their claim to have founded a durable order, that that order rested on a reversible relation of forces. It is indeed that characteristic – alongside the difference between oppression and extermination (which the Nazi 'final solution' has led theorists to project retrospectively on to the whole history of anti-Semitism) – that many writers have drawn upon to postulate an antithesis between colonial racism and anti-Semitism. These are thus presented as being two tendentially incompatible types of racism (hence the argument of some, not without a touch of Jewish nationalism, that 'anti-Semitism is not racism'): on the one hand, a racism which tends to eliminate an internal minority which is not merely 'assimilated', but constitutes an integral part of the culture and economy of the European nations since their beginnings and, on the other hand, a racism which both *de jure* and *de facto* continues to exclude a forcibly conquered minority from citizenship and from the dominant culture, and therefore to 'exclude' it indefinitely (which does not by any means prevent there being paternalism, the destruction of 'native' cultures and the imposition of the ways of life and thought of the colonizers on the 'elites' of the colonized nations).

We must, however, observe that the *exteriority* of the 'native' populations in colonization, or rather the representation of that state as *racial* exteriority, though it recuperates and assimilates into its discourse very old images of 'difference', is by no means a given state of affairs. It was in fact produced and reproduced within the very space constituted by conquest and colonization with its concrete structures of administration, forced labour and sexual oppression, and therefore on the basis of a certain *interiority*. Otherwise one could not explain the ambivalence of the dual movement of assimilation and exclusion of the 'natives' nor the way in which the subhuman nature attributed to the colonized comes to determine the self-image developed within the colonized nations in the period when the world was being divided up. The heritage of colonialism is, in reality, a fluctuating combination of continued exteriorization and 'internal exclusion'. One can also see this if one observes the way in which the imperialist superiority complex has been formed. The colonial castes of the various nationalities (British, French, Dutch, Portuguese and so on) *worked together* to forge the idea of 'White' superiority, of civilization as an interest that has to be defended against the savages. This representation – 'the White man's burden' – has contributed in a decisive way to moulding the modern notion of a supranational European or Western identity. It is no less true that the same castes were perpetually involved in what Kipling called the 'Great Game' – playing off, in other words, 'their' natives, rebellions against one another and, above and beyond this, all priding themselves, *in competition with one another*, on their particular humaneness, by projecting the image of racism on to the colonial practices of their rivals. French colonization proclaimed itself 'assimilatory', while British colonization saw itself as 'respectful of cultures'. The other White is also the bad White. Each White nation is spiritually 'the whitest': in other words, it is both the most elitist and the most universalistic, an apparent contradiction to which I return below.

When the pace of the decolonization process increased, these contradictions took on a new form. To judge it by its own ideals, decolonization has failed, the process being both incomplete and perverted. It has, however, in combination with other relatively independent events (the coming of the age of planetary weapons systems and communication networks), created a new political space. This is not merely a space in which strategies are formed, and capital, technologies and messages circulate, but a space in which entire populations subject to the law of the market come into contact physically and symbolically. Thus the equivocal interiority–exteriority configuration which had, since the period of colonial conquest, formed one of the structuring dimensions of racism, finds itself reproduced, expanded and re-activated. It is a commonplace to remark upon this in regard to those 'Third World within' effects which are produced by immigration from the former colonies or quasi-colonies into the capitalist 'centres'. But this form of *interiorization of the exterior* which marks out the horizon against which the representations of 'race' and 'ethnicity' are played out cannot be separated, other than abstractly, from apparently antithetical forms of *exteriorization of the interior*. And in particular it cannot be separated from those which result from the formation – after the more or less complete departure of the colonizers – of states which claim to be national (but only become so very unequally) throughout the immense periphery of the planet, with their explosive antagonisms between capitalist bourgeoisies or 'Westernized' state bourgeoisies and wretched masses, thrown back by this very fact upon 'traditionalism'.[6]

Benedict Anderson maintains that decolonization has not, so to speak, expressed itself in the Third World by the development of what a particular propaganda calls 'counter-racism' (anti-White or anti-European).[7] Let us concede that this was written before the recent developments in Islamic fundamentalism, the contribution of which to the flows of 'xenophobia' in our present conjuncture will certainly have to be assessed. Anderson's argument is, however, incomplete, for, though there may not be a 'Third-Worldist' counter-racism in Africa, Asia or Latin America, there is a plethora of devastating racisms, both institutional and popular, *between* 'nations', 'ethnic groups' and 'communities'. And the spectacle of these racisms, in its turn deformed by global communications, is continually feeding the stereotypes of White racism by keeping alive the old idea that three-quarters of humanity are incapable of governing themselves. Doubtless the background to these mimetic effects is constituted by the replacement of the old world of colonizing nations and their sphere of manoeuvre (the rest of humanity) by a new world which is formally organized into equivalent nation states (each represented in international institutions) but traversed by the constantly shifting frontier – irreducible to the frontiers between states – between two humanities which seem incommensurable, namely the humanity of destitution and that of 'consumption', the humanity of underdevelopment and that of overdevelopment. In appearance, humanity has been unified by the suppression of imperial hierarchies; in fact, however, it is only today that humanity exists as such, though split into tendentially incompatible masses. In the space of the world-economy, which has effectively become that of world politics and world ideology, the division between subhumans and super-humans is a structural but violently unstable one. Previously, the notion of humanity was merely an abstraction. But, to the question, 'What is man?' which – however aberrant its forms may appear to us – is insistently present in racist thought, there is today no response in which this split is not at work.[8]

What are we to conclude from this? The displacements to which I have just alluded are part of what, to borrow a term from Nietzsche, we might call the contemporary transvaluations of racism, which concern both the general economy of humanity's political groupings and its historical imaginary. They form what I have, above, called the singular development of racism which relativizes typologies and reworks accumulated experiences against the grain of what we believe to be the 'education of humanity'. In this sense, contrary to what is postulated in one of the most constant statements of racist ideology itself, it is not 'race' which is a biological or psychological human 'memory', but it is racism which represents one of the most insistent forms of the historical memory of modern societies. It is racism which continues to effect the imaginary 'fusion' of past and present in which the collective perception of human history unfolds.

This is why the question, which is perpetually being revived, of the irreducibility of anti-Semitism to colonial racism is wrongly framed. The two have never been totally independent and they are not immutable. They have a joint descent which reacts back upon our analysis of their earlier forms. Certain traces function constantly as a screen for others, but they also represent the 'unsaid' of those other traces. Thus the identification of racism with anti-Semitism – and particularly with Nazism – functions as an alibi: it enables the racist character of the 'xenophobia' directed against immigrants to be denied. Conversely, however, the (apparently quite gratuitous) association of anti-Semitism with anti-immigrant racism in the discourse of the xenophobic movements that are currently developing in Europe is not the expression of a generic anti-humanism, of a permanent structure of exclusion of the 'Other' in all its manifestations, nor the simple passive effect of a conservative political tradition (whether it be called nationalist or fascist). Much more specifically, and much more 'perversely', it organizes racist thought by giving it its conscious and unconscious models: the character of the Nazi extermination, which is strictly speaking unimaginable, thus comes to be lodged within the contemporary complex as the metaphorical expression of the desire for extermination which also haunts anti-Turkish or anti-Arab racism.[9]

The Field of Nationalism

Let us return, then, to the connection between nationalism and racism. And let us begin by acknowledging that the very category of nationalism is intrinsically ambiguous. This has to do, first of all, with the antithetical nature of the historical situations in which nationalist movements and policies arise. Fichte or Gandhi are not Bismarck; Bismarck or De Gaulle are not Hitler. And yet we cannot, by a mere intellectual decision, suppress the effect of ideological symmetry which imposes itself here on the antagonistic forces. We have no right whatever to equate the nationalism of the dominant with that of the dominated, the nationalism of liberation with the nationalism of conquest. Yet this does not mean we can simply ignore the fact that there is a common element – if only the logic of a situation, the structural inscription in the political forms of the modern world – in the nationalism of the Algerian FLN and that of the French colonial army, or today in the nationalism of the ANC and that of the Afrikaners. Let us take this to its extreme conclusion and say that this formal symmetry is not unrelated to the painful experience we have repeatedly undergone of seeing nationalisms of liberation transformed into nationalisms of domination (just as we have seen socialist revolutions turn around to produce state dictatorships), which has compelled us at regular intervals to inquire into the oppressive potentialities contained within every nationalism. Before coming to reside in words, the contradiction resides in history itself.[10]

Why does it prove to be so difficult to define nationalism? First, because the concept never functions alone, but is always part of a chain in which it is both the central and the weak link. This chain is constantly being enriched (the detailed modes of that enrichment varying from one language to another) with new intermediate or extreme terms: civic spirit, patriotism, populism, ethnicism, ethnocentrism, xenophobia, chauvinism, imperialism, jingoism ... I challenge anyone to fix once and for all, unequivocally, the differential meanings of these terms. But it seems to me that the overall figure can be interpreted fairly simply.

Where the *nationalism–nation* relation is concerned, the core of meaning opposes a 'reality', the nation, to an 'ideology', nationalism. This relation is, however, perceived very differently by different people, since several obscure questions underlie it: Is nationalist ideology the (necessary or circumstantial) reflection of the existence of nations? Or do nations constitute themselves out of nationalist ideologies (though it may mean that these latter, having attained their 'goal', are subsequently transformed)? Must the 'nation' itself – and naturally this question is not independent of the preceding ones – be considered as a 'state' or as a 'society' (a social formation)? Let us leave these issues in abeyance for a moment, together with the variants to which they may give rise by the introduction of terms such as city, people, nationality and so on.

As far as the relation between *nationalism and racism* is concerned at present, the core of meaning contrasts a 'normal' ideology and politics (nationalism) with an 'excessive' ideology and behaviour (racism), either to oppose the two or to offer the one as the truth of the other. Here again questions and other conceptual distinctions immediately arise. Rather than concentrating our attention upon racism, would it not be more appropriate to privilege the more 'objective' nationalism/ imperialism alternative? But this confrontation brings out the other possibilities: for example, that nationalism itself may be the ideologico-political effect of the imperialist character of nations or their survival into an imperialist age and environment. One may complicate the chain further by introducing notions like fascism and Nazism with their network of attendant questions: Are these both nationalisms? Are they both imperialisms? ...

In fact, and this is what all these questions bring out – the whole chain is inhabited by one fundamental question. As soon as 'somewhere' in this historico-political chain an intolerable, seemingly 'irrational' violence enters upon the scene, *where* are we to place that entry? Should we cut into a sequence in which only 'realities' are involved to locate it, or should we rather search among the 'ideological' conflicts? And should we consider violence as a perversion of a normal state of affairs, a deviation from the hypothetical 'straight line' of human history, or do we have to admit that it represents the truth of what has preceded it and therefore, from this point of view, the seeds of racism could be seen as lying at the heart of politics from the birth of nationalism onwards, or even indeed from the point where nations begin to exist?

Naturally, to all these questions, an extreme variety of responses are to be found, depending upon the viewpoint of the observers and the situations they reflect. In my view, however, in their very dispersion, they all revolve around a single dilemma: the notion of nationalism is constantly dividing. There is always a 'good' and a 'bad' nationalism. There is the one which ends to construct a state or a community and the one which tends to subjugate, to destroy; the one which refers to right and the one which refers to might; the one which tolerates other nationalisms and which may even argue in their defence and include them within a single historical perspective (the great dream of the 'Springtime of the Peoples') and the one which radically excludes them in an imperialist and racist perspective. There is the one which derives from love (even excessive love) and the one which derives from hate. In short, the internal split within nationalism seems as essential – and as difficult to pin down – as the step that leads from 'dying for one's fatherland' to 'killing for one's country' ... The proliferation of 'neighbouring' terms, whether they be synonyms or antonyms, is merely an exteriorization of this split. No one, in my view, has wholly escaped this reinscription of the dilemma within the very concept of nationalism itself (and when it has been evacuated within theory, it has re-entered by the door of practice), but it is particularly visible in the liberal tradition, which is probably to be explained by the very profound ambiguity of the relations between liberalism and nationalism over at least the last two centuries.[11] We also have to say that, by displacing it one or two degrees, racist ideologies may then mimic this dicussion and invade it themselves: is it not the function of notions like 'living space' to raise the question of the 'good side' of imperialism or racism? And is not the neo-racism we see proliferating today, from 'differentialist' anthropology to sociobiology, constantly concerned to distinguish what is supposed to be inevitable and, deep down, useful (a certain xenophobia which induces groups to defend their 'territories' and 'cultural identities' and to maintain the 'proper distance' between them) from what would be useless and in itself harmful (direct violence, acting out), though inevitable if one ignores the elementary exigencies of ethnicity?

How are we to break out of this circle? It is not enough simply to ask, as some recent analysts have done, that value judgements be rejected – that is, that judgement on the consequences of nationalism in different conjunctures be suspended –,[12] or, alternatively, to consider nationalism itself strictly as an ideological effect of the 'objective' process of constitution of nations (and nation states).[13] For the ambivalence of effects forms part of the very history of all nationalisms, and it is precisely this which has to be explained. From this point of view, the analysis of the place of racism in nationalism is decisive: though racism is not equally manifest in all racisms or in all the moments of their history, it none the less always represents a necessary tendency in their constitution. In the last analysis, the overlapping of the two goes back to the circumstances in which the nation states, established upon historically contested *territories*, have striven to control *population* movements, and to the very production of the 'people' as a political community taking precedence over class divisions.

At this point, however, an objection does arise regarding the very terms of the discussion. It is the objection Maxime Rodinson, among others, directs at all those – such as Colette Guillaumin – who insist upon a 'broad' definition of racism.[14] Such a definition seeks to take into account *all* forms of exclusion and depreciation, whether or not they are accompanied by biological theories. It seeks to get back beyond 'ethnic' racism to the origin of the 'race myth' and its genealogical discourse: the 'class racism' of the post-feudal aristocracy. And, most particularly, it seeks to include under the heading 'racism' all forms of minority oppression which, in a formally egalitarian society, lead in different ways to the 'racialization' of various social groups – not just ethnic groups, but women, sexual deviants, the mentally ill, subproletarians and so on – so as to be able to analyse the common mechanism of the naturalization of differences. In Rodinson's view, one ought, however, to choose: either one should make internal and external racism a tendency of nationalism and, beyond this, of ethnocentrism of which nationalism would be the modern form; or one could broaden the definition of racism in order to understand the psychological mechanisms (phobic projection, denial of the real Other overlaid with the signifiers of a phantasmatic alterity), but at the risk of dissolving its historical specificity.[15]

This objection can, however, be met. And it may even be met in such a way that the historical entanglement of nationalism and racism is made all the clearer; but on condition that one advances certain propositions which in part rectify the idea of a 'broad' definition of racism or at least make it more exact:

1. No nation, that is, no national state, has an ethnic basis, which means that nationalism cannot be defined as an ethnocentrism except precisely in the sense of the product of a *fictive* ethnicity. To reason any other way would be to forget that 'peoples' do not exist naturally any more than 'races' do, either by virtue of their ancestry, a community of culture or pre-existing interests. But they do have to institute in real (and therefore in historical) time their imaginary unity *against* other possible unities.

2. The phenomenon of 'depreciation' and 'racialization' which is directed simultaneously against different social groups which are quite different in 'nature' (particularly 'foreign' communities, 'inferior races', women and 'deviants') does not represent a juxtaposition of merely analogous behaviours and discourses applied to a potentially indefinite series of objects independent of each other, but *a historical system of complementary exclusions and dominations which are mutually interconnected.* In other words, it is not in practice simply the case that an 'ethnic racism' and a 'sexual racism' exist in parallel; racism and sexism function together and in particular, *racism always presupposes sexism.* In these conditions a general category of racism is not an abstraction which runs the risk of losing in historical precision and pertinence what it gains in universality; it is, rather, a more concrete notion of taking into account the necessary polymorphism of racism, its overarching function, its connections with the whole set of practices of social normalization and exclusion, as we might demonstrate by reference to neo-racism whose preferred target is not the 'Arab' or the 'Black', but the 'Arab (as) junky' or 'delinquent' or 'rapist' and so on, or equally, rapists and delinquents as 'Arabs' and 'Blacks'.

3. It is this broad structure of racism, which is heterogeneous and yet tightly knit (first in a network of phantasies and, second, through discourses and behaviours), which maintains a necessary relation with *nationalism* and contributes to constituting it by producing the fictive ethnicity around which it is organized.

4. If it is necessary to include in the structural conditions (both symbolic and institutional) of modern racism the fact that the societies in which racism develops are at the same time supposed to be 'egalitarian' societies, in other words, societies which (officially) disregard status differences between individuals, this sociological thesis (advanced most notably by L. Dumont) cannot be abstracted from the national environment itself. In other words, it is not the modern state which is 'egali-

tarian' but the modern (nationalist) nation-state, this equality having as
its internal and external limits the national community and, as its
essential content, the acts which signify it directly (particularly universal
suffrage and political 'citizenship'). It is, first and foremost, an equality
in respect of nationality.[16]

The discussion of this controversy (as of other similar controversies to
which we might refer[17]) is of considerable value to us here, since through
it we begin to grasp that the connection between nationalism and racism
is neither a matter of perversion (for there is no 'pure' essence of
nationalism) nor a question of formal similarity, but a question of historical articulation. What we have to understand is the specific difference of
racism and the way in which, in articulating itself to nationalism, it is, in
its difference, necessary to nationalism. This is to say, by the very same
token, that the articulation of nationalism and racism cannot be dis-
entangled by applying classical schemas of causality, whether mechanistic
(the one as the cause of the other, 'producing' the other according to the
rule of the proportionality of the effects to the cause) or spiritualistic
(the one 'expressing' the other, or giving it its meaning or revealing its
hidden essence). It requires a dialectics of the unity of opposites.
       Nowhere is this necessity more evident than in the debate, which is
forever being reopened, on the 'essence of Nazism', a positive magnet
for all the various forms of hermeneutics of social relations, in which the
political uncertainties of the present are mirrored (and transposed).[18]
       For some, Hitlerian racism is the culmination of nationalism: it
derives from Bismarck, if not indeed from German Romanticism or
Luther, from the defeat of 1918 and the humiliation of the Versailles
Diktat, and provides a project of absolute imperialism with its ideology
(*Lebensraum*, a German Europe). If the coherence of that ideology
seems analogous to the coherence of delirium, then one should see this
as precisely the explanation of its brief, but almost total hold on the
'mass' of the population, whatever their social origins, and on the
'leaders', whose blindness in the end plunged the nation to its doom.
Beyond all the 'revolutionary' deception and conjunctural twists and
turns, the enterprise of world domination was inherent in the
nationalism shared by masses and leaders alike.
       For others, such explanations are doomed always to miss the essential
point, however subtly they might analyse the social forces and intellectual traditions, events and political strategies, and however skilfully
they might relate the monstrous nature of Nazism to the anomalous
course of German history. It was precisely by regarding Nazism as
merely a nationalism analogous to their own – distinguished only by a
difference of degree – that public opinion and the political leaders in the

'democratic' nations of the time deluded themselves as to its goals and thought they could come to an arrangement with it or limit the havoc it might create. Nazism is exceptional (and perhaps shows up a possibility of transgression of the political rationality inscribed in the condition of modern man) because in it the logic of racism overwhelms all other factors, and imposes itself to the detriment of 'pure' nationalist logic, because 'race war', both internal and external, ends up by depriving 'national war' (whose goals of domination remain *positive* goals) of any coherence. Nazism could thus be seen as the very embodiment of that 'nihilism' of which it spoke itself, in which the extermination of the imaginary Enemy, who is seen as the incarnation of Evil (the Jew or the Communist) and self-destruction (more the annihilation of Germany than a confession of failure on the part of its 'racial elite', the SS caste and the Nazi party) meet.

We can see that in this controversy analytic discourses and value judgements are constantly intermingling. History sets itself up as diagnosis of the normal and the pathological and ends up echoing the discourse of its own object, demonizing Nazism which itself demonized its enemies and victims. Yet it is not easy to get out of this circle, since the essential point is not to reduce the phenomenon to conventional generalities, the *practical* impotence of which it precisely revealed. We have the contradictory impression that, with Nazi racism, nationalism both plumbs the greatest depths of its latent and, to borrow Hannah Arendt's expression, tragically 'ordinary' tendencies and yet *goes beyond* itself, and the ordinary form in which it is normally realized, that is, is normally institutionalized to penetrate in a lasting way the 'common sense' of the masses. On the one hand, we can see (admittedly after the event) the irrationality of a racial mythology which ends up dislocating the nation-state whose absolute superiority it proclaims. We can see this as proof that racism, as a complex which combines the banality of daily acts of violence and the 'historical' intoxication of the masses, the bureaucratism of the forced labour and extermination camps and the delirium of the 'world' domination of the 'master race', can no longer be considered a simple aspect of nationalism. But we then have to ask ourselves immediately: How are we to avoid this irrationality becoming its own cause, the exceptional character of Nazi anti-Semitism turning into a sacred mystery, into a speculative vision of history which represents history precisely as the history of Evil (and which, correlatively, represents its victims as the true Lamb of God)? It is not, however, in any way certain that doing the opposite and deducing Nazi racism from German nationalism frees us from all irrationalism. For we have to admit that only a nationalism of an 'extreme' intensity, a nationalism exacerbated by an 'exceptional' series of internal and external conflicts was able to idealize the goals of racism to the point of making the violence wrought by the great number of torturers possible and 'normalizing' this in the eyes of the great mass of other people. The combination of this banality and this idealism tends rather to reinforce the metaphysical idea that German nationalism might itself be 'exceptional' in history: though a paradigm of nationalism in its pathological content in relation to liberalism, it would in the end be irreducible to 'ordinary' nationalism. We here fall back then into the aporias described above of 'good' and 'bad' nationalism.

Now might we not rediscover, in respect of each conjuncture in which racism and nationalism are individualized in discourses, mass movements and specific policies, what the debate on Nazism emphatically exhibits? In this internal connectedness *and* this transgression of rational interests and ends, is there not *the same contradiction*, the terms of which we believe we can see once again in our present-day reality, for example when a movement which carries within it nostalgia for a 'New European Order' and 'colonial heroism' canvasses, as successfully as it has done, the possibility of a 'solution' to the 'immigrant problem'?

Generalizing these thoughts, I shall say then, first, that in the historical 'field' of nationalism, there is always a reciprocity of determination between this and racism.

This reciprocity shows itself initially in the way in which the development of nationalism and its official utilization by the state transforms antagonisms and persecutions that have quite other origins into racism in the modern sense (and ascribes the verbal markers of ethnicity to them). This runs from the way in which, since the times of the *Reconquista* in Spain, theological anti-Judaism was transposed into genealogical exclusion based on 'purity of blood' at the same time as the *raza* was launching itself upon the conquest of the New World, down to the way in which, in modern Europe, the new 'dangerous classes' of the international proletariat tend to be subsumed under the category of 'immigration', which becomes the main name given to race within the crisis-torn nations of the post-colonial era.

This reciprocal determination shows itself again in the way in which all the 'official nationalisms' of the nineteenth and twentieth centuries, aiming to confer the political and cultural unity of a nation on the heterogeneity of a pluri-ethnic state,[19] have used anti-Semitism: as if the domination of a culture and a more or less fictively unified nationality (for example, the Russian, German or Romanian) over a hierarchically ordered diversity of 'minority' ethnicities and cultures marked down for assimilation should be 'compensated' and mirrored by the racializing persecution of an absolutely singular *pseudo-ethnic group* (without their own territory and without a 'national' language) which represents the common internal enemy of all cultures and all dominated populations.[20]

Finally, it shows itself in the history of the national liberation struggles, whether they be directed against the old empires of the first period of colonization, against the dynastic multinational states or against the modern colonial empires. There is no question of reducing these processes to a single model. And yet it cannot be by chance that the genocide of the Indians became systematic immediately after the United States – the 'first of the new nations' in Lipset's famous expression – achieved independence.[21] Just as it cannot be by chance, to follow the illuminating analysis proposed by Bipan Chandra, that 'nationalism' and 'communalism' were formed together in India, and continue into the present to be inextricable (largely because of the early historical fusion of Indian nationalism with Hindu communalism).[22] Or again that independent Algeria made assimilating the 'Berbers' to 'Arabness' the key test of the nation's will in its struggle with the multicultural heritage of colonization. Or, indeed, that the State of Israel, faced with an internal and an external enemy and the impossible gamble of forging an 'Israeli nation' developed a powerful racism directed both against the 'Eastern' Jews (called 'Blacks') and the Palestinians, who were driven out of their lands and colonized.[23]

From this accumulation of entirely individual but historically linked cases there results what might be called the cycle of historical reciprocity of nationalism and racism, which is the temporal figure of the progressive domination of the system of nation-states over other social formations. Racism is constantly emerging out of nationalism, not only towards the exterior but towards the interior. In the United States, the systematic institution of segregation, which put a halt to the first civil rights movement, coincided with America's entry into world imperialist competition and with its subscribing to the idea that the Nordic races have a hegemonic mission. In France, the elaboration of an ideology of the 'French race', rooted in the past of 'the soil and the dead', coincides with the beginning of mass immigration, the preparation for revenge against Germany and the founding of the colonial empire. And nationalism emerges out of racism, in the sense that it would not constitute itself as the ideology of a 'new' nation if the official nationalism against which it were reacting were not profoundly racist: thus Zionism comes out of anti-Semitism and Third World nationalisms come out of colonial racism. Within this grand cycle, however, there is a multitude of individual cycles. Thus to take but one example, a crucial one in French national history, the defeat suffered by anti-Semitism after the Dreyfus Affair, which was symbolically incorporated into the ideals of the republican regime, opened up to a certain extent the possibility of a colonial 'good conscience' and made it possible for many years for the notion of

racism to be dissociated from that of colonization (at least in metro-
politan perceptions).

Secondly, however, I argue that *the gap subsists between the representations and practices of nationalism and racism.* It is a fluctuating gap
between the two poles of a contradiction and a forced identification –
and it is perhaps, as the Nazi example shows, when this identification is
apparently complete that the contradiction is most marked. Not a
contradiction between nationalism and racism as such, but a contradiction between determinate *forms*, between the political objectives of
nationalism and the crystallization of racism on a particular object, at a
particular moment: for example, when nationalism undertakes to
'integrate' a dominated, potentially autonomous population, as in
'French' Algeria or 'French' New Caledonia. From this point onwards, I
therefore concentrate on this gap and the paradoxical forms it may
assume, the better to understand the point that was emerging from most
of the examples to which I have referred: namely, that racism is not an
'expression' of nationalism, but *a supplement of nationalism* or more
precisely *a supplement internal to nationalism*, always in excess of it, but
always indispensable to its constitution and yet always still insufficient to
achieve its project, just as nationalism is both indispensable and always
insufficient to achieve the formation of the *nation* or the project of a
'nationalization' of society.

The Paradoxes of Universality

The fact that the theories and strategies of nationalism are always caught
up in the contradiction between universality and particularism is a
generally accepted idea which can be developed in an infinite range of
ways. In actual fact, nationalism is a force for uniformity and rationaliza-
tion and it also nurtures the fetishes of a national identity which derives
from the origins of the nation and has, allegedly, to be preserved from
any form of dispersal. What interests me here is not the general form of
this contradiction, but the way it is exhibited by racism.

In fact racism figures *both* on the side of the universal and the particular. The excess it represents in relation to nationalism, and therefore
the supplement it brings to it, tends both to universalize it, to correct its
lack of universality, and to particularize it, to correct its lack of specificity. In other words, racism actually adds to the ambiguous nature of
nationalism, which means that, through racism, nationalism engages in a
'headlong flight forward', a metamorphosis of its material contradictions
into ideal contradictions.[24]

Theoretically, speaking, racism is a philosophy of history or, more accurately, a *historiosophy* which makes history the consequence of a hidden secret revealed to men about their own nature and their own birth. It is a philosophy which makes visible the invisible cause of the fate of societies and peoples; not to know that cause is seen as evidence of degeneracy or of the historical power of the evil.[25] There are, of course, aspects of historiosophy in providentialist theologies, in philosophies of progress and also, indeed, in dialectical philosophies. Marxism is not exempt and this has played quite some part in keeping alive a semblance of symmetry between the 'class struggle' and the 'racial struggle', between the engine of progress and the enigma of evolution and therefore the possibilities of translating the one ideological universe into the other. This symmetry does, however, have very clear limits. I am not so much thinking here of the abstract antithesis between rationalism and irrationalism, nor that between optimism and pessimism, even though it is true (and crucial in practice) that most racist philosophies present themselves as inversions of the theme of progress in terms of decadence, degeneracy and the degradation of the national culture, identity and integrity.[26] But I think, in fact, that unlike a historiosophy of the racial or cultural struggle or the antagonism between the 'elite' and the 'masses', a historical dialectic can never present itself as the mere elaboration of a Manichaean theme. It has to explain not just the 'struggle' and the 'conflict', but the *historical constitution of the forces in struggle and the forms of struggle* or, in other words, ask critical questions in respect of its own representation of the course of history. From this point of view, the historiosophies of race and culture are radically acritical.

Certainly there is not *a* racist philosophy, particularly since racist thinking does not always assume a systematic form. Contemporary neo-racism directly confronts us today with a variety of historical and national forms: the myth of the 'racial struggle', evolutionist anthropology, 'differentialist' culturalism, sociobiology and so on. Around this constellation, there gravitate sociopolitical discourses and techniques such as demography, criminology, eugenics. We ought also to unravel the threads of the genealogy of the racist theories which, through Gobineau or Chamberlain, but also the 'psychology of peoples' and sociological evolutionism, go back to the anthropology and natural history of the Enlightenment,[27] and as far as what L. Sala-Molins calls 'White-biblical' theology.[28] To get to the heart of the matter as quickly as possible, I want first of all to recapitulate the intellectual operations that have always been at work – for more than three centuries now – in theoretical racism, operations that allow it to articulate itself to what we may call everyday racism's 'desire to know'.

First of all, there is the fundamental operation of *classification* – that

is, the reflection within the human species of the difference that constitutes it, the search for criteria by which men can be said to be 'men':
What makes them so? To what extent are they so? Of what kind are
they? Such classification is presupposed by any form of hierarchical
ranking. And it can lead to such a ranking, for the more or less coherent
construction of a hierarchical table of the groups which make up the
human race is a privileged representation of its unity in and through
inequality. It can also, however, be regarded as sufficient in itself, as
pure 'differentialism'. Or at least apparently so, since the criteria used
for differentiation can never be 'neutral' in a real context. They contain
within them sociopolitical values which are contested in practice and
which have to be imposed, in a roundabout way, by the use of ethnicity
or culture.[29]

Classification and hierarchy are operations of naturalization *par
excellence* or, more accurately, of projection of historical and social
differences into the realm of an imaginary nature. But we must not be
taken in by the self-evident character of the result. 'Human nature',
closely shadowed by a system of 'natural differences' within the human
species, in no way represents an unmediated category. In particular, it
necessarily has built into it sexual schemas, both on the 'effect' or
symptoms side ('racial characteristics', whether psychological or
somatic, are always metaphors for the difference between the sexes) and
on the 'cause' side (interbreeding, heredity). Hence the central importance of the criterion of *genealogy* which is anything but a category of
'pure' nature: it is a symbolic category articulated to relative juridical
notions and, first and foremost, to the legitimacy of filiation. There is
therefore a latent contradiction in the 'naturalism' of race, which has to
be overcome in a movement beyond this towards an originary, 'immemorial' 'super-nature', which is always already projected into an
imaginary divided between good and evil, innocence and perversion.[30]

This first aspect immediately introduces a second: every theoretical
racism draws upon *anthropological universals*. It is even, in a sense, the
way it selects and combines these that constitutes its development as a
doctrine. Among these universals we naturally find the notions of
'humanity's genetic inheritance' or 'cultural tradition', but we also find
more specific concepts such as human aggression or, conversely, 'preferential' altruism,[31] which brings us to the different variants of the ideas of
xenophobia, ethnocentrism and tribalism. We find here the possibility of
a double game which allows neo-racism to attack anti-racist criticism
from the rear, sometimes directly dividing and hierarchizing humanity
and, at others, turning into an explanation of the 'natural necessity for
racism' itself. And these ideas are in turn 'grounded' in other universals,
which are either sociological (for example, the idea that endogamy is a

condition and a norm of every human grouping, and therefore exogamy a cause of anxiety and something universally prohibited) or psychological (for example, suggestion and hypnotic contagion, concepts on which crowd psychology has traditionally fallen back).

In all these universals we can see the persistent presence of the same 'question': that of *the difference between humanity and animality*, the problematic character of which is re-utilized to interpret the conflicts within society and history. In classical Social Darwinism, we thus have the paradoxical figure of an evolution which has to extract humanity properly so-called (that is, culture, the technological mastery of nature – including the mastery of human nature: eugenics) from animality, but to do so by the means which characterized animality (the 'survival of the fittest') or, in other words, by an 'animal' competition between the different degrees of humanity. In contemporary sociobiology and ethology, the 'socio-affective' behaviours of individuals and, most importantly, of human groups (aggression and altruism) are represented as the indelible mark of animality within evolved humanity. In differentialist culturalism, one might think that this theme was totally absent. I believe it does exist, however, in an oblique form: in the frequent coupling of the discourse on cultural difference with that on ecology (as if the isolation of cultures were the precondition for the preservation of the 'natural milieu' of the human race) and, especially, in the thoroughgoing metaphorization of cultural categories in terms of individuality, selection, reproduction and interbreeding. Man's animality, animality within and against man – hence the systematic 'bestialization' of individuals and racialized human groups – is thus the means specific to theoretical racism for conceptualizing human historicity. A paradoxically static, if not indeed regressive, history, even when offering a stage for the affirmation of the 'will' of the superior beings.

Just as racist movements represent a paradoxical synthesis of the contradictory ideologies of revolution and reaction, which, in certain circumstances, is all the more effective for being paradoxical, so theoretical racism represents the ideal synthesis of transformation and fixity, of repetition and destiny. The 'secret', the discovery of which it endlessly rehearses, is that of a humanity eternally leaving animality behind and eternally threatened with falling into the grasp of animality. That is why, when it substitutes the signifier of culture for that of race, it has always to attach this to a 'heritage', and 'ancestry', a 'rootedness', all signifiers of the imaginary face-to-face relation between man and his origins.

It would therefore be very wide of the mark to believe that theoretical racism is incompatible with any form of transcendance, as has been argued by some recent critics of culturalism who, moreover, commit the same error in respect of nationalism.[32] On the contrary, racist theories necessarily contain an aspect of sublimation, an idealization of the species, the privileged figure of which is aesthetic; this is why that idealization necessarily culminates in the description and valorization of a certain type of man, demonstrating the human ideal, both in terms of body and of mind (from the 'Teuton' and the 'Celt' of old to the 'gifted child' of today's 'developed' nations). This ideal connects up both with the first man (non-degenerate) and the man of the future (the superman). This is a crucial point both in understanding the way in which racism and sexism are articulated (the importance of the phallic signifier in racism) and for seeing the connection between racism and the exploitation of labour and political alienation. The aestheticization of social relations is a crucial contribution of racism to the constitution of the projective field of politics. Even the idealization of the techno-cratic values of efficiency presupposes an aesthetic sublimation. It is no accident that the modern manager whose enterprises are to dominate the planet is simultaneously sportsman and womanizer. And the symbolic reversal which, in the socialist tradition, has, by contrast, valor-ized the figure of the worker as the perfect type of future humanity, as the 'transition' from extreme alienation to extreme potency, has been accompanied, as we know, by an intense aestheticization and sexualiz-ation, which has allowed it to be recuperated by fascism and which also forces us to ask what elements of racism re-surfaced historically in 'socialist humanism'.[33]

The remarkable constancy of these historical and anthropological themes allows us to begin to cast light on the ambiguous character of the relations which theoretical racism has maintained over two centuries with humanist (or universalist) ideologies. The critique of 'biological' racisms has given rise to the idea, which is especially widespread in France, that racism is, by definition, incompatible with humanism and therefore, theoretically speaking, an anti-humanism, since it valorizes 'life' to the detriment of properly human values, such as morality, knowledge, individual dignity. Now there is a confusion and a mis-understanding here. Confusion because the 'biologism' of the racial theories (from anthropometry to Social Darwinism and sociobiology) is not a valorization of life as such, still less an application of biology; rather it is a vitalized metaphor of certain sexualized social values: energy, decisiveness, initiative and generally all the virile representations of domination or, conversely, passivity, sensuality, femininity, or again, solidarity, *esprit de corps* and generally all the representations of the 'organic' unity of society along the lines of an endogamous 'family'. This vitalist metaphor is associated with a hermeneutics which makes somatic traits into symptoms of the psychological or cultural 'character'. Along-side this confusion, however, there is also a misunderstanding, because biological racism itself has never been a way of dissolving human specificity into the larger field of life, evolution or nature, but, on the contrary, a way of applying pseudo-biological notions to constitute the human race and improve it or preserve it from decline. Just as it is also closely allied to a morality of heroism and asceticism. It is here that the Nietzschean dialectic of the *Übermensch* and the 'higher man' may be illuminating. As Colette Guillaumin puts it so excellently: 'These categories, which are marked by biological difference, are situated within the human race and regarded as being so. This point is crucial. In fact, the human species is the key notion; it is in terms of this notion that racism has been and is, daily, constituted.'[34] It would not be so difficult to organize the struggle against racism in the intellectual sphere if the 'crime against humanity' were not being perpetrated in the name of and by means of a humanist discourse. It is perhaps above all this fact which confronts us with what, in another context, Marx called the 'bad side' of history, which does, however, constitute its reality.

The paradoxical presence of a humanist, universalist component in the ideological constitution of racism does, however, enable us also to cast some light on the profound ambivalence of the signifier of 'race' (and its current substitutes) from the point of view of national unity and identity.

As a supplement of particularity, racism first presents itself as a *super-nationalism*. Mere political nationalism is perceived as weak, as a conciliatory position in a universe of competition or pitiless warfare (the language of international 'economic warfare' is more widespread today than it has ever been). Racism sees itself as an 'integral' nationalism, which only has meaning (and chances of success) if it is based on the integrity of the nation, integrity both towards the outside and on the inside. What theoretical racism calls 'race' or 'culture' (or both together) is therefore a continued origin of the nation, a concentrate of the qualities which belong to the nationals 'as their own'; it is in the 'race of its children' that the nation could contemplate its own identity in the pure state. Consequently, it is around race that it must unite, with race – an 'inheritance' to be preserved from any kind of degradation – that it must identify both 'spiritually' and 'physically' or 'in its bones' (the same goes for culture as the substitute or inward expression of race).

This means, of course, that racism underlies the claims for annexation ('return') to the national 'body' of 'lost' individuals and populations (for example, the Sudeten or Tyrolean Germans) which is, as is well known, closely linked to what might be called the pan-ic developments of nationalism (Pan-Slavism, Pan-Germanism, Pan-Turanianism, Pan-Arabism, Pan-Americanism ...). Above all, however, it means that racism constantly induces an excess of 'purism' as far as the nation is concerned: for the nation to be itself, it has to be racially or culturally pure. It therefore has to isolate within its bosom, before eliminating or expelling them, the 'false', 'exogenous', 'cross-bred', 'cosmopolitan' elements. This is an obsessional imperative which is directly responsible for the racialization of social groups whose collectivizing features will be set up as stigmata of exteriority and impurity, whether these relate to style of life, beliefs or ethnic origins. But this process of forming the race into a super-nationality leads to an endless upping of the stakes. In theory, it ought to be possible to recognize by some sure criterion of appearance or behaviour those who are 'true nationals' or 'essential nationals', such as the 'French French', or the 'English English' (of whom Ben Anderson speaks with regard to the hierarchy of caste and the categorization of civil servants in the British Empire), the authentically 'Teutonic' German (cf. the distinction made by Nazism between *Volkszugehörigkeit* and *Staatsangehörigkeit*), or the authentic American-ness of the WASP, not to mention of course the Whiteness of the Afrikaner citizen. In practice, however, it has to be constituted out of juridical conventions or ambiguous cultural particularisms, by imaginarily denying other collectivizing features, other systems of irreducible 'differences', which sets the quest for nationality off once again through race towards an inaccessible goal. Moreover, it is often the case that the criteria invested with a 'racial' (and *a fortiori* cultural) significance in this way are, largely, criteria of social class or that ultimately they symbolically 'select' an elite which has *already* been selected by economic and political class inequalities, or that the dominated classes are those whose 'racial composition' and 'cultural identity' are the most questionable. These effects run directly counter to the nationalist objective, which is not to re-create an elitism, but to found a populism; not to cast suspicion upon the historical and social heterogeneity of the 'people', but to exhibit its essential unity.

This is why racism always tends to operate in an inverted fashion, drawing upon the projection mechanism we have already mentioned in regard to the role of anti-Semitism in European nationalisms: the racial-cultural identity of 'true nationals' remains invisible, but it can be inferred (and is ensured) *a contrario* by the alleged, quasi-hallucinatory visibility of the 'false nationals': the Jews, 'wogs', immigrants, 'Pakis', natives, Blacks ... In other words, it remains constantly in doubt and in danger; the fact that the 'false' is too visible will never guarantee that the 'true' is visible enough. By seeking to circumscribe the common essence of nationals, racism thus inevitably becomes involved in the obsessional quest for a 'core' of authenticity that cannot be found, shrinks the category of nationality and de-stabilizes the historical nation.[35] This can lead, in an extreme case, to the reversal of the racial phantasm: since it is impossible to *find* racial-national purity and guarantee its provenance from the origins of the people, it becomes necessary to *create* it in conformity with the ideal of a (super-)national superman. This is the meaning of Nazi eugenics. Yet we should add that the same orientation was inherent in all the sociotechnologies of human selection, indeed in a certain tradition of 'typically British' education, and that it is resurgent today in the 'educational' application of the psychology of differential mental abilities (whose ultimate weapon is IQ).

This also explains the rapidity with which the transition from super-nationalism to racism as *supranationalism* occurs. We must take absolutely seriously the fact that the racial theories of the nineteenth and twentieth centuries define communities of language, descent and tradition which do not, as a general rule, coincide with historical states, even though they always obliquely refer to one or more of these. This means that the dimension of universality of theoretical racism, the anthropological aspects of which we have sketched above, plays an essential role here: it permits a 'specific universalization' and therefore an idealization of nationalism. It is this aspect which I should like to examine in the last part of this chapter.[36]

The classical myths of race, in particular the myth of Aryanism, do not refer initially to the nation but to class, and they do so from an aristocratic perspective. In these conditions, the 'superior' race (or the superior races, the 'pure races' in Gobineau's writings) can never, by definition, coincide with the whole of the national population, nor be restricted to it.[37] Which means that the 'visible', institutional national collectivity must regulate its transformations by refernce to another, invisible collectivity, which transcends frontiers and is, by definition, transnational. But what was true of the aristocracy, and might seem to be the transient consequence of the modes of thought of a period in which nationalism was only beginning to assert itself, remains true of all later racist theories, whether their referent be biological (in fact, as we have seen, somatic) or cultural in nature. Skin colour, skull shape, intellectual predispositions or mind are beyond positive nationality; this is simply the other side of the obsession with purity. The consequence is the following paradox, which a number of those who have studied the question have run up against: there actually is a racist 'internationalism' or 'supranationalism' which tends to idealize timeless or transhistorical communities such as the 'Indo-Europeans', 'the West', 'Judaeo-Christian civilization' and therefore communities which are at the same time both closed and open, which have no frontiers or whose only frontiers are, as Fichte had it, 'internal' ones, inseparable from the individuals themselves or, more precisely, from their 'essence' (what was once called their 'soul'). In fact these are the frontiers of an ideal humanity.[38]

Here the excess of racism over nationalism, though it continues to be constitutive of nationalism, takes on a form that is the opposite of what we saw above: it stretches it out to the dimensions of an infinite totality. Hence the similarities to – and more or less caricatural borrowings from – theology, from 'gnosis'. Hence also the possibilities of a slide towards the racism of the universalist theologies where these are tightly bound to modern nationalism. This explains, above all, why a racial signifier has to transcend national differences and organize 'transnational' solidarities so as to be able, in return, to ensure the effectivity of nationalism. Thus anti-Semitism functioned on a European scale: each nationalism saw in the Jew (who was himself contradictorily conceived as both irreducibly inassimilable to others and as cosmopolitan, as member of an 'original' people and as rootless) its own specific enemy and the representative of all other 'hereditary enemies'; this meant, then, that all nationalisms were defined against the *same* foil, the same 'stateless other', and this has been a component of the very idea of Europe as the land of 'modern' nation-states or, in other words, of civilization. At the same time, the European or Euro-American nations, locked in a bitter struggle to divide up the world into colonial empires, recognized that they formed a community and shared an 'equality' through that very competition, a community and an equality to which they gave the name 'White'. We might adduce similar descriptions of the universalist extensions of Arab or Jewish-Israeli or Soviet nationality here. When historians speak of this universalist project within nationalism, meaning by that an aspiration towards – and a programme of – cultural imperialism (imposing an 'English', 'German', 'French', 'American' or 'Soviet' conception of man and universal culture on the whole of humanity) and yet evade the question of racism, their arguments are at best incomplete, for it is only as 'racism' – that is to say, only to the extent that the imperialist nation has been imagined and presented as the specific instrument of a more essential mission and destiny which other peoples cannot but recognize – that imperialism has been able to turn itself from a mere enterprise of conquest into an enterprise of universal domination, the founding of a 'civilization'.

From these reflections and hypotheses I shall draw two conclusions. The first is that, in these conditions, we should be less surprised that contemporary racist movements have given rise to the formation of international 'axes', to what Wilhelm Reich provocatively called 'nationalist internationalism'.[39] Reich's remark was provocative but accurate, for his concern was to understand the mimetic effects both of that paradoxical internationalism and of another one, which was increasingly tending to realize itself in the form of an 'internationalist nationalism' just as, following the example of the 'socialist homeland' and around it and beneath, the Communist parties were turning into 'national parties', a development which in some cases drew upon anti-Semitism. Just as decisive was the symmetry with which, since the middle of the nineteenth century, the two representations of history as 'class struggle' and 'race struggle' were ranged against each other, each of these being conceived as 'international civil wars' in which the fate of humanity was to be played out. Both were supranational in this sense, though the distinction between them, which cannot be evaded, was that the class struggle was supposed to dissolve nationalities and nationalisms, whereas the race struggle was supposed to establish for all time each nation's status and place in the hierarchy of nations, thus enabling nationalism to fuse specifically national and socially conservative elements (militant anti-socialism and anti-communism). It was as a supplement to universality, invested in the constitution of a supranationalism, that the ideology of the race struggle was able in a way to draw a line around the universalism of the class struggle and set against it a different 'conception of the world'.

My second conclusion is that theoretical racism is in no sense the absolute antithesis of humanism. Paradoxically, in the excess of signification and activism which marks the transition from nationalism to racism, while still remaining within nationalism, and which enables this latter to crystallize the violence that is specific to it, the aspect which wins out is universality. What makes us hesitate to admit this and draw the necessary conclusions from it is the confusion which continues to reign between a theoretical humanism and a practical humanism. If we identify this latter with a politics and an ethics of the defence of civil rights without limitations or exceptions, we can clearly see that racism and humanism are incompatible, and we have no difficulty in understanding why effective anti-racism has had to constitute itself as a 'logically coherent' humanism. This does not, however, mean that practical humanism is necessarily founded on theoretical humanism (that is, on a doctrine which makes man as a species the origin and end of declared and established rights). It can also be founded on a theology, on a non-religious form of wisdom subordinating the idea of man to the idea of nature or, which is decidedly different, on an analysis of social conflict and liberation movements which substitutes specific social relations for the general notions of man and the human race. Conversely, the necessary link between anti-racism and a practical humanism in no way prevents theoretical racism from also being a theoretical humanism. Which means that the conflict unfolds here within the ideological universe of humanism, where the outcome is decided on the basis of political criteria other than the simple distinction between the humanism of identity and the humanism of differences. Absolute

civic equality, taking precedence over the question of 'belonging' to a
particular state, represents a formulation decidedly more solid than
humanist generalities. This is why I believe we have to read the link
between these notions in a way that is the reverse of the traditional
reading; we have, so to speak, to 'set it back on its feet': a practical
humanism can only be achieved today if it is, first of all, an effective
anti-racism. This, admittedly, means pitting one idea of man against
another, but, indissociably from that, it means setting an internationalist
politics of citizenship against a nationalist one.[40]

Notes

1. The most thorough recent account is that by René Gallissot, *Misère de l'anti-racisme*, Editions Arcantère, Paris 1985.

2. Already, in her book *Race and Racism* of 1942 (republished by Routledge &
Kegan Paul, London 1983), this was the objective of Ruth Benedict. She does not,
however, really distinguish between nation, nationalism and culture, or rather she tends to
'culturalize' racism by the way of 'historicizing' it as an aspect of nationalism.

3. Cf., for example, Raoul Girardet's article 'Nation: 4. Le nationalisme', *Encyclopaedia universalis*.

4. As I have argued in an earlier study, 'Sujets ou citoyens? – Pour l'égalité', *Les Temps modernes*, Special number: *L'Immigration maghrébine en France*, 1984.

5. The category of delirium springs spontaneously to mind when one is attempting to
describe the complex of racism, by reason of the way in which racist discourse disavows the
real while projecting scenarios of aggression and persecution. It cannot, however, be
employed without correctives, on the one hand, because it runs the risk of masking the
activity of thought which racism always entails and, on the other hand, because the notion
of *collective delirium* comes very close to being a contradiction in terms.

6. Each of the classes of the 'new' nations of old colonial humanity thus projects its
social difference from the others in ethnico-cultural terms.

7. Benedict Anderson, *Imagined Communities: Reflections on the Origin and Spread
of Nationalism*, Verso, London 1983, pp. 129 *et seq.*

8. This specular structure seems to me essential: to the 'underdeveloped', the 'over-developed' are those who more than ever exhibit racist contempt; to the 'overdeveloped',
the 'underdeveloped' are mainly defined by the way they mutually despise one another.
For each group, racism is 'the work of the others' or, more precisely, the other is the site of
racism. But the frontier between 'overdevelopment' and 'underdevelopment' has begun to
shift about uncontrollably: no one can say exactly who is the other.

9. Hence the problems surrounding the 'process of educating memory' with which
anti-fascist organizations are trying to confront the current threat, particularly if they
believe that the potential of the Nazi model derives from the occulting of genocide. In this
regard, the activities of the 'revisionist' historians function as a real trap, since they are
essentially a way of endlessly speaking about the gas chambers in the highly ambivalent
mode of denial. Denouncing the concealment of the Nazi genocide by racists who really are
anti-Semites will unfortunately not be enough to allow a collective recognition of what
anti-Semitism and anti-Arabism have in common to emerge. However, unmasking the
nostalgia for Nazism within the leaders' speeches will also not be sufficient to enlighten the
'mass' of ordinary racists as to the displacement which they effect daily, but which largely
occurs without their knowledge. This is true, at least, as long as this indispensable
educational process does not extend to a complete explanation of contemporary racism as a
system of thought and a social relation, the condensed expression of a whole history.

10. For what is both a dogged and nuanced analysis of this contradiction, it would only be right to refer the reader to the whole of Maxime Rodinson's writings and, in particular, to the texts assembled in *Marxisme et monde musulman*, Editions de Seuil, Paris 1972 and *Peuple juif ou problème juif?*, Maspero, Paris 1981.

11. The primary question for liberal historians of nationalism (either as 'ideology' or as 'politics') is: 'Where and when does the transition from 'liberal nationalism' to 'imperialist nationalism' occur? Cf. Hannah Arendt, 'Imperialism', Part II of *The Origins of Totalitarianism*, André Deutsch, London 1986, and Hans Kohn, *The Idea of Nationalism. A Study of Its Origins and Background*, New York 1944. Their common answer to this question is that it occurs between the 'universalist' revolutions of the eighteenth century and the 'Romanticism' of the nineteenth, which begins in Germany and then extends over the whole of Europe and finally the whole world in the twentieth century. Examining the question more closely, however, it turns out that the French Revolution could already be said to contain within itself these two contradictory aspects. It is thus the French Revolution that caused nationalism to 'go off the rails'.

12. Cf. Tom Nairn's caveats in 'The Modern Janus', *New Left Review*, no. 94, 1975 (reprinted in *The Break-Up of Britain*, New Left Books, London 1977). See the critique by Eric Hobsbawm, 'Some Reflections on The Break-Up of Britain', *New Left Review*, no. 105, 1977.

13. Which is not only a Marxist position but also the thesis of other 'economistic' thinkers in the liberal tradition. Cf. Ernest Gellner, *Nations and Nationalism*, Oxford 1983.

14. Colette Guillaumin, *L'Idéologie raciste. Genèse et langage actuel*, Mouton, Paris/ The Hague 1972; M. Rodinson, 'Quelques thèses critiques sur la démarche poliakovienne', in M. Olender, ed., *Racisme, mythes et sciences*. See also M. Rodinson's article 'Nation: 3. Nation et idéologie', *Encyclopaedia universalis*.

15. This may usefully be compared with Erving Goffmann, *Stigma. Notes on the Management of Spoiled Identity*, Penguin, Harmondsworth 1968.

16. Cf. L. Dumont, *Essai sur l'individualisme*, Editions de Seuil, Paris 1983.

17. Cf. the debate between Tom Nairn and Benedict Anderson, in *The Break-Up of Britain* and *Imagined Communities*, on the relations between 'nationalism', 'patriotism' and 'racism'.

18. Cf. the excellent presentation by P. Ayçoberry in *La Question nazie. Essai sur les interprétations du national-socialisme, 1922–1975*, Editions de Seuil, Paris 1979.

19. Among other recent accounts, see Benedict Anderson, *Imagined Communities*, a happy parallel between the practices and discourses of Russification and Anglicization.

20. Cf. Léon Poliakov, *Histoire de l'antisémitisme*, new edn (Le Livre de Poche Pluriel), vol. II, pp. 259 *et seq.*: Madeleine Rebérioux, 'L'Essor du racisme nationaliste', in P. de Comarmond and C. Duchet, eds, *Racisme et société*, Maspero, Paris 1969.

21. Cf. R. Ertel and G. Fabre and E. Marienstras, *En marge. Les minorités aux Etats-Unis*, Maspero, Paris 1974, pp. 287 *et seq.*

22. Bipan Chandra, *Nationalism and Colonialism in Modern India*, Orient Longman, New Delhi 1979, pp. 287 *et seq.*

23. Cf. Haroun Jamous, *Israël et ses juifs. Essai sur les limites du volontarisme*, Maspero, Paris 1982.

24. It has often been thought possible to argue that nationalism, unlike the other great political theories of the nineteenth and twentieth centuries, lacked a theory and theorists (cf. Anderson, *Imagined Communities*; Isaiah Berlin, 'Nationalism – Past Neglect and Present Powers', in *Against the Current: Essays in the History of Ideas*, Oxford 1981). This is to forget that very often racism provides nationalism with its theories, just as it provides it with a daily stock of images, thus figuring at the two poles of the 'ideological movement'.

25. Cf. M. Rodinson on the function of *kerygma* in ideological movements: 'Nature et fonction des mythes dans les mouvements socio-politiques d'après deux exemples comparés: communisme marxiste et nationalisme arabe', *Marxisme et monde musulman*, pp. 245 *et seq.*

26. The introduction of the 'pessimistic' theme of degeneracy into Social Darwinism, when it clearly has no place in the Darwinian theory of natural selection, is an essential

stage in the ideological exploitation of the theory of evolution (playing on the double meaning of the notion of heredity). Not every racism is categorically pessimistic, though all are so hypothetically: the superior race (culture) is lost (and human civilization with it) if it ends up being 'swamped' by barbarians or lesser mortals. The differentialist version states that *all* races (cultures) are lost (and thus human civilization) if they all come to swamp each other with their diversity, if the 'order' which they constitute as distinct cultures dissipates, to be replaced by the entropy of a standardized 'mass culture'. Historical pessimism entails a voluntarist or 'decisionist' conception of politics: only a radical decision, expressing the antithesis which exists between pure will and the course of events, between men of will and men of passivity, can counter or indeed reverse the progress of decadence. Hence the way Marxism (and, more generally, socialism) comes dangerously close to these conceptions when it pushes its representation of historical determinism to the point of *catastrophism*, which, in its turn, entails a 'decisionist' conception of revolution.

27. Cf. especially the works of Michèle Duchet: *Anthropologie et histoire au siècle des Lumières*, Maspero, Paris 1971; 'Racisme et sexualité au XVIIIe siècle' in L. Poliakov *et al.*, *Ni juif ni grec. Entretiens sur le racisme* (II), Mouton, Paris/The Hague 1978; 'Du Noir au blanc, ou la cinquième génération' in L. Poliakov *et al. Le Couple interdit. Entretiens sur le racisme* (III), Mouton, Paris/The Hague 1980.

28. Cf. Louis Sala-Molins, *Le Code noir ou le calvaire de Canaan*, PUF, Paris 1987.

29. Differentialism displaces discrimination by transferring it from the immediate appearance of the groups being classified to the criteria of classification, thus constituting a 'fallback position' for racism. It also replaces the idea that 'races' are naturally given with the notion that 'racist attitudes' are naturally given. See this volume chapter 1, where I draw on recent analyses by C. Guillaumin, V. de Rudder, M. Barker and P. -A. Taguieff of racist discourse in France and Britain.

30. On nature as 'phantasmatic mother' in racist and sexist ideologies, cf. C. Guillaumin, 'Nature et histoire. A propos d'un "matérialisme"' in *Le Racisme, mythes et sciences*. On genealogy and heredity, cf. Pierre Legendre, *L'Inestimable objet de la transmission*, Fayard, Paris 1985.

31. Compare the way in which sociobiology hierarchizes 'altruistic sentiments': first the immediate family, then kin–kin altruism and lastly the ethnic community which is supposed to represent an extension of this. Cf. Martin Barker, *The New Racism. Conservatives and the Ideology of the Tribe*, Junction Books, London 1981.

32. Cf. A. Finkielkraut, *La Défaite de la pensée*, Gallimard, Paris 1987.

33. On Nazi thought as an aestheticization of politics, cf. Philippe Lacoue-Labarthe, *Heidegger, Art and Politics*, transl. C. Tirner, Basil Blackwell, Oxford 1990. Pierre Ayçoberry, *La Question nazie*, p. 31, notes that Nazi aesthetics 'has the function of obliterating the traces of the class struggle by situating each category firmly in its proper place in the racial community: the rooted peasant, the worker as athlete of production and women in the home'. Cf. also A.G. Rabinbach, 'L'Esthétique de la production sous le IIIe Reich', *Recherches*, nos 32–3, 1978.

34. Guillaumin, *L'Idéologie raciste*, p. 6.

35. This gives rise to a great deal of casuistry: if it has to be admitted that French nationality includes innumerable successive generations of migrants and descendants of migrants, their spiritual incorporation into the nation will be justified on the grounds of their capacity to be assimilated, this being understood as a predisposition to Frenchness. It will, however, always be possible (as it was with the *conversos* when they came before the Inquisition) to question whether their assimilation is not merely superficial, not pure simulation.

36. Hannah Arendt does not relate the 'secret meaning' perceived by a 'sixth sense', which she speaks of in the concluding chapter of *The Origins of Totalitarianism* (p. 471), to a process of idealization, but to the coercive force of terror which she sees as being inherent in the compulsion for 'ideological logicality'. Even less does she see it as connecting with a variety of humanism; it relates rather to the absorption of the human will into the anonymous movement of History or Nature, which the totalitarian movements see it as their task to 'speed up'.

37. On Gobineau, see especially the study by Colette Guillaumin, 'Aspects latents du racisme chez Gobineau', *Cahiers internationaux de sociologie*, vol. XLII, 1967.

38. One of the purest examples in contemporary literature is provided by the works of Ernst Jünger. See, for example, *Der gordische Knoten*, Klostermann, Frankfurt-am-Main 1953.

39. Cf. Wilhelm Reich, *Les Hommes dans l'Etat*, Payot, Paris 1978.

40. I have attempted to develop this position in a number of 'occasional' articles: 'Suffrage universel' (with Yves Bénot), *Le Monde*, 4 May 1983; 'Sujets ou citoyens? – Pour l'égalité'; 'La Société métissée', *Le Monde*, 1 December 1984; 'Propositions sur la citoyenneté', in C. Wihtol de Wenden, ed., *La Citoyenneté*, Edilig-Fondation Diderot, Paris 1988.

PART II

The Historical Nation

4

The Construction of Peoplehood: Racism, Nationalism, Ethnicity

Immanuel Wallerstein

Nothing seems more obvious than who or what is a people. Peoples have names, familiar names. They seem to have long histories. Yet any pollster knows that if one poses the open-ended question 'what are you?' to individuals presumably belonging to the same 'people', the responses will be incredibly varied, especially if the matter is not at that moment in the political limelight. And any student of the political scene knows that very passionate political debates hinge around these names. Are there Palestinians? Who is a Jew? Are Macedonians Bulgarians? Are Berbers Arabs? What is the correct label: Negro, Afro-American, Black (capitalized), black (uncapitalized)? People shoot each other every day over the question of labels. And yet, the very people who do so tend to deny that the issue is complex or puzzling or indeed anything but self-evident.

I should like to start by describing one recent debate about one particular people. It has the rare quality of being a relatively friendly debate, among people who assert they share common political objectives. It is a debate that was published in the explicit hope of resolving the issue amicably among comrades.

The setting is South Africa. The South African government has by law proclaimed the existence of four groups of 'peoples', each with a name: Europeans, Indians, Coloureds, Bantus. Each of these legal categories is complicated and contains multiple possible subgroups within it. The subgroups combined under one legal label are sometimes curious from the vantage point of an outsider. None the less, these labels have the force of law and have very specific consequences for individuals. Each resident of South Africa is classifed administratively into one of these four categories and as a result has different political and social rights. For example, he/she is required to live in a residential area assigned by the state to his category and in some cases to subcategories.

There are a large number of people in South Africa opposed to this process of legal categorization, which is known as apartheid. The history of their opposition shows, however, at least one significant shift of tactics with regard to the legal labels. Originally, those opposed to apartheid formed organizations within the framework of each separate category. These organizations then formed a political alliance and worked together. For example, in 1955, there occurred a very famous Congress of the People, cosponsored by four groups, each composed of persons belonging to one of the government's four categories of peoples. This Congress of the People issued a Freedom Charter calling for, among other things, the end of apartheid.

The largest of the four opposition organizations was the African National Congress (ANC), which represented what the government called Bantus, some 80 per cent of the total population falling under the state's jurisdiction. Somewhere in the 1960s or perhaps 1970s – it is not clear when – the ANC slipped into using the term 'African' for all those who were not 'Europeans' and thus included under the one label what the government called Bantus, Coloureds and Indians. Some others – it is not clear who – made a similar decision but designated this group as 'non-Whites' as opposed to 'Whites'. In any case, the consequence was to reduce a fourfold classification to a dichotomy.

The decision, if that is what it was, was not unambiguous, however. For example, the allied organization of the ANC among Indians, the South African Indian Congress (SAIC), continued to exist, though its president and others became simultaneously members of the SAIC and the ANC.

The category 'Coloured' has no doubt been the most nettlesome of the four. This 'group' was constituted historically out of descendants of various unions between African persons and European persons. It also included persons brought from the East Indies centuries ago, who came to be known as Cape Malays. The 'Coloureds' were mostly persons who in other parts of the world have been called 'mulattos' and who in the United States were always considered part of the 'Negro race', in terms of the now-defunct laws governing racial segregation.

In June 1984, Alex La Guma, member of the ANC and a Coloured from the government's point of view, wrote a letter to the editor of *Sechaba*, the official journal of the ANC. He posed the following issue:

I have noticed now in speeches, articles, interviews etc. in *Sechaba*, that I am called 'so-called Coloured' (sometimes with a small 'c'). When did the Congress decide to call me this? In South Africa I was active in the Congress Alliance and was a member of the Coloured People's Congress, not the 'so-called Coloured People's Congress'. When we worked for Congress of the People and the Freedom Charter we sang, 'We the Coloured people, we must struggle to exist....' I remember in those times some people of the so-called Unity Movement [a rival organization to the ANC] refer to so-called Coloured people, but not our Congress. The old copies of *Sechaba* do not show when it was decided to make this change, or why. Maybe governments, administrations, political and social dealings over centuries called me coloured. But clever people, the ethnologists and professors of anthropology and so on, did not bother to worry about who I really am.

Comrade Editor, I am confused. I need clarification. It makes me feel like a 'so-called' human, like a humanoid, those things who have all the characteristics of human beings but are really artificial. Other minority people are not called 'so-called.' Why me? It must be the 'curse of Ham.'

There were three responses to this letter. The first, also in the June issue, was from the editor:

As far as I can remember there is no decision taken in our movement to change from 'Coloured' to 'so-called Coloured'. All I know is that people at home – like Allan Boesak [Boesak is someone the government labels as Coloured] at the launch of the UDF [United Democratic Front, an anti-apartheid organization] – have been increasingly using the term, 'so-called Coloureds'. I suspect that what you have noticed is a reflection of this development.

Not long ago, *Sechaba* reviewed Richard Rive's book, *Writing Black*, and in that review we said:

Our strive for unity should not blind us from seeing the differences which if ignored can cause problems exactly for that unity we are striving to achieve. It is not enough to say the so-called Coloureds or to put the word Coloureds in inverted commas. A positive approach to this problem needs to be worked out because we are dealing with a group of people who are identifiable and distinguishable.

In other words, what we are saying in this review is that a discussion on this issue is necessary, and I think your letter may just as well be a starting point for such a discussion. Any comments on this issue are welcome.

In the August 1984 issue of *Sechaba*, there appeared a letter signed P.G. From the contents, it appears that P.G. is also someone labelled Coloured by the government. Unlike Alex La Guma, he rejects the term unequivocally.

In the Western Cape, I can remember the discussion we used to have about the term Coloured, when we met as groups of the Comrades Movement. These

were loosely organised groups of youth brought together in action and study
through the uprising of 1976, and who were largely pro-ANC. The term, 'so-
called Coloured', was commonly used amongst the youth in popular expression of rejection of apartheid terminology.

I am in full agreement with what was said in the *Sechaba* review of Richard
Rive's *Writing Black*, but would add that while, as you say, 'It is not enough
to say the "so-called Coloureds" or to put the word Coloureds in inverted
commas', it would be equally wrong to accept the term, 'Coloured'. I say this
especially in the light of the fact that most people are rejecting the term
'Coloured'. Congress people, UDF people, those in civic groups, church
groups and trade unions, leaders popular with the people speak of 'so-called
Coloured' without they, or the people they are speaking to, feeling like
humanoids. In fact the use of the term 'Coloured' is cited as making people
feel artificial. Coloured is a term which cries of lack of identity.

The term 'Coloured' did not evolve out of a distinctive group, but was
rather a label pinned on to a person whom the Population Registration Act of
1950 defines as 'who in appearance is obviously not White or Indian and who
is not a member of an aboriginal race or African tribe'. A definition based on
exclusion – that is, the isn't people.... The term 'Coloured' was given to what
the racists viewed as the marginal people. The term 'Coloured' was fundamental to the racist myth of the pure white Afrikaner. To accept the term
'Coloured' is to allow the myth to carry on....

Today, people are saying, 'We reject the racists' framework, we reject their
terminology,' and are beginning to build the NEW in defiance of the old, right
in the midst of the enemy. The term 'Coloured-Kleurling', like 'half-caste',
'Bruine Afrikaner' and 'South Africa's step-children', has been handed down
by the racists. Instead of some of us getting offended or taken aback by
adopting a very narrow interpretation of this usage, we should see the prefix
'so-called' as the first step in coming towards a solution of something which
has been a scourge for years.

We have got to move on from the term 'so-called Coloured' in a positive
way. People are now saying that we have the choice of what we will be called,
and most, in the spirit of the nation in the making, opt for 'South African'.
The debate can take many forms, but not a reverting to acceptance of the
Baasskap term. If one really needs a sub-identity to that of being a South
African, maybe through popular debate the question could be sorted out.

In the September 1984 issue of *Sechaba*, Arnold Selby, someone
labelled by the government as a European, entered the debate utilizing a
set of categories that distinguished between 'nations' and 'national
minorities':

Let's start the ball rolling viewing some established and accepted facts:

(a) As yet there is no such thing as a South African nation;
(b) The African majority is an oppressed nation, the Coloured people and

the Indian people are distinct identifiable oppressed national minorities, the White population comprises the minority oppressor nation;

(c) The Coloured, Indian and White national minorities are not homogeneous but embrace other national or ethnic groups. For example, the Lebanese community is in the main classified and regards itself as White, the Malay and Griqua people regard themselves as part of the Coloured nation, the Chinese minority finds some of its number classified as White, others as Asian and others as Coloured;

(d) The key to South Africa's future and the solution of the national question lies in the national liberation of the African nation. The victory of our national democratic revolution, headed by the African National Congress bringing with it the national liberation of the African nation, will set in motion the process for the birth of a South African nation.

As stated in (b) above, the Coloured people comprise a distinct identifiable oppressed national minority. But the definition, 'Coloured', the terminology arising therefrom and its usage in the practice of daily life did not emerge from the natural social causes, nor were they chosen by the Coloured people. They were imposed upon the Coloured people by the successive regimes which came in the wake of successive waves of aggressions, penetration and settlement of South Africa by the European bourgeois nations, in both their trading and imperialist phases, and after the founding of the aggressor South African state in 1910....

Now let me come to the tendency on the part of some of us to talk about the 'so-called' Coloured people. This, I believe, arises from two real factors with which we are faced.

First is the question of our work abroad. Other countries and nations have different conceptions about the term 'Coloured people', which are far out of keeping with the reality of the nationally oppressed Coloured national minority in our country. When we speak about our country and its struggle and the role and place of the Coloured people in this struggle we have to explain who the Coloured people are, hence we often find ourselves using the words 'so-called' (please note inverted commas) to emphasise the aggressors' imposition of the term. Like one could say the 'so-called' Indians when referring to the original inhabitants of what is now the USA. This gives a clearer picture to those abroad who want to know more about our liberation struggle.

Secondly, I do not believe that the tendency of some at home to use the words 'so-called' means a rejection of our generally accepted term 'Coloured people'. To my way of thinking the words are used to stress the growing unity of the oppressed Coloured and Indian national minorities with the oppressed majority African nation. The usage of these words, I believe, indicates an identification with Black rather than Coloured separation from Black. At the same time the usage distances the Coloured people from the White oppressor minority nation. Time without number the oppressor White minority nation has sought without success to get acceptance of the idea that the Coloured people are an inferior off-shoot of the White nation, to which it is naturally allied. The usage of 'so-called' means a rejection of the aggressor's attempts to get acceptance of such racist ideology clothed in scientific terminology.

Whether we use 'so-called' or not, the reality is that there is an oppressed Coloured national minority in our country. In my opinion, under today's conditions, it is not incorrect to use 'so-called' provided it is done in the proper context to convey the true meaning and is put in inverted commas. Under no circumstances can there be a rejection of the reality of the existence of the Coloured people as an oppressed minority nation.

Note that Selby's position is really quite different from P.G.'s. While both accept the use of 'so-called' before 'Coloured', P.G. does it because there is no such thing as Coloureds. Selby thinks Coloureds exist as a people, of a variety of people he calls 'national minorities', but defends the use of 'so-called' as a tactic in political communication.

Finally, in the November 1984 issue, La Guma responds, unrepentant:

[PG] says that 'so-called Coloured' was used in popular expression of rejection of 'apartheid terminology'. Yet later he says that 'most, in the spirit of a nation in the making, opt for "South African"'. But, Comrade Editor, he does not tell us who gave our country the official name of South Africa? On what or whose authority? There are some who, rejecting this 'terminology', call the country 'Azania' (again, on whose authority?) and maybe they would call the rest of the population 'so-called South Africans'. But it would seem that even though the Boer anthem refers to *Suid-Afrika*, the name of South Africa is accepted. Yet for any minority (even so-called) to assume the right to call themselves South African for their own studied convenience seems to me to be somewhat undemocratic, if not downright presumptuous, since the right naturally belongs to the majority.

I regret to say that I did not know (as PG seems to say) that the term 'Coloured' emerged as a result of the definition laid down by the Population Registration Act or the Group Areas Act. I was born long before these Acts, so our people must be a little older than that. And we should not believe that all the awful experiences described by PG (divided families, rejection, etc.) are only suffered by us. Mixed race or marginal communities in other parts of the world suffer similar trials and tribulations.

Now PG even says 'so-called' is not good enough, but neither is 'Coloured', which adds to my confusion, Comrade Editor. But it is not being called Coloured that has been 'a scourge for years', but the way our people have been and are being treated, whatever they are called, just as the term 'Asiatic' or 'Indian' in itself does not mean scourged.... While I wait patiently for the outcome of PG's 'mass debate', I would still like to know what I am today. So, Comrade Editor, call me what the devil you like, but for God's sake don't call me 'so-called.'

I have cited this exchange at some length to show first of all that even the most amicable of debates is quite passionate; and secondly, to show

how difficult the issue is to resolve on either historical or logical grounds. Is there a Coloured people, or a Coloured national minority, or a Coloured ethnic group? Was there ever? I can say that some people think there is and/or was, others do not, still others are indifferent, and still others are ignorant of the category.

Ergo, what? If there is some essential phenomenon, a Coloured people, we should be able to come to terms about its parameters. But if we find that we cannot come to terms about this name designating a 'people' or indeed about virtually any other name designating some people, maybe this is because peoplehood is not merely a construct but one which, in each particular instance, has constantly changing boundaries. Maybe a people is something that is supposed to be inconstant in form. But if so, why the passion? Maybe because no one is supposed to comment upon the inconstancy. If I am right, then we have a very curious phenomenon indeed – one whose central features are the reality of inconstancy and the denial of this reality. Very complicated, indeed bizarre, I should say! What is there in the historical system in which we are located that would give rise to such a curious social process? Perhaps there is a quark to locate.

I propose to address this issue in successive steps. Let us first review briefly the existing views in social science about peoplehood. Let us then see what there is in the structure and processes of this historical system that might have produced such a concept. Finally, let us see if there is some conceptual reformulation that might be useful.

To start with the literature of the historical social sciences, one must note that the term 'people' is actually used somewhat infrequently. Rather the three commonest terms are 'race', 'nation' and 'ethnic group', all presumably varieties of 'peoples' in the modern world. The last of these three is the most recent and has replaced in effect the previously widely used term of 'minority'. Of course, each of these terms has many variants, but none the less I think both statistically and logically these are the three modal terms.

A 'race' is supposed to be a genetic category, which has a visible physical form. There has been a great deal of scholarly debate over the past 150 years as to the names and characteristics of races. This debate is quite famous and, for much of it, infamous. A 'nation' is supposed to be a sociopolitical category, linked somehow to the actual or potential boundaries of a state. An 'ethnic group' is supposed to be a cultural category, of which there are said to be certain continuing behaviours that are passed on from generation to generation and that are *not* normally linked in theory to state boundaries.

The three terms are used with incredible inconsistency, of course, leaving quite aside the multitude of other terms utilized. (We have already seen, in the above debate, one person designate as a 'national minority' what others might have called an 'ethnic group'.) Most users of the terms use them, all three of them, to indicate some persisting phenomenon which, by virtue of its continuity, not only has a strong impact on current behaviour but also offers a basis for making present-day political claims. That is, a 'people' is said to be or act as it does because of either its genetic characterstics, or its sociopolitical history, or its 'traditional' norms and values.

The whole point of these categories seems to be to enable us to make claims based upon the past against the manipulable 'rational' processes of the present. We may use these categories to explain why things are the way they are and shouldn't be changed, or why things are the way they are and cannot be changed. Or conversely we may use them to explain why the present structures should indeed be superseded in the name of deeper and more ancient, *ergo* more legitimate, social realities. The temporal dimension of pastness is central to and inherent in the concept of peoplehood.

Why does one want or need a past, an 'identity'? This is a perfectly sensible question to ask and is even, on occasion, asked. Notice, for example, that P.G. in the cited debate advocates discarding the appellation 'Coloured' in favour of a larger category 'South African' and then says: 'If one really needs a sub-identity to that of being a South African....' If ... implies why.

Pastness is a mode by which persons are persuaded to act in the present in ways they might not otherwise act. Pastness is a tool persons use against each other. Pastness is a central element in the socialization of individuals, in the maintenance of group solidarity, in the establishment of or challenge to social legitimation. Pastness therefore is pre-eminently a moral phenomenon, therefore a political phenomenon, always a contemporary phenomenon. That is of course why it is so inconstant. Since the real world is constantly changing, what is relevant to contemporary politics is necessarily constantly changing. *Ergo*, the content of pastness necessarily constantly changes. Since, however, pastness is by definition an assertion of the constant past, no one can ever admit that any particular past has ever changed or could possibly change. The past is normally considered to be inscribed in stone and irreversible. The real past, to be sure, is indeed inscribed in stone. The social past, how we understand this real past, on the other hand, is inscribed at best in soft clay.

This being the case, it makes little difference whether we define pastness in terms of genetically continuous groups (races), historical sociopolitical groups (nations) or cultural groups (ethnic groups). They are all peoplehood constructs, all inventions of pastness, all contemporary

political phenomena. If this is so, however, we then have another
analytic puzzle. Why should three different modal terms have developed
when one term might have served? There must be some reason for the
separation of one logical category into three social categories. We have
but to look at the historical structure of the capitalist world-economy to
find it.

Each of the three modal terms hinges on one of the basic structural
features of the capitalist world-economy. The concept of 'race' is related
to the axial division of labour in the world-economy, the core–periphery
antinomy. The concept of 'nation' is related to the political superstructure of this historical system, the sovereign states that form and
derive from the interstate system. The concept of 'ethnic group' is
related to the creation of household structures that permit the maintenance of large components of non-waged labour in the accumulation of
capital. None of the three terms is directly related to class. That is
because 'class' and 'peoplehood' are orthogonally defined, which as we
shall see is one of the contradictions of this historical system.

The axial division of labour within the world-economy has engen-
dered a spatial division of labour. We speak of a core–periphery
antinomy as constitutive of this division of labour. Core and periphery
strictly speaking are relational concepts that have to do with differential
cost structures of production. The location of these different production
processes in spatially distant zones is not an inevitable and constant
feature of the relationship. But it tends to be a normal one. There are
several reasons for this. To the extent that peripheral processes are
associated with primary production – which has in fact been historically
true, although far less today than previously – then there is constraint on
the geographical relocatability of these processes, associated with
environmental conditions for cultivation or with geological deposits.
Second, in so far as there are political elements in maintaining a set of
core–periphery relationships, the fact that products in a commodity
chain cross political frontiers facilitates the necessary political processes,
since the control of frontier transit is among the greatest real powers the
states actually exercise. Third, the concentration of core processes in
states different from those in which peripheral processes are concentrated tends to create differing internal political structures in each, a
difference which in turn becomes a major sustaining bulwark of the
inegalitarian interstate system that manages and maintains the axial
division of labour.

Hence, to put the matter simply, we tend over time to arrive at a situation in which some zones of the world are largely the loci of core
production processes and others are largely the loci of peripheral
production processes. Indeed, although there are cyclical fluctuations in

the degree of polarization, there is a secular trend towards a widening of this gap. This world-wide spatial differentiation took the political form primarily of the expansion of a Europe-centred capitalist world-economy into one that eventually covered the globe. This came to be known as the phenomenon of the 'expansion of Europe'.

In the evolution of the human species on the planet Earth, there occurred in a period preceding the development of settled agriculture, a distribution of genetic variants such that at the outset of the development of the capitalist world-economy, different genetic types in any one location were considerably more homogeneous than they are today.

As the capitalist world-economy expanded from its initial location primarily in Europe, as concentrations of core and peripheral production processes became more and more geographically disparate, 'racial' categories began to crystallize around certain labels. It may be obvious that there are a large series of genetic traits that vary, and vary considerably, among different persons. It is not at all obvious that these have to be coded as falling into three, five or fifteen reified groupings we call 'races'. The number of categories, indeed the fact of any categorization, is a social decision. What we observe is that, as the polarization increased, the number of categories became fewer and fewer. When W.E.B. Du Bois said in 1900 that 'the problem of the twentieth century is the problem of the color line', the colours to which he was referring came down in reality to White and non-White.

Race, and therefore racism, is the expression, the promoter and the consequence of the geographical concentrations associated with the axial division of labour. That this is so has been made stunningly clear by the decision of the South African state in the last twenty years to designate visiting Japanese businessmen not as Asians (which local Chinese are considered to be) but rather as 'honorary White'. In a country whose laws are supposed to be based on the permanence of genetic categories, apparently genetics follows the election returns of the world-economy. Such absurd decisions are not limited to South Africa. South Africa merely got itself into the box of putting absurdities on paper.

Race is not, however, the only category of social identity we use. It apparently is not enough; we use nation as well. As we said, nation derives from the *political* structuring of the world-system. The states that are today members of the United Nations are all creations of the modern world-system. Most of them did not even exist either as names or as administrative units more than a century or two ago. For those very few that can trace a name and a continuous administrative entity in roughly the same geographical location to a period prior to 1450 – there are fewer of these than we think: France, Russia, Portugal, Denmark, Sweden, Switzerland, Morocco, Japan, China, Iran, Ethiopia are perhaps the least ambiguous cases – it can still be argued that even these states came into existence as modern sovereign states only with the emergence of the present world-system. There are some other modern states that can trace a more discontinuous history of the use of a name to describe a zone – for example, Greece, India, Egypt. We get on to still thinner ice with such names as Turkey, Germany, Italy, Syria. The fact is, if we look forward from the vantage-point of 1450 at many entities that then existed – for example, the Burgundian Netherlands, the Holy Roman Empire, the Mogul Empire – we find we have today in each case not one state but at the very least three sovereign states that can argue some kind of political, cultural, spatial descent from these entities.

And does the fact that there are now three states mean that there are three nations? Is there a Belgian, a Dutch, a Luxembourg nation today? Most observers seem to think so. If there is, is this not because there came into existence *first* a Dutch state, a Belgian state, a Luxembourg state? A systematic look at the history of the modern world will show, I believe, that in almost every case statehood preceded nationhood, and not the other way around, despite a widespread myth to the contrary.

To be sure, once the interstate system was functioning, nationalist movements did arise in many zones demanding the creation of new sovereign states, and these movements sometimes achieved their objectives. But two caveats are in order. These movements, with rare exceptions, arose within already constructed administrative boundaries. Hence it could be said that a state, albeit a non-independent one, preceded the movement. And secondly, it is debatable how deep a root 'nation' as a communal sentiment took before the actual creation of the state. Take for example the case of the Sahrawi people. Is there a Sahrawi nation? If you ask Polisario, the national liberation movement, they will say yes, and add that there has been one for a thousand years. If you ask the Moroccans, there never has been a Sahrawi nation, and the people who live in what was once the colony of the Spanish Sahara were always part of the Moroccan nation. How can we resolve this difference intellectually? The answer is that we cannot. If by the year 2000 or perhaps 2020, Polisario wins the current war, there will have been a Sahrawi nation. And if Morocco wins, there will not have been. Any historian writing in 2100 will take it as a settled question, or more probably still as a non-question.

Why should the establishment of any particular sovereign state within the interstate system create a corresponding 'nation', a 'people'? This is not really difficult to understand. The evidence is all around us. States in this system have problems of cohesion. Once recognized as sovereign, the states frequently find themselves subsequently threatened by both internal disintegration and external aggression. To the extent that

'national' sentiment develops, these threats are lessened. The governments in power have an interest in promoting this sentiment, as do all
sorts of subgroups within the state. Any group who sees advantage in
using the state's legal powers to advance its interests against groups
outside the state or in any subregion of the state has an interest in
promoting nationalist sentiment as a legitimation of its claims. States
furthermore have an interest in administrative uniformity that increases
the efficacy of their policies. Nationalism is the expression, the promoter
and the consequence of such state-level uniformities.

There is another, even more important reason for the rise of
nationalism. The interstate system is not a mere assemblage of so-called
sovereign states. It is a hierarchical system with a pecking order that is
stable but changeable. That is to say, slow shifts in rank order are not
merely possible, but historically normal. Inequalities that are significant
and firm but not immutable are precisely the kind of processes that lead
to ideologies able to justify high rank but also to challenge low rank.
Such ideologies we call nationalisms. For a state not to be a nation is for
that state to be outside the game of either resisting or promoting the
alteration of its rank. But then that state would not be part of the interstate system. Political entities that existed outside of and/or prior to the
development of the interstate system as the political superstructure of a
capitalist world-economy did not need to be 'nations', and were not.
Since we misleadingly use the same word, 'state', to describe both these
other political entities and the states created within the interstate system,
we often miss the obvious inevitable link between the statehood of these
latter 'states' and their nationhood.

If we then ask what is served by having two categories – races and
nations – instead of one, we see that while racial categorization arose
primarily as a mode of expressing and sustaining the core–periphery
antinomy, national categorization arose originally as a mode of
expressing the competition between states in the slow but regular
permutation of the hierarchical order and therefore of the detailed
degree of advantage in the system as opposed to the cruder racial classification. In an over-simplified formula, we could say that race and
racism unifies intrazonally the core zones and the peripheral zones in
their battles with each other, whereas nation and nationalism divides
core zones and peripheral zones intrazonally in the more complex intra-
zonal as well as interzonal competition for detailed rank order. Both
categories are claims to the right to possess advantage in the capitalist
world-economy.

If all this were not enough, we have created the category of the ethnic
group, the erstwhile minority. For there to be minorities, there needs to
be a majority. It has long been noticed by analysts that minorityhood is

not necessarily an arithmetically based concept; it refers to the degree of social power. Numerical majorities can be social minorities. The location within which we are measuring this social power is not of course the world-system as a whole, but the separate states. The concept 'ethnic group' is therefore as linked in practice to state boundaries, as is the concept 'nation', despite the fact that this is never included in the definition. The difference is only that a state tends to have *one* nation and *many* ethnic groups.

The capitalist system is based not merely on the capital–labour antinomy that is permanent and fundamental to it but on a complex hierarchy within the labour segment in which, although all labour is exploited because it creates surplus-value that is transferred to others, some labourers 'lose' a larger proportion of their created surplus-value than others. The key institution that permits this is the household of part-lifetime wage labourers. These households are constructed in such a way that these wage workers may receive less in hourly wages than what is, on a proportionate calculation, the cost of the reproduction of labour. This is a very widespread institution, covering the majority of the world's work force. I shall not repeat here the arguments for this analysis which have been made elsewhere.[1] I merely wish to discuss its consequences in terms of peoplehood. Wherever we find wage workers located in different kinds of household structures from more highly paid workers located in more 'proletarianized' household structures to less highly paid ones located in more 'semiproletarianized' household structures, we tend to find at the same time that these varieties of household structures are located inside 'communities' called 'ethnic groups'. That is, along with an occupational hierarchy comes the 'ethnicization' of the work force within a given state's boundaries. Even without a comprehensive legal framework to enforce this, as in South Africa today or the United States yesterday, there has been a very high correlation everywhere of ethnicity and occupation, provided one groups 'occupations' into broad and not narrow categories.

There seem to be various advantages to the ethnicization of occu-pational categories. Different kinds of relations of production, we may assume, require different kinds of normal behaviour by the work force. Since this behaviour is not in fact genitally determined, it must be taught. Work forces need to be socialized into reasonably specific sets of attitudes. The 'culture' of an ethnic group is precisely the set of rules into which parents belonging to that ethnic group are pressured to socialize their children. The state or the school system can do this of course. But they usually seek to avoid performing that particularistic function alone or too overtly, since it violates the concept of 'national' equality for them to do so. Those few states willing to avow such a violation are under constant pressure to renounce the violation. But 'ethnic groups' not only *may* socialize their respective members differently from each other; it is the very definition of ethnic groups that they socialize in a particular manner. Thus what is illegitimate for the state to do comes in by the rear window as 'voluntary' group behaviour defending a social 'identity'.

This therefore provides a legitimation to the hierarchical reality of capitalism that does not offend the formal equality before the law which is one of its avowed political premises. The quark for which we were looking may be there. Ethnicization, or peoplehood, resolves one of the basic contradictions of historical capitalism – its simultaneous thrust for theoretical equality and practical inequality – and it does so by utilizing the mentalities of the world's working strata.

In this effort, the very inconstancy of peoplehood categories of which we have been speaking turns out to be crucially important. For while capitalism as a historical system requires constant inequality, it also requires constant restructuring of economic processes. Hence what guarantees a particular set of hierarchical social relations today may not work tomorrow. The behaviour of the work force must change without undermining the legitimacy of the system. The recurrent birth, restructuring and disappearance of ethnic groups is thereby an invaluable instrument of flexibility in the operation of the economic machinery.

Peoplehood is a major institutional construct of historical capitalism. It is an essential pillar, and as such has grown more and more important as the system has developed greater density. In this sense it is like sovereign statehood, which is also an essential pillar, and has also grown more and more important. We are growing more, not less, attached to these basic *Gemeinschaften* formed within our world-historical *Gesellschaft*, the capitalist world-economy.

Classes are really quite a different construct from peoples, as both Marx and Weber knew well. Classes are 'objective' categories, that is, analytic categories, statements about contradictions in an historical system, and not descriptions of social communities. The issue is whether and under what circumstances a class community can be created. This is the famous *an sich/für sich* distinction. Classes *für sich* have been a very elusive entity.

Perhaps, and here is where we will end, the reason is that the constructed 'peoples' – the races, the nations, the ethnic groups – correlate so heavily, albeit imperfectly, with 'objective class'. The consequence has been that a very high proportion of class-based political activity in the modern world has taken the form of people-based political activity. The percentage will turn out to be even higher than we usually think if we look closely at so-called 'pure' workers' organizations that quite frequently have had implicit and *de facto* 'people' bases, even while utilizing a non-people, purely class terminology.

For more than a hundred years, the world Left has bemoaned its dilemma that the world's workers have all too often organized themselves in 'people' forms. But this is not a soluble dilemma. It derives from the contradictions of the system. There cannot be *für sich* class activity that is entirely divorced from people-based political activity. We see this in the so-called national liberation movements, in all the new social movements, in the anti-bureaucratic movements in socialist countries.

Would it not make more sense to try to understand peoplehood for what it is – in no sense a primordial stable social reality, but a complex, clay-like historical product of the capitalist world-economy through which the antagonistic forces struggle with each other. We can never do away with peoplehood in this system nor relegate it to a minor role. On the other hand, we must not be bemused by the virtues ascribed to it, or we shall be betrayed by the ways in which it legitimates the existing system. What we need to analyse more closely are the possible directions in which, as peoplehood becomes ever more central to this historical system, it will push us, at the system's bifurcation point, towards various possible alternative outcomes in the uncertain process of the transition from our present historical system to the one or ones that will replace it.

Note

1. Wallerstein, *Historical Capitalism*, New Left Books, London 1983 and 'Household Structures and Labour-Force Formation in the Capitalist World-Economy', this volume, pp. 107–112.

5

The Nation Form:
History and Ideology

Etienne Balibar

... a 'past' that has never been present, and which never will be.
Jacques Derrida, *Margins of Philosophy*

The history of nations, beginning with our own, is always already presented to us in the form of a narrative which attributes to these entities the continuity of a subject. The formation of the nation thus appears as the fulfilment of a 'project' stretching over centuries, in which there are different stages and moments of coming to self-awareness, which the prejudices of the various historians will portray as more or less decisive – where, for example, are we to situate the origins of France? with our ancestors the Gauls? the Capetian monarchy? the revolution of 1789? – but which, in any case, all fit into an identical pattern: that of the self-manifestation of the national personality. Such a representation clearly constitutes a retrospective illusion, but it also expresses constraining institutional realities. The illusion is twofold. It consists in believing that the generations which succeed one another over centuries on a reasonably stable territory, under a reasonably univocal designation, have handed down to each other an invariant substance. And it consists in believing that the process of development from which we select aspects retrospectively, so as to see ourselves as the culmination of that process, was the only one possible, that is, it represented a destiny. Project and destiny are the two symmetrical figures of the illusion of national identity. The 'French' of 1988 – one in three of whom has at least one 'foreign'[1] ancestor – are only collectively connected to the subjects of King Louis XIV (not to speak of the Gauls) by a succession of contingent events, the causes of which have nothing to do either with the destiny of 'France', the project of 'its kings' or the aspirations of 'its people'.

This critique should not, however, be allowed to prevent our perceiving the continuing power of myths of national origins. One perfectly conclusive example of this is the French Revolution, by the very fact of the contradictory appropriations to which it is continually subjected. It is possible to suggest (with Hegel and Marx) that, in the history of every modern nation, wherever the argument can apply, there is never more than one single founding revolutionary event (which explains both the permanent temptation to repeat its forms, to imitate its episodes and characters, and the temptation found among the 'extreme' parties to suppress it, either by proving that national identity derives from before the revolution or by awaiting the realization of that identity from a *new* revolution which would complete the work of the first). The myth of origins and national continuity, which we can easily see being set in place in the contemporary history of the 'young' nations (such as India or Algeria) which emerged with the end of colonialism, but which we have a tendency to forget has also been fabricated over recent centuries in the case of the 'old' nations, is therefore an effective ideological form, in which the imaginary singularity of national formations is constructed daily, by moving back from the present into the past.

From the 'Pre-National' State to the Nation-State

How are we to take this distortion into account? The 'origins' of the national formation go back to a multiplicity of institutions dating from widely differing periods. Some are in fact very old: the institution of state languages that were distinct both from the sacred languages of the clergy and from 'local' idioms – initially for purely administrative purposes, but subsequently as aristocratic languages – goes back in Europe to the High Middle Ages. It is connected with the process by which monarchical power became autonomous and sacred. Similarly, the progressive formation of absolute monarchy brought with it effects of monetary monopoly, administrative and fiscal centralization and a relative degree of standardization of the legal system and internal 'pacification'. It thus revolutionized the institutions of the *frontier* and the *territory*. The Reformation and Counter-Reformation precipitated a transition from a situation in which church and state competed (rivalry between the ecclesiastical state and the secular one) to a situation in which the two were complementary (in the extreme case, in a state religion).

All these structures appear retrospectively to us as pre-national, because they made possible certain features of the nation-state, into which they were ultimately to be incorporated with varying degrees of modification. We can therefore acknowledge the fact that the national formation is the product of a long 'pre-history'. This pre-history, however, differs in essential features from the nationalist myth of a linear destiny. First, it consists of a multiplicity of qualitatively distinct events spread out over time, none of which implies any subsequent event. Second, these events do not of their nature belong to the history of *one* determinate nation. They have occurred within the framework of political units other than those which seem to us today endowed with an original ethical personality (this, just as in the twentieth century the state apparatuses of the 'young nations' were prefigured in the apparatuses of the colonial period, so the European Middle Ages saw the outlines of the modern state emerge within the framework of 'Sicily', 'Catalonia' or 'Burgundy'). And they do not even belong by nature to the history of the *nation*-state, but to other rival forms (for example, the 'imperial' form). It is not a line of necessary evolution but a series of conjunctural relations which has inscribed them after the event into the pre-history of the nation form. It is the characteristic feature of states of all types to represent the order they institute as eternal, though practice shows that more or less the opposite is the case.

The fact remains that all these events, on condition they are repeated or integrated into new political structures, have effectively played a role in the genesis of national formations. This has precisely to do with their institutional character, with the fact that they cause the state to intervene in the form which it assumed at a particular moment In other words, *non-national* state apparatuses aiming at quite other (for example, dynastic) objectives have progressively produced the elements of the nation-state or, if one prefers, they have been involuntarily 'nationalized' and have begun to nationalize society – the resurrection of Roman law, mercantilism and the domestication of the feudal aristocracies are all examples of this. And the closer we come to the modern period, the greater the constraint imposed by the accumulation of these elements seems to be. Which raises the crucial question of the *threshold* of irreversibility.

At what moment and for what reasons has this threshold been crossed – an event which, on the one hand, caused the configuration of a *system* of sovereign states to emerge and, on the other, imposed the progressive diffusion of the nation form to almost all human societies over two centuries of violent conflict? I admit that this threshold (which it is obviously impossible to identify with a single date[2]) corresponds to the development of the market structures and class relations specific to modern capitalism (in particular, the proletarianization of the labour force, a process which gradually extracts its members from feudal and corporatist relations). Nevertheless this commonly accepted thesis needs qualifying in several ways.

It is quite impossible to 'deduce' the nation form from capitalist relations of production. Monetary circulation and the exploitation of wage labour do not logically entail a single determinate form of state. Moreover, the realization space which is implied by accumulation – the world capitalist market – has within it an intrinsic tendency to transcend any national limitations that might be instituted by determinate fractions of social capital or imposed by 'extra-economic' means. May we, in these conditions, continue to see the formation of the nation as a 'bourgeois project'? It seems likely that this formulation – taken over by Marxism from liberal philosophies of history – constitutes in its turn a historical myth. It seems, however, that we might overcome this difficulty if we return to Braudel and Wallerstein's perspective – the view which sees the constitution of nations as being bound up not with the abstraction of the capitalist market, but with its concrete historical form: that of a 'world-economy' which is always already hierarchically organized into a 'core' and a 'periphery', each of which have different methods of accumulation and exploitation of labour power, and between which relations of unequal exchange and domination are established.[3]

Beginning from the core, national units form out of the overall structure of the world-economy, as a function of the role they play in that structure in a given period. More exactly, they form against one another as competing instruments in the service of the core's domination of the periphery. This first qualification is a crucial one, because it substitutes for the 'ideal' capitalism of Marx and, particularly, of the Marxist economists, a 'historical capitalism' in which a decisive role is played by the early forms of imperialism and the articulation of wars with colonization. In a sense, every modern nation is a product of colonization: it has always been to some degree colonized or colonizing, and sometimes both at the same time.

However, a second qualification is necessary. One of the most important of Braudel and Wallerstein's contributions consists in their having shown that, in the history of capitalism, *state forms other than the national have emerged* and have for a time competed with it, before finally being repressed or instrumentalized: the form of empire and, most importantly, that of the transnational politico-commercial complex, centred on one or more cities.[4] This form shows us that there was not a single inherently 'bourgeois' political form, but several (we could take the Hanseatic League as an example, but the history of the

United Provinces in the seventeenth century is closely determined by this alternative which echoes through the whole of its social life, including religious and intellectual life). In other words, the nascent capitalist bourgeoisie seems to have 'hesitated' – depending on circumstances – between several forms of hegemony. Or let us rather say that there existed *different bourgeoisies*, each connected to different sectors of exploitation of the resources of the world-economy. If the 'national bourgeoisies' finally won out, even before the industrial revolution (though at the cost of 'time-lags' and 'compromises' and therefore of fusions with other dominant classes), this is probably both because they needed to use the armed forces of the existing states externally and internally, and because they had to subject the peasantry to the new economic order and penetrate the countryside, turning it into a market where there were consumers of manufactured goods and reserves of 'free' labour power. In the last analysis, it is therefore the concrete configurations of the class struggle and not 'pure' economic logic which explain the constitution of nation-states, each with its own history, and the corresponding transformation of social formations into national formations.

The Nationalization of Society

The world-economy is not a self-regulating, globally invariant system, whose social formations can be regarded as mere local effects; it is a system of constraints, subject to the unforeseeable dialectic of its internal contradictions. It is globally necessary that control of the capital circulating in the whole accumulation space should be exercised from the core; but there has always been struggle over the *form* in which this concentration has been effected. The privileged status of the nation form derives from the fact that, locally, that form made it possible (at least for an entire historical period) for struggles between heterogeneous classes to be controlled and for not only a 'capitalist class' but the *bourgeoisies* proper to emerge from these – state bourgeoisies both capable of political, economic and cultural hegemony and *produced* by that hegemony. The dominant bourgeoisie and the bourgeois social formations formed one another reciprocally in a 'process without a subject', by restructuring the state in the national form and by modifying the status of all the other classes. This explains the simultaneous genesis of nationalism and cosmopolitanism.

However simplified this hypothesis may be, it has one essential consequence for the analysis of the nation as a historical form: we have to renounce linear developmental schemas once and for all, not only where modes of production are concerned, but also in respect of political forms. There is, then, nothing to prevent us from examining whether in a new phase of the world-economy rival state structures to that of the nation-state are not tending to form once again. In reality, there is a close implicit connection between the illusion of a necessary unilinear evolution of social formations and the uncritical acceptance of the nation-state as the 'ultimate form' of political institution, destined to be perpetuated for ever (have failed to give way to a hypothetical 'end of the state').[5]

To bring out the relative indeterminacy of the process of constitution and development of the nation form, let us approach matters from the perspective of a consciously provocative question: *For whom today is it too late?* In other words, which are the social formations which, in spite of the global constraint of the world-economy and of the system of state to which it has given rise, can no longer completely effect their transformation into nations, except in a purely juridical sense and at the cost of interminable conflicts that produce no decisive result? An a priori answer, and even a general answer, is doubtless impossible, but it is obvious that the question arises not only in respect of the 'new nations' created after decolonization, the transnationalization of capital and communications, the creation of planetary war machines and so on, but also in respect of 'old nations' which are today affected by the same phenomena.

One might be tempted to say that it is too late for those independent states which are formally equal and represented in the institutions which are precisely styled 'international' to become self-centred nations, each with its national language(s) of culture, administration and commerce, with its independent military forces, its protected internal market, its currency and its enterprises competing on a world scale and, particularly, with its ruling bourgeoisie (whether it be a private capitalist bourgeoisie or a state *nomenklatura*), since in one way or another every bourgeoisie is a state bourgeoisie. Yet one might also be tempted to say the opposite: the field of the reproduction of nations, of the deployment of the nation form is no longer open today except in the old peripheries and semiperipheries; so far as the old 'core' is concerned, it has, to varying degrees, entered the phase of the decomposition of national structures which were connected with the old forms of its domination, even if the outcome of such a decomposition is both distant and uncertain. It clearly seems, however, if one accepts this hypothesis, that the nations of the future will not be like those of the past. The fact that we are today seeing a general upsurge of nationalism everywhere (North and South, East and West) does not enable us to resolve this kind of dilemma: it is part of the formal universality of the international system of states. Contemporary nationalism, whatever its language, tells us nothing of the real age of the nation form in relation to 'world time'.

In reality, if we are to cast a little more light on this question, we must take into account a further characteristic of the history of national formations. This is what I call the *delayed nationalization of society*, which first of all concerns the old nations themselves – so delayed is it, it ultimately appears as an endless task. A historian like Eugen Weber has shown (as have other subsequent studies) that, in the case of France, universal schooling and the unification of customs and beliefs by inter-regional labour migration and military service and the subordination of political and religious conflicts to patriotic ideology did not come about until the early years of the twentieth century.[6] His study suggests that the French peasantry was only finally 'nationalized' at the point when it was about to disappear as the majority class (though this disappearance, as we know, was itself retarded by the protectionism that is an essential characteristic of national politics). The more recent work of Gérard Noiriel shows in its turn that, since the end of the nineteenth century, 'French identity' has continually been dependent upon the capacity to integrate immigrant populations. The question arises as to whether that capacity is today reaching its limit or whether it can in fact continue to be exercised in the same form.[7]

In order completely to identify the reasons for the relative stability of the national formation, it is not sufficient, then, merely to refer to the initial threshold of its emergence. We must also ask how the problems of unequal development of town and countryside, colonization and de-colonization, wars and the revolutions which they have sometimes sparked off, the constitution of supranational blocs and so on have in practice been surmounted, since these are all events and processes which involved at least a risk of class conflicts drifting beyond the limits within which they had been more or less easily confined by the 'consensus' of the national state. We may say that in France as, *mutatis mutandis*, in the other old bourgeois formations, what made it possible to resolve the contradictions capitalism brought with it and to begin to remake the nation form at a point when it was not even completed (or to prevent it from coming apart before it was completed), was the institution of the *national-social state*, that is, of a state 'intervening' in the very repro-duction of the economy and particularly in the formation of individuals, in family structures, the structures of public health and, more generally, in the whole space of 'private life'. This is a tendency that was present from the very beginnings of the nation form – a point to which I return below – but one which has become dominant during the nineteenth and twentieth centuries, the result of which is entirely to subordinate the existence of the individuals of all classes to their status as citizens of the nation-state, to the fact of their being 'nationals' that is.[8]

Producing the People

A social formation only reproduces itself as a nation to the extent that, through a network of apparatuses and daily practices, the individual is instituted as *homo nationalis* from cradle to grave, at the same time as he or she is instituted as *homo œconomicus, politicus, religiosus* ... That is why the question of the nation form, if it is henceforth an open one, is, at bottom, the question of knowing under what historical conditions it is possible to institute such a thing: by virtue of what internal and external relations of force and also by virtue of what symbolic forms invested in elementary material practices? Asking this question is another way of asking oneself to what transition in civilization the nationalization of societies corresponds, and what are the figures of individuality between which nationality moves.

The crucial point is this: What makes the nation a 'community'? Or rather in what way is the form of community instituted by the nation distinguished specifically from other historical communities?

Let us dispense right away with the antitheses traditionally attached to that notion, the first of which is the antithesis between the 'real' and the 'imaginary' community. *Every social community reproduced by the functioning of institutions is imaginary*, that is to say, it is based on the projection of individual existence into the weft of a collective narrative, on the recognition of a common name and on traditions lived as the trace of an immemorial past (even when they have been fabricated and inculcated in the recent past). But this comes down to accepting that, under certain conditions, *only* imaginary communities are real.

In the case of national formations, the imaginary which inscribes itself in the real in this way is that of the 'people'. It is that of a community which recognizes itself in advance in the institution of the state, which recognizes that state as 'its own' in opposition to other states and, in particular, inscribes its political struggles within the horizon of that state – by, for example, formulating its aspirations for reform and social revolution as projects for the transformation of 'its national state'. Without this, there can be neither 'monopoly of organized violence' (Max Weber), nor 'national-popular will' (Gramsci). But such a people does not exist naturally, and even when it is tendentially constituted, it does not exist for all time. No modern nation possesses a given 'ethnic' basis, even when it arises out of a national independence struggle. And, moreover, no modern nation, however 'egalitarian' it may be, corresponds to the extinction of class conflicts. The fundamental problem is therefore to produce the people. More exactly, it is to make the people produce itself continually as national community. Or again, it is to produce the effect of unity by virtue of which the people will appear, in everyone's eyes, 'as a people', that is, as the basis and origin of political power.

Rousseau was the first to have explicitly conceived the question in these terms 'What makes a people a people?' Deep down, this question is no different from the one which arose a moment ago: How are individuals nationalized or, in other words, socialized in the dominant form of national belonging? Which enables us to put aside from the outset another artificial dilemma: it is not a question of setting a collective identity against individual identities. *All identity is individual,* but there is no individual identity that is not historical or, in other words, constructed within a field of social values, norms of behaviour and collective symbols. Individuals never identify with one another (not even in the 'fusional' practices of mass movements or the 'intimacy' of affective relations), nor, however, do they ever acquire an isolated identity, which is an intrinsically contradictory notion. The real question is how the dominant reference points of individual identity change over time and with the changing institutional environment.

To the question of the historical production of the people (or of national individuality) we cannot merely be content to rely with a description of conquests, population movements and administrative practices of 'territorialization'. The individuals destined to perceive themselves as the members of a single nation are either gathered together externally from diverse geographical origins, as in the nations formed by immigration (France, the USA) or else are brought mutually to recognize one another within a historical frontier which contained them all. The people is constituted out of various populations subject to a common law. In every case, however, a model of their unity must 'anticipate' that constitution: the process of unification (the effectiveness of which can be measured, for example, in collective mobilization in wartime, that is, in the capacity to confront death collectively) presupposes the constitution of a specific ideological form. It must at one and the same time be a mass phenomenon and a phenomenon of individuation, must effect an 'interpellation of individuals as subjects' (Althusser) which is much more potent than the mere inculcation of political values or rather one that integrates this inculcation into a more elementary process (which we may term 'primary') of fixation of the affects of love and hate and representation of the 'self'. That ideological form must become an a priori condition of communication between individuals (the 'citizens') and between social groups – not by suppressing all differences, but by relativizing them and subordinating them to itself in such a way that it is the symbolic difference between 'ourselves' and 'foreigners' which wins out and which is lived as irreducible. In other words, to use the terminology proposed by Fichte in his

Reden an die deutsche Nation of 1808, the 'external frontiers' of the state have to become 'internal frontiers' or – which amounts to the same thing – external frontiers have to be imagined constantly as a projection and protection of an internal collective personality, which each of us carries within ourselves and enables us to inhabit the space of the state as a place where we have always been – and always will be – 'at home'.

What might that ideological form be? Depending on the particular circumstances, it will be called patriotism or nationalism, the events which promote its formation or which reveal its potency will be recorded and its origin will be traced back to political methods – the combination of 'force' and 'education' (as Machiavelli and Gramsci put it) – which enable the state to some extent to fabricate public consciousness. But this fabrication is merely an external aspect. To grasp the deepest reasons for its effectiveness, attention will turn then, as the attention of political philosophy and sociology have turned for three centuries, towards the analogy of *religion*, making nationalism and patriotism out to be a religion – if not indeed *the* religion – of modern times.

Inevitably, there is some truth in this – and not only because religions, formally, in so far as they start out from 'souls' and individual identities, institute forms of community and prescribe a social 'morality'; but also because theological discourse has provided models for the idealization of the nation and the sacralization of the state, which make it possible for a bond of sacrifice to be created between individuals, and for the stamp of 'truth' and 'law' to be conferred upon the rules of the legal system.[9] Every national community must have been represented at some point or another as a 'chosen people'. Nevertheless, the political philo-sophies of the Classical Age had already recognized the inadequacy of this analogy, which is equally clearly demonstrated by the failure of the attempts to constitute 'civil religions', by the fact that the 'state religion' ultimately only constituted a transitory form of national ideology (even when this transition lasted for a long time and produced important effects by superimposing religious on national struggles) and by the interminable con-flict between theological universality and the universality of nationalism.

In reality, the opposite argument is correct. Incontestably, national ideology involves ideal signifiers (first and foremost the very *name* of the nation or 'fatherland') on to which may be transferred the sense of the sacred and the affects of love, respect, sacrifice and fear which have cemented religious communities; but that transfer only takes place because *another type* of community is involved here. The analogy is itself based on a deeper difference. If it were not, it would be impossible to understand why national identity, more or less completely integrating the forms of religious identity, ends up tending to replace it, and forcing it itself to become 'nationalized'.

Fictive Ethnicity and Ideal Nation

I apply the term 'fictive ethnicity' to the community instituted by the nation-state. This is an intentionally complex expression in which the term fiction, in keeping with my remarks above, should not be taken in the sense of a pure and simple illusion without historical effects, but must, on the contrary, be understood by analogy with the *persona ficta* of the juridical tradition in the sense of an institutional effect, a 'fabric-ation'. No nation possesses an ethnic base naturally, but as social formations are nationalized, the populations included within them, divided up among them or dominated by them are ethnicized – that is, represented in the past or in the future *as if* they formed a natural community, possessing of itself an identity of origins, culture and inter-ests which transcends individuals and social conditions.[10]

Fictive ethnicity is not purely and simply identical with the *ideal nation* which is the object of patriotism, but it is indispensable to it, for, without it, the nation would appear precisely only as an idea or an arbitrary abstraction; patriotism's appeal would be addressed to no one. It is fictive ethnicity which makes it possible for the expression of a pre-existing unity to be seen in the state, and continually to measure the state against its 'historic mission' in the service of the nation and, as a consequence, to idealize politics. By constituting the people as a fictively ethnic unity against the background of a universalistic representation which attributes to each individual one – and only one – ethnic identity and which thus divides up the whole of humanity between different ethnic groups corresponding potentially to so many nations, national ideology does much more than justify the strategies employed by the state to control populations. It inscribes their demands in advance in a sense of belonging in the double sense of the term – both what it is that makes one belong to oneself and also what makes one belong to other fellow human beings. Which means that one can be interpellated, as an individual, *in the name of* the collectivity whose name one bears. The naturalization of belonging and the sublimation of the ideal nation are two aspects of the same process.

How can ethnicity be produced? And how can it be produced in such a way that it does not appear as fiction, but as the most natural of origins? History shows us that there are two great competing routes to this: language and race. Most often the two operate together, for only their complementarity makes it possible for the 'people' to be repre-sented as an absolutely autonomous unit. Both express the idea that the national character (which might also be called its soul or its spirit) is immanent in the people. But both offer a means of transcending actual individuals and political relations. They constitute two ways of rooting historical populations in a fact of 'nature' (the diversity of languages and the diversity of races appearing predestined), but also two ways of giving a meaning to their continued existence, of transcending its contingency. By force of circumstance, however, at times one or the other is dominant, for they are not based on the development of the same institutions and do not appeal to the same symbols or the same idealizations of the national identity. The fact of these different articulations of, on the one hand, a predominantly linguistic ethnicity and, on the other, an ethnicity that is predominantly racial has obvious political consequences. For this reason, and for the sake of clarity of analysis, we must begin by examining the two separately.

The language community seems the more abstract notion, but in reality it is the more concrete since it connects individuals up with an origin which may at any moment be actualized and which has as its content the *common act* of their own exchanges, of their discursive communication, using the instruments of spoken language and the whole, constantly self-renewing mass of written and recorded texts. This is not to say that that community is an immediate one, without internal limits, any more than communication is in reality 'transparent' between all individuals. But these limits are always relative: even if it were the case that individuals whose social conditions were very distant from one another were never in direct communication, they would be bound together by an uninterrupted chain of intermediate discourses. They are not isolated – either *de jure* or *de facto.*

We should, however, certainly not allow ourselves to believe that this situation is as old as the world itself. It is, on the contrary, remarkably recent. The old empires and the *Ancien Régime* societies were still based on the juxtaposition of linguistically separate populations, on the super-imposition of mutually incompatible 'languages' for the dominant and the dominated and for the sacred and profane spheres. Between these there had to be a whole system of translations.[11] In modern national formations, the translators are writers, journalists and politicians, social actors who speak the language of the 'people' in a way that seems all the more natural for the very degree of distinction they thereby bring to it. The translation process has become primarily one of internal translation between different 'levels of language'. Social differences are expressed and relativized as different ways of speaking the national language, which supposes a common code and even a common norm.[12] This latter is, as we know, inculcated by universal schooling, whose primary function it is to perform precisely this task.

That is why there is a close historical correlation between the national formation and the development of schools as 'popular' institutions, not limited to specialized training or to elite culture, but serving to underpin

the whole process of the socialization of individuals. That the school
should also be the site of the inculcation of a nationalist ideology – and
sometimes also the place where it is contested – is a secondary phenomenon, and is, strictly speaking, a less indispensable aspect. Let us simply
say that schooling is the principal institution which produces ethnicity as
linguistic community. It is not, however, the only one: the state,
economic exchange and family life are also schools in a sense, organs of
the ideal nation recognizable by a common language which belongs to
them 'as their own'. For what is decisive here is not only that the
national language should be recognized as the official language, but,
much more fundamentally, that it should be able to appear as the very
element of the life of a people, the *reality* which each person may appropriate in his or her own way, without thereby destroying its identity.
There is no contradiction between the instituting of *one* national
language and the daily discrepancy between – and clash of – 'class
languages' which precisely are not different languages. In fact, the two
things are complementary. All linguistic practices feed into a single 'love
of the language' which is addressed not to the textbook norm nor to
particular usage, but to the 'mother tongue' – that is, to the ideal of a
common origin projected back beyond learning processes and specialist
forms of usage and which, by that very fact, becomes the metaphor for
the love fellow nationals feel for one another.[13]

One might then ask oneself, quite apart from the precise historical
questions which the history of national languages poses – from the difficulties of their unification or imposition, and from their elaboration into
an idiom that is both 'popular' and 'cultivated' (a process which we
know to be far from complete today in all nation-states, in spite of the
labours of their intellectuals with the aid of various international bodies)
– *why the language community is not sufficient* to produce ethnicity.

Perhaps this has to do with the paradoxical properties which, by
virtue of its very structure, the linguistic signifier confers on individual
identity. In a sense, it is always in the element of language that individuals are interpellated as subjects, for every interpellation is of the
order of discourse. Every 'personality' is constructed with words, in
which law, genealogy, history, political choices, professional qualifi-
cations and psychology are set forth. But the linguistic construction of
identity is by definition *open*. No individual 'chooses' his or her mother
tongue or can 'change' it at will. Nevertheless, it is always possible to
appropriate several languages and to turn oneself into a different kind of
bearer of discourse and of the transformations of language. The
linguistic community induces a terribly constraining ethnic memory
(Roland Barthes once went so far as to call it 'fascist'), but it is one
which none the less possesses a strange plasticity: it immediately natural-

izes new acquisitions. It does so *too quickly* in a sense. It is a collective memory which perpetuates itself at the cost of an individual forgetting of 'origins'. The 'second generation' immigrant – a notion which in this context acquires a structural significance – inhabits the national language (and through it the nation itself) in a manner as spontaneous, as 'hereditary' and as imperious, so far as affectivity and the imaginary are concerned, as the son of one of those native heaths which we think of as so very French (and most of which not so long ago did not even have the national language as their daily parlance). One's 'mother' tongue is not necessarily the language of one's 'real' mother. The language community is a community *in the present*, which produces the feeling that it has always existed, but which lays down no destiny for the successive generations. Ideally, it 'assimilates' anyone, but holds no one. Finally, it affects all individuals in their innermost being (in the way in which they constitute themselves as subjects), but its historical particularity is bound only to interchangeable institutions. When circumstances permit, it may serve different nations (as English, Spanish and even French do) or survive the 'physical' disappearance of the people who used it (like 'ancient' Greek and Latin or 'literary' Arabic). For it to be tied down to the frontiers of a particular people, it therefore needs an extra degree [*un supplément*] of particularity, or a principle of closure, of exclusion.

This principle is that of being part of a common race. But here we must be very careful not to give rise to misunderstandings. All kinds of somatic or psychological features, both visible and invisible, may lend themselves to creating the fiction of a racial identity and therefore to representing natural and hereditary differences between social groups either within the same nation or outside its frontiers. I have discussed elsewhere, as have others before me, the development of the marks of race and the relation they bear to different historical figures of social conflict. What we are solely concerned with here is the symbolic kernel which makes it possible to equate race and ethnicity ideally, and to represent unity of race to oneself as the origin or cause of the historical unity of a people. Now, unlike what applied in the case of the linguistic community, it cannot be a question here of a practice which is really common to *all* the individuals who form a political unit. We are not dealing with anything equivalent to communication. What we are speaking of is therefore a second-degree fiction. This fiction, however, also derives its effectiveness from everyday practices, relations which immediately structure the 'life' of individuals. And, most importantly, whereas the language community can only create equality between individuals by simultaneously 'naturalizing' the social inequality of linguistic practices, the race community dissolves social inequalities in an even more ambivalent 'similarity'; it ethnicizes the social difference which is an expression of irreconcilable antagonisms by lending it the form of a division between the 'genuinely' and the 'falsely' national.

I think we may cast some light on this paradox in the following way. The symbolic kernel of the idea of race (and of its demographic and cultural equivalents) is the schema of genealogy, that is, quite simply the idea that the filiation of individuals transmits from generation to generation a substance both biological and spiritual and thereby inscribes them in a temporal community known as 'kinship'. That is why, *as soon as* national ideology enunciates the proposition that the individuals belonging to the same people are interrelated (or, in the prescriptive mode, that they should constitute a circle of extended kinship), we are in the presence of this second mode of ethnicization.

The objection will no doubt be raised here that such a representation characterizes societies and communities which have nothing national about them. But, it is precisely on this point that the particular innovation hinges by which the nation form is articulated to the modern idea of race. This idea is correlative with the tendency for 'private' genealogies, as (still) codified by traditional systems of preferential marriage and lineage, to disappear. The idea of a racial community makes its appearance when the frontiers of kinship dissolve at the level of the clan, the neighbourhood community and, theoretically at least, the social class, to be imaginarily transferred to the threshold of nationality: that is to say, when nothing prevents marriage with any of one's 'fellow citizens' whatever, and when, on the contrary, such a marriage seems the only one that is 'normal' or 'natural'. The racial community has a tendency to represent itself as one big family or as the common envelope of family relations (the community of 'French', 'American' or 'Algerian' families).[14] From that point onward, each individual has his/her family, whatever his/her social condition, but the family – like property – becomes a contingent relation between individuals. In order to consider this question further, we ought therefore to turn to a discussion of the history of the family, an institution which here plays a role every bit as central as that played by the school in the discussion above, and one that is ubiquitous in the discourse of race.

The Family and the School

We here run up against the lacunae in family history, a subject which remains prey to the dominant perspective of laws relating to marriage on the one hand and, on the other, of 'private life' as a literary and anthropological subject. The great theme of the recent history of the family is the emergence of the 'nuclear' or small family (constituted by the parental couple and their children), and here discussion is focused on whether it is a specifically 'modern' phenomenon (eighteenth and nine-teenth centuries) connected with bourgeois forms of sociality (the thesis of Ariès and Shorter) or whether it is the result of a development, the basis of which was laid down a long time before by ecclesiastical law and the control of marriage by the Christian authorities (Goody's thesis).[15] In fact, these positions are not incompatible. But, most importantly, they tend to push into the shade what is for us the most crucial question: the correlation which has gradually been established since the institution of public registration and the codification of the family (of which the Code Napoléon was the prototype) between the dissolution of relations of 'extended' kinship and the penetration of family relations by the inter-vention of the nation-state, which runs from legislation in respect of inheritance to the organization of birth control. Let us note here that in contemporary national societies, except for a few genealogy 'fanatics' and a few who are 'nostalgic' for the days of the aristocracy, genealogy is no longer either a body of theoretical knowledge or an object of oral memory, nor is it recorded and conserved *privately*: today *it is the state which draws up and keeps the archive of filiations and alliances.*

Here again we have to distinguish between a deep and a superficial level. The superficial level is familialist discourse (constitutive of con-servative nationalism), which at a very early stage became linked with nationalism in political tradition – particularly within the French tra-dition. The deep level is the simultaneous emergence of 'private life', the 'intimate (small) family circle' *and* the family policy of the state, which projects into the public sphere the new notion of population and the demographic techniques for measuring it, of the supervision of its health and morals, of its reproduction. The result is that the modern family circle is quite the opposite of an autonomous sphere at the frontiers of which the structures of the state would halt. It is the sphere in which the relations between individuals are immediately charged with a 'civic' function and made possible by constant state assistance, beginning with relations between the sexes which are aligned to procreation. This is also what enables us to understand the anarchistic tone that sexually 'deviant' behaviour easily takes on in modern national formations, whereas in earlier societies it more usually took on a tone of religious heresy. Public health and social security have replaced the father confessor, not term for term, but by introducing both a new 'freedom' and a new assistance, a new mission and therefore also a new demand. Thus, as lineal kinship, solidarity between generations and the economic functions of the extended family dissolve, what takes their place is neither a natural micro-society nor a purely 'individualistic' contractual relation, but a nationalization of the family, which has as its counterpart the identification of the national community with a symbolic kinship, circumscribed by rules of pseudo-endogamy, and with a tendency not so much to project itself into a sense of having common antecedents as a feeling of having common descendants.

That is why the idea of eugenics is always latent in the reciprocal relation between the 'bourgeois' family and a society which takes the nation form. That is why nationalism also has a secret affinity with sexism: not so much as a manifestation of the same authoritarian tradition but in so far as the inequality of sexual roles in conjugal love and child-rearing constitutes the anchoring point for the juridical, economic, educational and medical mediation of the state. Finally also, that is why the representation of nationalism as a 'tribalism' – the sociologists' grand alternative to representing it as a religion – is both mystificatory and revealing. Mystificatory because it imagines nationalism as a regression to archaic forms of community which are in reality incompatible with the nation-state (this can be clearly seen from the incompleteness of the formation of a nation wherever powerful lineal or tribal solidarities still exist). But it is also revealing of the substitution of one imaginary of kinship for another, a substitution which the nation effects and which underpins the transformation of the family itself. It is also what forces us to ask ourselves to what extent the nation form can continue to reproduce itself indefinitely (at least as the dominant form) once the transformation of the family is 'completed' – that is to say, once relations of sex and procreation are completely removed from the genealogical order. We would then reach the limit of the material possibilities of conceiving what human 'races' are and of investing that particular representation in the process of producing ethnicity. But no doubt we have not reached that point yet.

Althusser was not wrong in his outline definition of the 'Ideological State Apparatuses' to suggest that the kernel of the dominant ideology of bourgeois societies has passed from the family–church dyad to the family–school dyad.[16] I am, however, tempted to introduce two correctives to that formulation. First, I shall not say that a particular institution of this kind in itself constitutes *an* 'Ideological State Apparatus': what such a formulation adequately designates is rather the combined functioning of *several* dominant institutions. I shall further propose that the contemporary importance of schooling and the family unit does not derive solely from the functional place they take in the reproduction of labour power, but from the fact that they subordinate that reproduction to the constitution of a fictive ethnicity – that is, to the articulation of a linguistic community and a community of race implicit in population policies (what Foucault called by a suggestive but ambiguous term the system of 'bio-powers').[17] School and family perhaps have other aspects or deserve to be analysed from other points of view. Their history begins well before the appearance of the nation form and may continue beyond it. But what makes them together constitute the dominant ideological apparatus in bourgeois societies – which is expressed in their growing interdependence and in their tendency to divide up the time devoted to the training of individuals exhaustively between them – is their national importance, that is, their immediate importance for the production of ethnicity. In this sense, there is only *one* dominant 'Ideological State Apparatus' in bourgeois social formations, using the school and family institutions for its own ends – together with other institutions grafted on to the school and the family – and the existence of that apparatus is at the root of the hegemony of nationalism.

We must add one remark in conclusion on this hypothesis. Articulation – even complementarity – does not mean harmony. Linguistic ethnicity and racial (or hereditary) ethnicity are in a sense mutually exclusive. I suggested above that the linguistic community is open, whereas the race community appears in principle closed (since it leads – theoretically – to maintaining indefinitely, until the end of the generations, outside the community or on its 'inferior' 'foreign' margins those who, by its criteria, are not authentically national). Both are ideal representations. Doubtless race symbolism combines the element of anthropological universality on which it is based (the chain of generations, the absolute of kinship extended to the whole of humanity) with an imaginary of segregation and prohibitions. But in practice migration and intermarriage are constantly transgressing the limits which are thus projected (even where coercive policies criminalize 'interbreeding'). The real obstacle to the mixing of populations is constituted rather by class differences which tend to reconstitute caste phenomena. The hereditary substance of ethnicity constantly has to be redefined: yesterday it was 'German-ness', 'the French' or 'Anglo-Saxon' race, today it is 'European-ness' or 'Western-ness', tomorrow perhaps the 'Mediterranean race'. Conversely, the openness of the linguistic community is an ideal openness, even thought it has as its material support the possibility of translating from one language to another and therefore the capacity of individuals to increase the range of their linguistic competence.

Though formally egalitarian, belonging to the linguistic community – chiefly because of the fact that it is mediated by the institution of the school – immediately re-creates divisions, differential norms which also overlap with class differences to a very great degree. The greater the role taken on by the education system within bourgeois societies, the more do differences in linguistic (and therefore literary, 'cultural' and techno-

logical) competence function as caste differences, assigning different
'social destinies' to individuals. In these circumstances, it is not
surprising that they should immediately be associated with forms of
corporal *habitus* (to use Pierre Bourdieu's terminology) which confer on
the act of speaking in its personal, non-universalizable traits the function
of a racial or quasi-racial mark (and which still occupy a very important
place in the formulation of 'class racism'): 'foreign' or 'regional' accent,
'popular' style of speech, language 'errors' or, conversely, ostentatious
'correctness' immediately designating a speaker's belonging to a particular population and spontaneously interpreted as reflecting a specific
family origin and a hereditary disposition.[18] The production of ethnicity
is also the racialization of language and the verbalization of race.

It is not an irrelevant matter – either from the immediate political
point of view or from the point of view of the development of the nation
form, or its future role in the instituting of social relations – that a particular representation of ethnicity should be dominant, since it leads to
two radically different attitudes to the problem of integration and
assimilation, two ways of grounding the juridical order and nationalizing
institutions.[19]

The French 'revolutionary nation' accorded a privileged place to the
symbol of language in its own initial process of formation; it bound
political unity closely to linguistic uniformity, the democratization of the
state to the coercive repression of cultural 'particularisms', local *patois*
being the object on which it became fixated. For its part, the American
'revolutionary nation' built its original ideals on a double repression:
that of the extermination of the Amerindian 'natives' and that of the
difference between free 'White' men and 'Black' slaves. The linguistic
community inherited from the Anglo-Saxon 'mother country' did not
pose a problem – at least apparently – until Hispanic immigration
conferred upon it the significance of class symbol and racial feature.
'Nativism' has always been implicit in the history of French national
ideology until, at the end of the nineteenth century, colonization on the
one hand, and an intensification of the importation of labour and the
segregation of manual workers by means of their ethnic origin on the
other, led to the constitution of the phantasm of the 'French race'. It
was, by contrast, very quickly made explicit in the history of American
national ideology, which represented the formation of the American
people as the melting-pot of a new race, but also as a hierarchical
combination of the different ethnic contributions, at the cost of difficult
analogies between European or Asian immigration and the social
inequalities inherited from slavery and reinforced by the economic
exploitation of the Blacks.[20]

These historical differences in no sense impose any necessary outcome – they are rather the stuff of political struggles – but they deeply modify the conditions in which problems of assimilation, equality of rights, citizenship, nationalism and internationalism are posed. One might seriously wonder whether in regard to the production of fictive ethnicity, the 'building of Europe' – to the extent that it will seek to transfer to the 'Community' level functions and symbols of the nation-state – will orientate itself *predominantly* towards the institution of a 'European co-lingualism' (and if so, adopting which language) or *predominantly* in the direction of the idealization of 'European demographic identity' conceived mainly in opposition to the 'southern populations' (Turks, Arabs, Blacks).[21] Every 'people', which is the product of a national process of ethnicization, is forced today to find its own means of going beyond exclusivism or identitarian ideology in the world of transnational communications and global relations of force. Or rather: every individual is compelled to find in the transformation of the imaginary of 'his' or 'her' people the means to leave it, in order to communicate with the individuals of other peoples with which he or she shares the same interests and, to some extent, the same future.

Notes

1. See Gérard Noiriel, *Le Creuset français. Histoire de l'immigration XIXe–XXe siècles*, Editions du Seuil, Paris 1988.

2. If one did, however, have to choose a date symbolically, one might point to the middle of the sixteenth century: the completion of the Spanish conquest of the New World, the break-up of the Habsburg Empire, the end of the dynastic wars in England and the beginning of the Dutch War of Independence.

3. Fernand Braudel, *Civilization and Capitalism*, vol. 2, *The Wheels of Commerce*, transl. Siân Reynolds, Collins, London 1982, and vol. 3, *The Perspective of the World*, transl. Siân Reynolds, Collins, London 1984; Immanuel Wallerstein, *The Modern World-System*, vol. 1, *Capitalist Agriculture and the Origin of the European World-Economy in the Sixteenth Century*, Academic Press, London 1974, and vol. 2, *Mercantilism and the Consolidation of the European World-Economy*, Academic Press, London 1980.

4. See Braudel, *The Perspective of the World*, pp. 97–105; Wallerstein, *Capitalist Agriculture*, pp. 165 *et seq.*

5. From this point of view, there is nothing surprising about the fact that the 'orthodox' Marxist theory of the linear succession of modes of production became the official doctrine in the USSR at the point when nationalism triumphed there, particularly as it made it possible for the 'first socialist state' to be represented as the new universal nation.

6. Eugen Weber, *Peasants into Frenchmen*, Stanford University Press, Stanford, CA 1976.

7. Gérard Noiriel, *Longwy, Immigrés et prolétaires, 1880–1980*, PUF, Paris 1984; *Le Creuset français*.

8. For some further remarks on this same point, see my study, 'Propositions sur la citoyenneté', in C. Wihtol de Wenden, ed., *La Citoyenneté*, Edilig-Fondation Diderot, Paris 1988.

9. On all these points, the work of Kantorowicz is clearly of crucial signficance: see *Mourir pour la patrie et autres textes*, PUF, Paris 1985.

10. I say 'included within them', but I should also add 'or excluded by them', since the ethnicization of the 'others' occurs simultaneously with that of the 'nationals': there are no longer any historical differences other than ethnic ones (thus the Jews also have to be a 'people'). On the ethnicization of colonized populations, see J.-L. Amselle and E. M'Bokolo, *Au cœur de l'ethnie: ethnies, tribalisme et Etat en Afrique*, La Découverte, Paris 1985.

11. Ernest Gellner (*Nations and Nationalism,*, Blackwell, Oxford 1983) and Benedict Anderson (*Imagined Communities*, Verso, London 1983), whose analyses are as opposed as 'materialism' and 'idealism', both rightly stress this point.

12. See Renée Balibar, *L'Institution du français. Essai sur le colingualisme des Carolingiens à la République*, PUF, Paris 1985.

13. Jean-Claude Milner offers some very stimulating suggestions on this point, though more in *Les Noms indistincts* (Seuil, Paris 1983), pp. 43 *et seq.* than in *L'Amour de la langue* (Seuil, Paris 1978). On the 'class struggle'/'language struggle' alternative in the USSR at the point when the policy of 'socialism in one country' became dominant, see F. Gadet, J.-M. Gaymann, Y. Mignot and E. Roudinesco, *Les Maîtres de la langue*, Maspero, Paris 1979.

14. Let us add that we have here a sure *criterion* for the commutation between racism and nationalism: every discourse on the fatherland or nation which associates these notions with the 'defence of the family' – not to speak of the birth rate – is already ensconced in the universe of racism.

15. Philippe Ariès, *L'Enfant et la vie familiale sous l'Ancien Régime*, Plon, Paris 1960, revised edn 1975 (*Centuries of Childhood*, transl. Robert Baldick, London, Cape 1962); Edward Shorter, *The Making of the Modern Family*, Basic Books, New York 1975; Jack Goody, *The Development of the Family and Marriage in Europe*, Cambridge University Press, Cambridge 1983.

16. See Louis Althusser, 'Ideology and State Ideological Apparatuses', *Lenin and Philosophy and Other Essays*, New Left Books, London 1971.

17. Michel Foucault, *The History of Sexuality*, vol. I, transl. Robert Hurley, Allen Lane, London 1977.

18. See P. Bourdieu, *Distinction*, transl. Richard Nice, Routledge & Kegan Paul, London 1984: *Ce que parler veut dire: l'économie des échanges linguistiques*, Fayard, Paris 1982; and the critique by the 'Révoltes logiques' collective (*L'Empire du sociologue*, La Découverte, Paris 1984), which bears essentially on the way that Bourdieu *fixes* social roles as 'destinies' and immediately attributes to the antagonism between them a function of reproducing the 'totality' (the chapter on language is by Françoise Kerleroux).

19. See some most valuable remarks on this point in Françoise Gadet and Michel Pêcheux, *La Langue introuvable*, Maspero, Paris 1981, pp. 38 *et seq.* ('L'anthropologie linguistique entre le Droit et la Vie').

20. On American 'nativism', see R. Ertel, G. Fabre and E. Marienstras, *En marge. Les minorités aux Etats-Unis*, Maspero, Paris 1974, pp. 25 *et seq.*, and Michael Omi and Howard Winant, *Racial Formation in the United States. From the 1960s to the 1980s*, Routledge & Kegan Paul, London 1986, p. 120. It is interesting to see a movement developing today in the United States (directed against Latin American immigration) calling for English to be made the *official* language.

21. Right at the heart of this alternative lies the following truly crucial question: will the administrative and educational institutions of the future 'United Europe' accept Arabic, Turkish or even certain Asian or African languages on an equal footing with French, German and Portuguese, or will those languages be regarded as 'foreign'?

6

Household Structures and Labour-Force Formation in the Capitalist World-Economy

Immanuel Wallerstein

Households make up one of the key institutional structures of the capitalist world-economy. It is always an error to analyse social institutions transhistorically, as though they constituted a genus of which each historical system produced a variant or species. Rather, the multiple institutional structures of a given historical system (a) are in fundamental ways unique to that system, and (b) are part of an inter-related *set* of institutions that constitute the operational structures of the system.

The historical system in this case is the capitalist world-economy as a single evolving historical entity. The households located in that system can most fruitfully be understood by analysing how they fit into the set of institutions of that system rather than by comparing them to hypothetically parallel institutions (often bearing the same nominal designation) in other historical systems. Indeed, one can reasonably doubt whether there was anything parallel to our 'household' in previous systems (but the same could be said of such institutional concepts as 'state' or 'class'). The use of such terms as 'households' transhistorically is at best an analogy.

Rather than compare putative sets of characteristics of possibly parallel institutions, let us rather pose the problem from inside the ongoing capitalist world-economy. The endless accumulation of capital is the defining characteristic and *raison d'être* of this system. Over time, this endless accumulation pushes towards the commodification of everything, the absolute increase of world production, and a complex and sophisticated social division of labour. The objective of accumulation presupposes a system of polarizing distribution in which the majority of the world population serves as a labour force producing surplus-value, which is somehow distributed among the remaining minority of the world population.

From the point of view of the accumulators of capital, what problems are posed by the ways in which this world labour force is produced and reproduced? I think the accumulators can be seen to have three main concerns:

1. They benefit by having a labour force whose use is variable in time. That is to say, individual entrepreneurs will want to have expenditures only directly related to production and therefore will not wish to pay a rental fee for future option on unused labour time. On the other hand, when they wish to produce, they also wish to have persons willing to work. The variation in time may be decade to decade, year to year, week to week, or even hour to hour.

2. They will benefit by having a labour force whose use is variable in space. That is to say, individual entrepreneurs will wish to locate or relocate their enterprises according to some considerations of costs (the costs of transport, the historical costs of labour-power and so on) without being unduly constrained by the existing geographical distribution of the world's labour force. The variation in space can be continent to continent, rural to urban, or one particular immediate locus to another.

3. They will benefit by having the cost-level of the labour force as low as possible. That is to say, individual entrepreneurs will want their direct costs (in the form of wages, of indirect monetary payments and of payments in kind) to be minimized, at least over the middle term.

Each of these preferences to which individual entrepreneurs must adhere (on pain of their elimination from the economic arena through bankruptcy) lies in partial contradiction with the interests of the accumulators of capital as a world class. As a world class, accumulators need to ensure that the world labour force be reproduced at a numerical level related to the level of world production, and that this world labour force not so organize itself as a class force that it will threaten the existence of the system as such. Thus, as a world class, certain kinds of redistribution (to ensure an adequate level of world-wide effective demand, to ensure long-term reproduction of the world labour force and to guarantee an adequate political defence mechanism for the system by allowing cadres to receive a part of the surplus) all may seem necessary steps.

The problem then is what kinds of institutions would, from the point of view of the accumulators of capital (in their contradictory capacities as a set of competing individuals and as a collective class), be optimal in terms of labour-force formation? We shall suggest several ways in which the historical development of 'household' structures have been consonant with this objective. The contradictory needs of entrepreneurs as individuals and entrepreneurs as a class can best be reconciled if the determinants of labour-force supply have a molasses-like consistency: the institutions ooze (that is, they respond flexibly to various pressures of the 'market') but they ooze slowly. The 'household' as it has historically developed under capitalism seems to have precisely this character. Its boundaries are malleable but have none the less a short-term firmness embedded in both economic self-interest and the social psychology of its members.

There are three major ways in which the boundaries have been kept gently malleable. First of all, there has been a steady pressure to break the link between household organization and territoriality. In the early phase, this was the pressure, long observed, to detach more and more people from a commitment (physical, legal and emotional) to a particular small unit of land. In the second phase, usually temporally later, this has been the pressure to diminish but never entirely eliminate co-residentiality as the basis of the legal and sociopsychological commitments to a pooled income structure. (It is this phenomenon that has been perceived, largely incorrectly in my view, as the rise of the nuclear family.)

Second, as the capitalist world-economy has evolved over time, it has become more and more clear that the social division of production has been predicated on a partially waged world labour force. This 'partialism' was double. There was (a) a dispersion of the world's households along a curve representing the percentage of total productive work that was remunerated by wages. I suspect that a proper statistical analysis for the world-economy as a whole would show that this curve has got less skewed and more bell-like over historical time. And (b) virtually no households inside the capitalist world-economy have been located on the far ends of the curve. This means that virtually every individual household's mode of remuneration was that of 'partial' wage labour.

Third, the households' forms of participation in the labour force were stratified, and increasingly so, in terms of ethnicity/peoplehood and gender. But the ideology of equal opportunity was simultaneously increasingly asserted and implemented. The way these two thrusts were reconciled was that the actual stratification was flexible, since the boundary lines of ethnicity (including the rules for endogamy) were themselves malleable. While the boundary lines for gender were less malleable than those for ethnicity, it was none the less possible to redefine constantly which occupational roles fell on each side of the gender-stratification dividing line.

Note that, in each of these aspects (territoriality, wage labour and ethnic and gender stratification), the structure was one involving a tension – the break from territoriality but some role for coresidentiality, a waged labour system but only a partial one, ethnic and gender stratification system but one moderated by an ideology of equal opportunity. It is precisely this tension, this 'intermediateness', that enabled the accumulators to manipulate (but only up to a point) the world labour force. It was the very same tension that created both the vigour and the ambiguities of the response of the world labour force – a response in terms of social consciousness (loyalties to a people, a class, a household) and in terms of political consciousness (involvement in movements).

The efficacy of the household from the point of view of the accumulators can be seen if it is contrasted with two hypothetical alternatives as an income-pooling unit (commensality in the figurative sense). One is a 'community' (a commune) of 50 or 100 or even more persons. The second is an isolated very small unit (a single person or a nuclear family with no children of adult status). The community was of course a frequent unit of social reproduction in prior historical systems. There have been occasional (mostly unsuccessful) attempts to replicate units of such size within the capitalist world-economy. The very small units of course occurred but seemed also to be strongly resisted as somehow 'unviable'.

It is empirically the case that actual income-pooling households have tended to be intermediate in size. In order to avoid too small units, households have often moved beyond the kinship networks to incorporate non-kin. In order to avoid the too large units, both social and legal limits to mutual obligations have grown up. Why should such a tendency to intermediateness – in size as well as composition – have prevailed?

The chief disadvantage, it would seem, of the too small units was that the level of wage-income necessary to ensure collective reproduction was clearly higher than for the intermediate units. Where the level of wages was too low, the households themselves sought to enlarge their boundaries for survival. But this was clearly in the interest of the accumulators as well.

The chief disadvantage, it would seem, of the too large units was that the level of work-output required to ensure survival was too low. On the one hand, accumulators did not like this because it diminished pressure to enter the wage-labour market. On the other hand, members of the labour force found that it created a strain between those members of the community who felt they could profit from some immediate mobility and those who did not. One could 'move' a household. It was very difficult to 'move' a community.

Institutional structures are not givens. They tend to be loci of, indeed objects of, contradictory attempts to shape them. There were two primary struggles surrounding the institution of the household. The first was the frequently opposed interests of the workers grouped together in a household and the accumulators who had power in a given locality and/or state. The second was the contradiction between the objectives pursued by the accumulators in terms of household structures and their frequent need to engage in behaviour that undermined these objectives. Let us consider each in turn.

The household as an income-pooling unit can be seen as a fortress both of accommodation to and resistance to the patterns of labour-force allocation favoured by accumulators. As more and more responsibility for reproduction of the work force moved away from the 'community' towards the 'household' as constrained by the 'state', the very malleability of the institution (in terms of membership, boundaries, location and combination of forms of labour), which was so useful to capitalists, was also useful in resisting or circumventing the pressures in the short term. Indeed, until the rise of the movements, and even after that, household decision-making was perhaps the principal everyday political weapon available to the world's labour force. What have frequently been analysed as atavistic thrusts were often sociopolitical parries in defence of given use values or simply efforts to minimize the rate of exploitation. The fact that the demands of the households varied erratically (e.g. sometimes in favour of more women moving into waged labour, sometimes against it) can in fact be readily explained if we look on such demands as tactical rather than strategic, as immediate responses to an immediate political situation.

The actual forms of conflict between the household as a locus of political resistance by the world labour force and the accumulators controlling economic and state structures, and how this varies systematically over time and place, is a topic worthy of much elaboration. I shall not do it here. Rather I turn to the impact of the contradiction within the basic economic mechanisms of capitalism itself. Capitalism involves commodification, but as we have emphasized, only partial commodification. Further commodification, however, has in fact been a regular mechanism for getting out of the cyclical stagnations of the world-economy. The result can be summed up as follows: Despite themselves, and against their own long-term interests, accumulators constantly push to the commodification of everything, and in particular of everyday life. The description of the secular process of the commodification of everyday life has compromised a large part of social science efforts for two centuries. In the long run, this secular process guarantees the demise of the system. In the meantime, it gets translated into household struc-

tures whose internal dynamics have been, are increasingly, commodi-
fied, from the preparation of food, to the cleaning and repair of home
appurtenances and clothing, to custodial care, to nursing care, to
emotional repair. With the increasing commodification of everyday life
has gone a decline in coresidentiality and kinship as determinative of the
boundaries. The end point of this secular pressure is not, however, it
seems to me, the 'individual' or the 'nuclear family' but a unit whose
cohesiveness is increasing predicated on the income-pooling function it
performs.

Marshall Berman has used as the title of his book on the experience
of modernity Marx's metaphor in the *Manifesto*: 'All that is solid melts
into air.'[1] This comes as the conclusion of Marx's analysis of the relent-
less 'revolutionizing' of the means and relations of production. The
passage continues, 'All that is holy is profaned', and then culminates in
what I think is the most relevant passage for us in the context: 'And man
is at last compelled to face with sober senses his real conditions of life
and his relations with his kind.' In many ways this has just begun to
happen. It is the income-pooling lifetime proletarian household –
torn from its once indissoluble link to territory, to kinship and to co-
residentiality – that does the most to strip bare the real conditions of life.
That is why it becomes politically impossible to keep them at this
minimum level. The very expansion of commodification is itself the most
profound politicization. If all that is holy if profaned, then there remains
no justification for the unequal distribution of reward. Even the individualistic reaction of 'more for me' translates into 'at least my fair share'.
This is the most radical political message imaginable.

In this way, it becomes clear why the efforts of the accumulators have
always been to create an 'intermediate' household – to break with the
older 'community' forms of labour-force organization to be sure, but still
to retard the inexorable if slow pace of proletarianization. It is no
accident therefore that today issues surrounding family life, gender
rights and the organization of everyday life remain central political
issues. Indeed, these issues are becoming more acute precisely because
of the secular advance of proletarianization, which is regarded with deep
distrust by the accumulators but often also with confused dismay by the
world's work forces, whose social movements have developed such
ambivalent positions on the subject. And yet it is the key in many ways
to the structuring of class consciousness and therefore to the potential of
these movements themselves.

Note

1. *All That is Solid Melts into Air*, Verso, London 1983.

PART III

Classes: Polarization and Overdetermination

7

Class Conflict in the Capitalist World-Economy

Immanuel Wallerstein

Social class was not a concept invented by Karl Marx. The Greeks knew it and it re-emerged in eighteenth-century European social thought and in the writings that followed the French Revolution. Marx's contribution was threefold. First, he argued that *all* history is the history of the class struggle. Second, he pointed to the fact that a class *an sich* was not necessarily a class *für sich*. Third, he argued that the fundamental conflict of the capitalist mode of production was that between bourgeois and proletarian, between the owners and the non-owners of the means of production. (This is in contrast to the suggestion that the key antagonism is between a productive and non-productive sector, in which active owners were grouped with workers as productive persons as opposed to non-productive rentiers.)

As class analysis came to be used for revolutionary ends, non-revolutionary thinkers by and large put it aside, many if not most fervidly rejecting its legitimacy. Each of Marx's three major contentions on class has been subject to violent controversy ever since.

To the argument that class conflict was the fundamental form of group conflict, Weber responded by arguing that class was only one of three dimensions along which groups were formed, the other two being status and ideology, and that these three dimensions were more or less equal in relevance. Many of Weber's disciples went further and insisted that it was status-group conflict that was primary or 'primordial'.

To the argument that classes existed *an sich* whether or not, at given points of time, they were *für sich*, various social psychologists insisted that the only meaningful construct was a so-called 'subjective' one.

Individuals were members of only such classes as they considered themselves to be.

To the argument that the bourgeoisie and the proletariat were the two essential, polarized groups in the capitalist mode of production, many analysts responded by arguing that more than two 'classes' existed (citing Marx himself), and that 'polarization' was diminishing over time rather than increasing.

Each of these counter-arguments to the Marxian premises had the effect, to the extent that they were accepted, of vitiating the political strategy derived from the original Marxist analysis. One riposte therefore has been to point to the ideological bases of these counter-arguments, which of course was done many times. But since ideological distortions involve theoretical incorrectness, it is in fact in the long run more effective, both intellectually and politically, to concentrate on discussing the theoretical usefulness of the competing concepts.

In addition, the running assault on the Marxian premisses about class and class conflict have combined with the realities of the world to create internal intellectual uncertainty in the Marxist camp, which has taken three forms over time: debate on the significance of the so-called 'national question'; debate on the role of specified social strata (particularly the 'peasantry' and the 'petty bourgeoisie' and/or the 'new working class'); debate on the utility of concepts of global spatial hierarchization ('core' and 'periphery') and the allied concept of 'unequal exchange'.

The 'national question' first began to plague Marxist (and socialist) movements in the nineteenth century, especially within the Austro-Hungarian and Russian empires. The 'peasant question' came to the fore between the two world wars with the Chinese Revolution. The dependent role of the 'periphery' became a central issue after the Second World War, in the wake of Bandung, decolonization and 'Third Worldism'. These three 'questions' are in fact variants of a single theme: how to interpret the Marxian premisses; what in fact are the bases of class formation and class consciousness in the capitalist world-economy as it has historically evolved; and how does one reconcile descriptions of the world in terms of these premisses with the ongoing political definitions of the world by the participating groups.

I propose, in view of these historical debates, to discuss what the nature of the capitalist mode of production tells us about who in fact are bourgeois and proletarians, and what are the *political* consequences of the various ways both bourgeois and proletarians have fitted into the capitalist division of labour.

What is capitalism as a mode of production? This is not an easy question, and for that reason is not in fact a widely discussed one. It seems to me that there are several elements that combine to constitute the 'model'. Capitalism is the *only* mode of production in which the *maximization* of surplus-creation is rewarded *per se*. In every historical system, there has been *some* production for *use*, and *some* production for *exchange*, but only in capitalism are all producers rewarded primarily in terms of the exchange value they produce and penalized to the extent they neglect it. The 'rewards' and 'penalties' are mediated through a structure called the 'market'. It is a structure but not an institution. It is a structure moulded by *many* institutions (political, economic, social, even cultural), and it is the principal arena of economic struggle.

Not only is surplus maximized for its own sake, but those who use the surplus to accumulate more capital to produce still more surplus are further rewarded. Thus the pressure is for constant expansion, although the individualist premiss of the system simultaneously renders *constant* expansion impossible.

How does the search for profit operate? It operates by creating legal protections for individual firms (which can range in size from individuals to quite large organizations, including parastatal agencies) to appropriate the surplus-value created by the labour of the primary producers. Were all or most of this surplus-value, however, consumed by the few who owned or controlled the 'firms', we would not have capitalism. This is in fact approximately what had happened in various pre-capitalist systems.

Capitalism involves in addition structures and institutions which reward primarily that subsegment of the owners and controllers who use the surplus-value only *in part* for their own consumption, and in another (usually larger) part for further investment. The structure of the market ensures that those who do not accumulate capital (but merely consume surplus-value) lose out economically over time to those who do accumulate capital.

We may thereupon designate as the bourgeoisie those who receive a part of the surplus-value they do not themselves create and use some of it to accumulate capital. What defines the bourgeois is not a particular profession and not even the legal status of proprietor (although this was historically important) but the fact that the bourgeois obtains, either as an individual or a member of some collectivity, a part of the surplus that he did not create and is in the position to invest (again either individually or as part of a collectivity) some of this surplus in capital goods.

There is a very large gamut of organizational arrangements which can permit this, of which the classic model of the 'free entrepreneur' is only one. Which organizational arrangements prevail at particular moments of time in particular states (for these arrangements are dependent on the legal framework) is a function of the state of development of the world-economy as a whole (and the role of a particular state in that world-economy) on the one hand, and the consequent forms of class struggle in the world-economy (and within the particular state) on the other. Hence, like all other social constructs, the 'bourgeoisie' is not a static phenomenon. It is the designation of a class in the process of perpetual re-creation and hence of constant change of form and composition.

At one level, this is so obvious (at least given certain epistemological premises) that it is a truism. And yet the literature is cram packed with evaluations of whether or not some local group was or was not 'bourgeois' (or 'proletarian') in terms of a model organizational arrangement derived from some other place and time in the historical development of the capitalist world-economy. *There is no ideal type.* (Curiously enough, though the 'ideal type' is a Weberian methodological concept, many Weberians in practice realize this, and *per contra* many Marxists in fact constantly utilize 'ideal types'.)

If we accept that there is no ideal type, then we cannot define (that is, abstract) in terms of attributes, but only in terms of processes. How does an individual become a bourgeois, remain a bourgeois, cease being a bourgeois? The basic way one becomes a bourgeois is achievement in the market. How one gets in a position to achieve initially is a subordinate question. The routes are various. There is the Horatio Alger model: differentiation out of the working classes by dint of extra effort. (This is remarkably similar to Marx's 'truly revolutionary' road from feudalism to capitalism.) There is the Oliver Twist model: co-option because of talent. There is the Horace Mann model: demonstration of potential via performance in formal education.

But the road to the diving board is minor. Most bourgeois become bourgeois by inheritance. The access to the swimming pool is unequal and sometimes capricious. But the crucial question is: can a given individual (or firm) swim? Being a bourgeois requires skills not everyone has: shrewdness, hardness, diligence. At any given time, a certain percentage of bourgeois fail in the market.

More importantly, however, there is a large group that succeeds many if not most of whom aspire to enjoy the rewards of their situation. One of the potential rewards is in fact not to have to compete as hard in the market. But since the market presumably originally provided the income, there is a structured pressure to find ways of maintaining income level without maintaining a corresponding level of work input. This is the effort – the social and political effort – to transform achievement into status. Status is nothing more than the fossilization of the rewards of past achievement.

The problem for the bourgeoisie is that the dynamic of capitalism is located in the economy and not in the political or cultural institutions. Therefore, there are always new bourgeois without status, laying claim to entry to status. And since high status is worthless if too many persons have it, the *nouveaux riches* (the new achievers) are always seeking to oust others to make room for themselves. The obvious target is that subsegment of the old achievers who are coasting on their acquired status but no longer perform in the market.

Ergo, at any one time, there are always three segments of the bourgeoisie: the 'nouveaux riches'; the 'coasters'; and the descendants of bourgeois who are still performing adequately in the market. To appreciate the relations of these three subgroups, we must bear in mind that almost always the third category is the largest one, and usually larger than the other two combined. This is the basic source of the relative stability and 'homogeneity' of the bourgeois class.

There are, however, moments of time when the number of 'nouveaux riches' and 'coasters' as a percentage of the bourgeoisie rises. I think these are usually moments of economic contraction which see both rising bankruptcies and increasing concentration of capital.

As such moments, it has usually been the case that a political quarrel *internal to the bourgeoisie* becomes quite acute. It is often defined terminologically as the fight of 'progressive' elements versus 'reactionary' ones, in which the 'progressive' groups demand that institutional 'rights' and access be defined or redefined in terms of performance in the market ('equality of opportunity'), and 'reactionary' groups lay emphasis on the maintenance of previously acquired privilege (so-called 'tradition'). I think the English Revolution is a very clear instance of this kind of intrabourgeois conflict.

What makes the analysis of such political struggles so open to contention and the real outcome so often ambiguous (and essentially 'conservative') is the fact that the largest segment of the bourgeoisie (even during the conflict) have claims to privilege both in 'class' terms and in 'status' terms. That is, as individuals and subgroups they do not stand to lose automatically, whichever of the two definitions prevail. Typically, therefore, they are politically indecisive or oscillating and seek after 'compromises'. And if they cannot immediately achieve these compromises because of the passions of the other subgroup, they bide their time until the moment is ripe. (Hence 1688–89 in the case of England.)

While an analysis of such intrabourgeois conflicts in terms of the rhetoric of the contending groups would be misleading. I am not suggesting that such conflicts are unimportant or irrelevant to the ongoing processes of the capitalist world-economy.

Such intrabourgeois conflicts are precisely part of the recurring 'shake-downs' of the system which economic contractions force, part of the mechanism of renewing and revitalizing the essential motor of the system, the accumulation of capital. Such conflicts purge the system of a certain number of useless parasites, bring sociopolitical structures into closer consonance with the changing economic networks of activity, and provide an ideological veneer to ongoing structural change. If one wants to call this 'progress', one may. I myself would prefer to reserve the term for more basic kinds of social transformations.

These other social transformations of which I speak are not the consequence of the evolving character of the bourgeoisie but of the evolving character of the proletariat. If we have defined the bourgeoisie as those who receive surplus-value they do not themselves create and use some of it to accumulate capital, it follows that the proletariat are those who yield part of the value they have created to others. In this sense there exists in the capitalist mode of production only bourgeois and proletarians. The polarity is structural.

Let us be quite clear what this approach to the concept of proletarian does. It eliminates as a *defining* characteristic of the proletarian the payment of *wages* to the producer. It starts instead from another perspective. The producer creates value. What happens to this value? There are three logical possibilities. He 'owns' (and therefore keeps) *all* of it, *part* of it or *none* of it. If he does not keep all of it, but therefore 'transfers' some or all of it to someone else (or to some 'firm'), he receives in return either nothing, goods, money, or goods plus money.

If the producer truly keeps *all* the value produced by him over his lifetime, he is not participating in the capitalist system. But such a producer is a far rarer phenomenon within the boundaries of the capitalist world-economy than we commonly admit. The so-called 'subsistence farmer' quite frequently turns out on closer inspection in fact to be transferring surplus-value to someone by some means.

If we eliminate this group, the other logical possibilities form a matrix of eight varieties of proletarians, only one of which meets the classic model: the worker who transfers all the value he has created to the 'owner' and receives in return money (i.e., wages). In other boxes of the matrix, we can place such familiar types as petty producer (or 'middle peasant'), tenant farmer, sharecropper, peon, slave.

Of course there is another dimension which is part of the definition of each of the 'types'. There is the question of the degree to which performing the role in a particular fashion is accepted by the worker under the pressures of the market (which we cynically call 'free' labour) or because of the exigencies of some political machinery (which we more frankly call 'forced' or 'coerced' labour). A further issue is the length of the contract – by the day, the week, the year or for life. A third issue is whether the producer's relationship to a given owner could be transferred to another owner without the producer's assent.

The degree of constraint and the length of contract cross-cut the mode of payment. For example, the *mita* in seventeenth-century Peru was wage-labour that was forced but of specified duration. Indentured labour was a form of labour in which the producer transferred all the value created, receiving in return largely goods. It was of limited duration. The peon transferred all value, received in theory money but in practice goods, and the contract was in theory annual but in practice lifetime. The difference between a peon and a slave was in the 'theory' to be sure, but in two respects in the practice. First, a landlord could 'sell' a slave but not usually a peon. Second, if an outsider gave money to a peon, he was legally able to terminate his 'contract'. This was not true for a slave.

I have not constructed a morphology for its own sake but to clarify some *processes* of the capitalist world-economy. There are great differences between the various forms of labour in terms of their economic and political implications.

Economically, I think it can be said, for all labour processes that can be supervised simply (that is, at minimal cost), wage labour is probably the most highly paid of the forms of labour. And therefore wherever possible, the receiver of surplus-value would prefer not to relate to the producer as a wage-earner but as something else. To be sure, labour processes that require more costly supervision are less costly if some of the surplus that would otherwise be spent on supervisory costs is turned back to the producer. The easiest way to do this is via wages and this is the historic (and ongoing) source of the wage system.

Since wages are a relatively costly mode of labour from the point of view of the bourgeoisie, it is easy to understand why wage labour has *never* been the exclusive, and until relatively recently not even the principal, form of labour in the capitalist world-economy.

Capitalism, however, has its contradictions. One basic one is that what is profitable in the short run is not necessarily what is profitable in the long run. The ability of the system as a whole to expand (necessary to maintain the rate of profit) regularly runs into the bottleneck of inadequate world demand. One of the ways this is overcome is by the social transformation of some productive processes from non-wage-labour to wage-labour processes. This tends to increase the portion of produced value the producer keeps and thereby to increase world demand. As a result, the overall world-wide *percentage* of wage-labour as a form of labour has been steadily increasing throughout the history of the capitalist world-economy. This is what is referred to usually as 'proletarianization'.

The form of labour also makes a great difference politically. For it can be argued that as real income of the producer rises, and as formal legal rights expand, it follows *up to a point* that proletarian class consciousness expands. I say up to a point, because at a certain level of expansion of income and 'rights', the 'proletarian' becomes in reality a 'bourgeois', *living off the surplus-value of others,* and the most immediate effect of this is on class consciousness. The twentieth-century bureaucrat/professional is a clear instance of this qualitative shift, which is in fact sometimes visible in the life patterns of particular cohorts.

Even if this way of approaching the categories 'bourgeois' and 'proletarian' speak clearly to the role of 'peasants' or 'petty bourgeois' or 'new working class', what, one may ask, is its relevance for the 'national' question and for the concepts of 'core' and 'periphery'.

To speak to this, we have to look at a currently popular question, the role of the state in capitalism. The fundamental role of the state as an institution in the capitalist world-economy is to augment the advantage of some against others in the market – that is, to *reduce* the 'freedom' of the market. Everyone is in favour of this, as long as they are the beneficiaries of the 'distortion', and everyone opposed to the extent that they lose. It is all a matter of whose ox is being gored.

The modes of augmenting advantage are many. The state can transfer income by taking it from some and giving it to others. The state can restrict access to the market (of commodities or of labour) which favour those who thereby share in the oligopoly or oligopsony. The state can restrain persons from organizing to change the actions of the state. And, of course, the state can act not only within its jurisdiction but beyond it. This may be licit (the rules concerning transit over boundaries) or illicit (interference in the internal affairs of another state). Warfare is of course one of the mechanisms used.

What is crucial to perceive is that the state is a special kind of organization. Its 'sovereignty', a notion of the modern world, is the claim to the monopolization (regulation) of the legitimate use of force within its boundaries, and it is in a relatively strong position to interfere effectively with the flow of factors of production. Obviously also it is possible for particular social groups to alter advantage by altering state boundaries; hence both movements for secession (or autonomy) and movements for annexation (or federation).

It is this realistic ability of states to interfere with the flow of factors of production that provides the political underpinnings of the structural division of labour in the capitalist world-economy as a whole. Normal market considerations may account for recurring initial thrusts to specialization (natural or sociohistorical advantages in the production of one or another commodity), but it is the state system which encrusts, enforces and exaggerates the patterns, and it has regularly required the use of state machinery to revise the pattern of the world-wide division of labour.

Furthermore, the ability of states to interfere with flows becomes differentiated. That is, core states become stronger than peripheral states, and use this differential power to maintain a differential degree of interstate freedom of flow. Specifically, core states have historically arranged that world-wide and over time money and goods have flowed more 'freely' than labour. The reason for doing this is that core states have thereby received the advantages of 'unequal exchange'.

In effect, unequal exchange is simply a part of the world-wide process of the appropriation of surplus. We analyse falsely if we try to take literally the model of *one* proletarian relating to *one* bourgeois. In fact, the surplus-value that the producer creates passes through a series of persons and firms. It is therefore the case that *many* bourgeois *share* the surplus-value of *one* proletarian. The exact share of different groups in the chain (property owner, merchants, intermediate consumers) is subject to much historical change and is itself a principal analytical variable in the functioning of the capitalist world-economy.

This chain of the transfer of surplus-value frequently (often? almost always?) traverses national boundaries and, when it does, state operations intervene to tilt the sharing among bourgeois towards those bourgeois located in core states. This is unequal exchange, a mechanism in the overall process of the appropriation of surplus-value.

One of the sociogeographic consequences of this system is the uneven distribution of the bourgeoisie and proletariat in different states, core states containing a higher percentage nationally of bourgeois than peripheral states. In addition, there are systematic differences in *kinds* of bourgeois and proletarians located in the two zones. For example, the percentage of wage-earning proletarians is systematically higher in core states.

Since states are the primary arena of political conflict in a capitalist world-economy, and since the functioning of the world-economy is such that national class composition varies widely, it is easy to perceive why the politics of states differentially located in relation to the world-economy should be so dissimilar. It is also then easy to perceive that using the political machinery of a given state to change the social composition and world-economic function of national production does not *per se* change the capitalist world-system as such.

Obviously, however, these various national thrusts to a change in structural position (which we often misleadingly call 'development') do in fact affect − indeed in the long run do in fact transform − the world-system. But they do so via the intervening variable of their impact on world-wide class consciousness of the proletariat.

Core and periphery, then, are simply phrases to locate one crucial part of the system of surplus appropriation by the bourgeoisie. To over-

simplify, capitalism is a system in which the surplus-value of the proletarian is appropriated by the bourgeois. When this proletarian is
located in a different country from this bourgeois, one of the mechanisms that has affected the process of appropriation is the manipulation of
controlling flows over state boundaries. This results in patterns of
'uneven development' which are *summarized* in the concepts of core,
semiperiphery and periphery. This is an intellectual tool to help analyse
the multiple forms of class conflict in the capitalist world-economy.

8

Marx and History:
Fruitful and Unfruitful Emphases

Immanuel Wallerstein

As a general rule, most analysts (and particularly Marxist analysts) tend to emphasize the more dubious historiographical ideas of Marx, and in the process then tend to neglect what were his most original and fruitful ideas. It is perhaps what one should expect, but it is not very helpful.

To each his Marx, they say, and this is no doubt true. In fact, I'd add to each his two Marxes, as the debates of the last thirty years concerning the young Marx, the epistemological break, etc., are there to remind us. My two Marxes are not chronologically successive. They grow out of what seems to me a fundamental internal contradiction in Marx's epistemology, which results in two different historiographies.

On the one hand, Marx is the supreme rebel against bourgeois liberal thought, with its anthropology centred on the concept of human nature, its Kantian categorical imperatives, its beliefs in the slow but inevitable improvement in the human condition, its preoccupation with the individual in search of liberty. Against this whole set of concepts, Marx suggested the existence of multiple social realities, each with its different structure, located in distinct worlds, each world being defined by its mode of production. The point was to uncover the way these modes of production functioned behind their ideological screens. It followed that a belief in 'universal laws' precisely kept one from recognizing the particularities of each mode of production, of discovering the secrets of its functioning, and thus of examining clearly the paths of history.

On the other hand, Marx accepted universalism in so far as he accepted the idea of an inevitable historical march towards progress, with its linear anthropology. His modes of production seemed to be lined up, like schoolboys – by height, that is, according to the degree of development of the forces of production. (This is in fact the source of the acute embarrassment caused by the concept of the Asiatic mode of production, which seemed to play the role of a rambunctious schoolboy who refused to follow the rules and line up properly.)

This second Marx is obviously far more acceptable to liberals, and it is with this Marx they have been prepared to come to terms, both intellectually and politically. The other Marx is far more bothersome. The liberals fear and reject that Marx; indeed they deny him intellectual legitimacy. Devil or hero, the first Marx is the only one who seems to me interesting and who still has something to say to us today.

What is at stake in this distinction between the two Marxes is the different expectations of capitalist development which one derives from the opposing historical myths. We can construct our story of capitalism around one of two protagonists: the triumphant bourgeois, or the impoverished masses. Which of these two is the key figure of the five centuries of the history of the capitalist world-economy? How shall we assess the epoch of historical capitalism? As globally positive because it leads, dialectically, to its negation and its *Aufhebung*? Or as globally negative because it brings about the immiserization of the large majority of the world's population?

That this choice of optic is reflected in every detailed analysis seems to me quite evident. I will cite but one example, that of a passing remark by a contemporary author. I cite it precisely because it is a remark made in passing, thus innocently, one might say. In a learned and perceptive discussion of Saint-Just's views on economics during the French Revolution, the author concludes that it would be appropriate to describe Saint-Just as 'anti-capitalist', and that this description could in fact be extended to include industrial capitalism. Then he adds: 'In this sense, one might say, that Saint-Just is less progressive than some of his predecessors or contemporaries.'[1] But why 'less' progressive rather than 'more' progressive? That is the nub of the issue.

Marx was of course a man of the Enlightenment, a Smithian, a Jacobin, a Saint-Simonian. He said so himself. He was deeply imbued with the doctrines of bourgeois liberalism, as were all good left intellectuals of the nineteenth century. That is, he shared with all his associates the sort of permanent, almost instinctive protest against anything that smelled of the *Ancien Régime* – privilege, monopoly, seigneurial rights, idleness, piety, superstition. In opposition to this world whose day was done, Marx was in favour of whatever was rational, serious, scientific, productive. Hard work was virtue.

Even to the extent that Marx had some reservations about this new ideology (and he didn't have many), he found it tactically useful to assert an allegiance to these values, and then use them politically against the liberals, hanging them by their own petard. For it wasn't very difficult for him to show that the liberals cast off their own principles whenever order was threatened in their states. It was thus an easy ploy for Marx to hold the liberals to their word, to push the logic of liberalism to its end point, and thus to make the liberals swallow the medicine they were prescribing for everyone else. It could be argued that one of Marx's prime slogans was more liberty, more equality, more fraternity.

No doubt from time to time he was tempted to make a leap of imagination into an anti-Saint-Simonian future. But he quite evidently hesitated to go very far in this direction, fearing perhaps that he would add grist to the mill of utopian and anarchist voluntarism which he had always found distasteful and indeed pernicious. It is precisely that Marx, Marx the bourgeois liberal, whose views we should approach with much scepticism.

It is instead the other Marx, the Marx who saw history as complex and sinuous, the Marx who stressed the analysis of the specificity of different historical systems, the Marx who was thus the critic of capitalism as a historical system, whom we ought to bring back to front stage. What did that Marx find when taking a close look at the historical process of capitalism? He found not only the class *struggle*, which was after all the phenomenon of 'all hitherto existing society', but also class *polarization*. That was his most radical and most daring hypothesis, and thereupon the hypothesis that has been the most vigorously denounced.

In the beginning, Marxist parties and thinkers brandished this concept which, because it was catastrophist, seemed to ensure the future. But, at least since 1945, anti-Marxist intellectuals have found it relatively easy to demonstrate that, far from being immiserized, industrial workers in Western countries were living far better than their grandparents and that, consequently, there had been no immiserization, even relative, not to speak of absolute.

Furthermore, they were right. And no one knew this better than the industrial workers themselves, who were the prime social base of left parties in industrial countries. This being so, Marxist parties and thinkers began to beat a retreat on this theme. Perhaps it wasn't a rout, but at least they became hesitant to broach the subject. Bit by bit, the references to polarization and immiserization (just as to the withering away of the state) diminished radically or disappeared, refuted so it seemed by history itself.

Thus occurred a sort of unplanned and disorderly dropping of one of the most perspicacious insights our Marx had had, for Marx was far more astute about the *longue durée* than we often give him credit for being. The fact is that polarization is a historically correct hypothesis, not a false one, and one can demonstrate this empirically, provided we use as the unit of calculation the only entity which really matters for capitalism, the capitalist world-economy. Within this entity there has been over four centuries not merely a relative but even an absolute polarization of classes. And if this is the case, wherein lies the progressiveness of capitalism?

Needless to say, we have to specify what we mean by polarization. The definition is by no means self-evident. First of all, we have to distinguish between social distribution of material wealth (broadly defined) on the one hand, and the social bifurcation that is the result of the twin processes of proletarianization and bourgeoisification on the other.

As far as the distribution of wealth is concerned, there are various ways to calculate it. We have to decide initially upon the unit of calculation, not only the spatial unit (we have already indicated above our preference for the world-economy over the national state or the enterprise), but also the temporal unit. Are we talking of distribution over an hour, a week, a year, thirty years? Each calculation might give different, even incompatible, results. In point of fact, the majority of people are interested in two temporal calculations. One is that of the very short term, which might be called the survival calculation. The other might be called the lifetime calculation, used for measuring the quality of life, the social assessment of the everyday life one has actually lived.

The survival calculation is by nature variable and ephemeral. It is the lifetime calculation which offers us the best measure, objectively and subjectively, of whether or not there has been material polarization. We need to make comparisons of these lifetime calculations that are intergenerational and long term. Intergenerational comparisons, however, do not mean here comparisons within a single lineage, because that intrudes a factor that is irrelevant from the perspective of the world-system as a whole, which is the social mobility rate in particular zones of the world-economy. Rather we should compare parallel strata of the world-economy at successive historical moments, each stratum being measured over the lifetimes of the cohort. The question to ask is whether for a given stratum the lifetime experience at one historical moment is easier or harder than at another, and whether or not there has occurred over time an increased gap between the higher strata and the lower.

The calculation should involve not merely total lifetime revenue but also this revenue divided by total lifetime hours of work devoted to its acquisition (in whatever form) so as to get figures which could serve as the basis of comparative analysis. One must also consider the life-span, but preferably one calculated from age one or even age five (in order to eliminate the effect of those improvements in sanitation which may have lowered the infant mortality rate without necessarily affecting the health of adults). Finally, one should work into the calculation (or index) the various ethnocides which, by depriving many persons of any descendants, played a role in improving the lot of certain others.

If one finally obtained some reasonable figures, calculated over the long run and across the whole world-economy, I believe these figures would demonstrate clearly that over the last four hundred years there has been a significant material polarization within the capitalist world-economy. To make myself quite clear, I am suggesting that the large (still rural) majority of the populations of the world-economy works harder and longer today for less reward than 400 years ago.

I have no intention of idealizing the life of the masses of earlier epochs; I merely wish to assess the overall level of their human possibilities compared with their present-day descendants. The fact that skilled workers in a Western country are better off than *their* ancestors says little about the standards of living of an unskilled worker in Calcutta today, not to speak of that of a Peruvian or Indonesian agricultural casual worker.

It may be perhaps objected that I am being too 'economistic' in using as the measure of a Marxist concept like proletarianization the balance-sheet of material revenue. After all, it is argued by some, what matters are the relations of production. No doubt this is a fair comment. Let us look, therefore, at polarization as a social bifurcation, a transformation of multiple relations into the single antinomy of bourgeois and proletarian. Let us look, that is, not only at proletarianization (a standby of the Marxist literature) but also at bourgeoisification (its logical counterpart, which is however seldom discussed in this same literature).

In this case too we must specify what we mean by these terms. If by definition a bourgeois can only be a typical industrialist of Frengland at the beginning of the nineteenth century, and a proletarian can only be the person who works in this industrialist's factory, then it is quite certain that there has not been much of a class polarization in the history of the capitalist system. One might even make a case that polarization has been reduced. However, if one means by a true bourgeois and a true proletarian all those who live off *current* revenue, that is, without depending on income from inherited sources (capital, property, privileges, etc.), the distinction being one between those (the bourgeois) who live off the surplus-value which the others (the proletarians) create, without much dual role-playing by individuals, then one can argue indeed that over the centuries more and more persons have come to be located unambiguously in one or the other category and that this is the consequence of a structural process which is far from completed.

It will clarify the argument to look at these processes close up. What actually happens in 'proletarianization'? Workers throughout the world live in small groups of income-pooling 'households'. These groups, which are neither necessarily nor totally kin-related nor necessarily co-residential, rarely do without some wage-income. But they equally rarely subsist exclusively on their wage-income. They add to wage-income from petty commodity production, rents, gifts and transfer payments, and (not least) subsistence production.

Thus they pool multiple sources of income, in of course very different proportions in different places and times. We can think of proletarian-ization thus as the process of increasing dependence on wage-income as a percentage of the whole. It is totally ahistorical to think that a house-hold goes suddenly from zero per cent to one hundred per cent depend-ence on wages. More likely, given households shift, sometimes in brief periods, from say a twenty-five per cent dependence to a fifty per cent dependence. This is for example what happened more or less in that locus classicus, the English enclosures of the eighteenth century.

Who gains by proletarianization? It is far from sure that it is the capitalists. As the percentage of a household's income coming from wages increases, the level of wages must simultaneously be *increased* and not decreased in order for it to approach the *minimum* level required for reproduction. Perhaps you will think such an argument absurd. If these workers had not previously received the minimum wage necessary for their physical survival, how could they have survived? It is not in fact, however, absurd. For if the wage-income is but a small proportion of total household income, the employer of the wage worker is able to pay a *subminimal* hourly wage, forcing the other 'components' of total household income to 'make up' the difference between the wage paid and the minimum needed for survival. Thus the work required to obtain supraminimal income from subsistence labour or petty commodity production in order to 'average out' at a minimum level for the whole household serves in effect as a 'subsidy' for the employer of the wage labourer, a transfer to this employer of additional surplus-value. This is what explains the scandalously low wage-scales of the peri-pheral zones of the world-economy.

The essential contradiction of capitalism is well known. It is that between the interest of the capitalist as individual entrepreneur seeking to maximize his profits (and hence minimize his costs of production, including wages) and his interest as a member of a class which cannot make money unless its members can realize their profits, that is, sell what they produce. Hence capitalists need buyers, and this can often mean that they need to increase the cash revenue of workers.

I shall not review here the mechanisms by which the repeated stag-nations of the world-economy lead to discontinuous but necessary (that is, step-like) increases of the purchasing power of some (each time new) sector of the (world) population. I will only say that one of the most important of these mechanisms of increasing real purchasing power is the process we are calling proletarianization. Although proletarianization may serve the short-term interest (the short term only) of the capitalists as a class, it goes against their interests as individual employers, and hence normally proletarianization occurs despite them and not because of them. The demand for proletarianization comes rather from the other side. Workers organize themselves in various ways and thereby achieve some of their demands, which in fact permits them to reach the threshold of a true wage-based minimum income. That is, by their own efforts, workers become proletarianized, and then shout victory!

The true character of bourgeoisification is similarly quite different from what we've been led to believe. The classic Marxist sociological portrait of the bourgeois is fraught with the epistemological contradictions at the base of Marxism itself. On the one hand, Marxists suggest that the bourgeois-entrepreneur-progressive is the opposite of the aristocrat-rentier-idler. And, among bourgeois, a contrast is drawn between the merchant capitalist who buys cheaply and sells dearly (hence speculator-financial manipulator-idler) and the industrialist who 'revolutionizes' the relations of production. This contrast is all the sharper if this industrialist has taken the 'truly revolutionary' path to capitalism, that is, if this industrialist resembles the hero of liberal legends, a little man who by dint of effort has become a big man. It is in this incredible but deeply rooted manner that Marxists have become some of the best purveyors of the celebration of the capitalist system.

This description almost makes one forget the other Marxist thesis on the exploitation of the worker which takes the form of the extraction of surplus-value from the workers by this very same industrialist who then, logically, joins the ranks of the idlers, along with the merchant and the 'feudal aristocrat'. But if they are all alike in this essential way, why on earth should we spend so much time spelling out the differences, discussing the historical evolution of categories, the presumed regressions (for example, the 'aristocratization' of bourgeoisies who desire to *vivre noblement*), the treasons (of some bourgeoisies who refuse, it appears, 'to play their historic role')?

But is this a correct sociological portrait? Just like the workers who live in households which merge revenue from multiple sources (only one being wages), the capitalists (especially big ones) live in enterprises which in reality merge revenues from many sources of investment – rents, speculation, trading profits, 'normal' production profits, financial manipulation. Once these revenues are in money form, they're all the same for the capitalists, a means of pursuing that incessant and infernal accumulation to which they are condemned.

At this point the psycho-sociological contradictions of their position enters the picture. A long time ago, Weber noted that the logic of Calvinism contradicts the 'psycho-logic' of man. The logic tells us that it is impossible for man to know the fate of his soul because if he could know the intentions of the Lord, by that very fact he would be limiting God's power, and God would no longer be omnipotent. But psychologically man refuses to accept that he can in no way affect his destiny. This contradiction led to the Calvinist theological 'compromise'. If one couldn't *know* the intentions of the Lord, one could at least *recognize* a negative decision via 'external signs', without necessarily drawing the inverse conclusion in the absence of such signs. The moral thus became: leading an upright and prosperous life is a necessary but not sufficient condition for salvation.

This very same contradiction is still faced by the bourgeois today, albeit in more secular garb. Logically, the Lord of the capitalists requires that the bourgeois do nothing but accumulate. And he punishes those who violate this commandment by forcing them sooner or later into bankruptcy. But it's not really all that much fun to do nothing but accumulate. One wants occasionally to taste the fruits of accumulation. The demon of the 'feudal-aristocractic' idler, locked up in the bourgeois soul, emerges from the shadows, and the bourgeois seeks to *vivre noblement*. But, in order to *vivre noblement*, one must be a rentier in a broad sense, that is, have sources of revenue which require little effort to obtain, which are 'guaranteed' politically, and which can be 'inherited'.

Thus, what is 'natural', what each privileged participant in this capitalist world 'seeks', is not to move from the status of rentier to entrepreneur, but precisely the opposite. Capitalists don't want to become 'bourgeois'. They infinitely prefer to become 'feudal aristocrats'.

If capitalists are none the less becoming more and more bourgeoisified, it is not because of their will, but despite it. This is quite parallel to the proletarianization of the workers, which occurs not because of but despite the will of the capitalists. Indeed the parallelism goes even further. If the process of bourgeoisification proceeds, it is in part due to the contradictions of capitalism, and in part due to the pressures of the workers.

Objectively, as the capitalist system spreads, becomes more rationalized, brings about greater concentration, competition becomes stiffer and stiffer. Those who neglect the imperative of accumulation suffer even more rapidly, surely and ferociously the counter-attacks of competitors. Thus each lapsus in the direction of 'aristocratization' is ever more severely penalized *in the world market*, requiring an internal rectification of the 'enterprise', especially if it is large and (quasi-)nationalized.

Children who seek to inherit the direction of an enterprise must now receive an external, intensive, 'universalist' training. Little by little, the role of the technocratic manager has expanded. It is this manager who personifies the bourgeoisification of the capitalist class. A state bureaucracy, provided that it could really monopolize the extraction of surplus-value, would personify it to perfection, making *all* privilege dependent on *current* activity rather than partially on individual or class inheritance.

It is quite clear that this process is being pushed forward by the working class. All their efforts to take over the levers of economic life and to eliminate injustice tend to constrain capitalists and make them retreat towards bourgeoisification. Feudal-aristocratic idleness becomes too obvious and too politically dangerous.

It is in this fashion that the historiographical prognosis of Karl Marx is working itself out: the polarization into two great classes of bourgeois and proletarians, both materially and socially. But why does this whole distinction matter, between the fruitful and unfruitful historiographical emphases that may be derived from reading Marx? It matters a great deal when one comes to the question of theorizing the 'transition' to socialism, in fact of theorizing 'transitions' in general. The Marx who spoke of capitalism as 'progressive' vis-à-vis what was before also talks of bourgeois revolutions, of the bourgeois revolution, as a sort of keystone of the multiple 'national' transitions from feudalism to capitalism.

The very concept of a bourgeois 'revolution', leaving aside its doubtful empirical qualities, leads us to think of a proletarian revolution to which somehow it is tied, both as precedent and prerequisite. Modernity becomes the sum of these two successive 'revolutions'. To be sure, the succession is neither painless nor gradual; rather it is violent and disjunctive. But it is none the less inevitable, just as the succession of capitalism to feudalism has been. These concepts imply a whole strategy for the struggle of the working classes, a strategy filled with moral blame for bourgeois who neglect their historic roles.

But if there are no bourgeois 'revolutions', but merely internecine struggles of rapacious capitalist sectors, there is neither a model to copy, nor sociopolitical 'backwardness' to overcome. It may even be the case that the whole 'bourgeois' strategy is one to shy away from. If the 'transition' from feudalism to capitalism was neither progressive nor revolutionary, if instead this transition had been a great rescue of dominant strata which permitted them to reinforce their control over the working masses and increase the level of exploitation (we are now speaking the language of the other Marx), we might conclude that even if today *a* transition is inevitable, it is not *inevitably* a transition to socialism (that is, a transition to an egalitarian world in which production is for use value). We might conclude that the key question today is the direction of the global transition.

That capitalism will in the not too distant future know its demise seems to me both certain and desirable. It is easy to demonstrate this by an analysis of its 'objective' endogenous contradictions. That the nature of our future world remains an open question, depending on the outcome of current struggles, seems to me equally certain. The strategy of transition is in fact the key to our destiny. We are not likely to find a good strategy by giving ourselves over to an apologia of the historical progressiveness of capitalism. That kind of historiographical emphasis runs the risk of implying a strategy which will lead us to a 'socialism' that is no more progressive than the current system, an avatar so to speak of this system.

Note

1. Charles-Albert Michalet, 'Economie et politique chez Saint-Just. L'exemple de l'inflation', *Annales historiques de la Revolution française*, vol. LV, no. 191, 1968, pp. 105–6.

9

The Bourgeois(ie) as Concept and Reality

Immanuel Wallerstein

Définir le bourgeois? Nous ne serions pas d'accord.

Ernest Labrousse (1955)

In the mythology of the modern world, the quintessential protagonist is the bourgeois. Hero for some, villain for others, the inspiration or lure for most, he has been the shaper of the present and the destroyer of the past. In English, we tend to avoid the term 'bourgeois', preferring in general the locution 'middle class' (or classes). It is a small irony that despite the vaunted individualism of Anglo-Saxon thought, there is no convenient singular form for 'middle class(es)'. We are told by the linguists that the term appeared for the first time in Latin form, *burgensis*, in 1007 and is recorded in French as *burgeis* as of 1100. It originally designated the inhabitant of a *bourg*, an urban area, but an inhabitant who was 'free'.[1] Free, however, from what? Free from the obligations that were the social cement and the economic nexus of a feudal system. The bourgeois was *not* a peasant or serf, but he was also *not* a noble.

Thus, from the start there was both an anomaly and an ambiguity. The anomaly was that there was no logical place for the bourgeois in the hierarchical structure and value-system of feudalism with its classical three orders, themselves only becoming crystallized at the very moment that the concept of 'bourgeois' was being born.[2] And the ambiguity was that bourgeois was then (as it remains today) both a term of honour and a term of scorn, a compliment and a reproach. Louis XI, it is said, took pride in the honorific 'bourgeois of Berne'.[3] But Molière wrote his scathing satire on 'le bourgeois gentilhomme', and Flaubert said: 'J'appelle bourgeois quiconque pense bassement.'

Because the medieval bourgeois was neither lord nor peasant, he

135

came eventually to be thought of as a member of an intermediary class, that is, a middle class. And thereby commenced another ambiguity. Were all urban dwellers bourgeois, or only some? Was the artisan a bourgeois, or only a petty bourgeois, or not a bourgeois at all? As the term came to be used, it was in practice identified with a certain level of income – that of being well off – which implied both the possibilities of consumption (style of life) and the possibilities of investment (capital).

It is along these two axes – consumption and capital – that the usage developed. On the one hand, the style of life of a bourgeois could be contrasted with that of either the noble or the peasant/artisan. Vis-à-vis the peasant/artisan, a bourgeois style of life implied comfort, manners, cleanliness. But vis-à-vis the noble, it implied a certain absence of true luxury and a certain awkwardness of social behaviour (viz. the idea of the *nouveau riche*). Much later, when urban life became richer and more complex, the style of life of a bourgeois could also be set against that of an artist or an intellectual, representing order, social convention, sobriety and dullness in contrast to all that was seen as spontaneous, freer, gayer, more intelligent, eventually what we today call 'counter-cultural'. Finally, capitalist development made possible the adoption of a pseudo-bourgeois style of life by a proletarian, without the latter simultaneously adopting the economic role as capitalist, and it is to this that we have given the label 'embourgeoisement'.

But if the bourgeois as Babbitt has been the centrepiece of modern cultural discourse it is the bourgeois as capitalist that has been the centrepiece of modern politico-economic discourse. The bourgeois has meant the one who has capitalized means of production, hiring workers for wages who in turn have made things to be sold on a market. To the extent that the revenue from sales is greater than costs of production including wages, we speak of there being profit, presumably the objective of the bourgeois capitalist. There have been those who have celebrated the virtues of this social role – the bourgeois as creative entre-preneur. And there have been those who have denounced the vices of this social role – the bourgeois as parasitical exploiter. But admirers and critics have generally combined to agree that the bourgeois, this bourgeois the capitalist, has been the central dynamic force of modern economic life, for all since the nineteenth century, for many since the sixteenth century, for a few even longer than that.

Nineteenth-Century Definitions

Just as the concept 'bourgeois' has meant an intermediate stratum between noble/landowner and peasant/artisan, so the bourgeois era, or bourgeois society, came to be defined in two directions, backwards in time as progress over feudalism, and forwards in time vis-à-vis the promise (or threat) of socialism. This definition was itself a phenomenon of the nineteenth century, which thought of itself and has been thought of ever since by most people as the century of bourgeois triumph, the quintessential historical moment for the bourgeois – as concept, and as reality. What represents bourgeois civilization more in our collective consciousness than Victorian Britain, workshop of the world, heartland of the white man's burden, on which the sun never set – responsible, scientific, civilized?

Bourgeois reality – both its cultural and its politico-economic reality – has thus been something we have all known intimately and which has been described in remarkably similar ways by the three great ideological currents of the nineteenth century – conservatism, liberalism and Marxism. In their conceptions of the bourgeois, all three have tended to agree upon his occupational function (in earlier times usually a merchant, but later an employer of wage labour and owner of the means of production, primarily one whose workers were producer of goods), his economic motor (the profit motive, the desire to accumulate capital) and his cultural profile (non-reckless, rational, pursuing his own interests). One would have thought that with such unanimity emerging in the nineteenth century around a central concept, we would all have proceeded to use it without hesitation and with little debate. Yet Labrousse tells us that we shall not agree on a definition, and he therefore exhorts us to look closely at empirical reality, casting as wide a net as possible. Furthermore, although Labrousse made his exhortation in 1955, I do not have the impression that the world scholarly community took up his challenge. Why should this be? Let us look at five contexts in which, in the work of historians and other social scientists, the concept of bourgeois(ie) has been used in ways that result in discomfort – if not theirs, then that of many of their readers. Perhaps by analysing the discomforts, we will find clues for a better fit between concept and reality.

1. Historians frequently describe a phenomenon designated as the 'aristocratization of the bourgeoisie'. Some have argued, for example, that this occurred in the United Provinces in the seventeenth century.[4] The system in *Ancien Régime* France of a '*noblesse de robe*' created by the venality of office was virtually an institutionalization of this concept. It is, of course, what Thomas Mann described in *Buddenbrooks* – the typical path of transformation in the social patterns of a wealthy family dynasty, from great entrepreneur to economic consolidator to patron of the arts, and eventually these days to either decadent roué or hedonistic-idealistic dropout.

What is it we are supposed to be noticing? That, for some reason and at a certain biographical moment, a bourgeois seems to renounce both his cultural style and his politico-economic role in favour of an 'aristocratic' role, which since the nineteenth century has not necessarily been that of titled nobility but simply that of old wealth. The traditional formal symbol of this phenomenon has been the acquisition of the landed estate, marking the shift from bourgeois factory owner/urban resident to noble landowner/rural resident.

Why should a bourgeois do this? The answer is obvious. In terms of social status, in terms of the cultural discourse of the modern world, it has always been true – from the eleventh century to today – that it is somehow 'better' or more desirable to be an aristocrat than a bourgeois. Now, this is remarkable on the face of it, for two reasons. One, we are constantly told by everyone that the dynamic figure in our politico-economic process is and has been – since the nineteenth century, since the sixteenth century, since perhaps even longer – the bourgeois. Why would one want to give up being centre-stage in order to occupy an ever more archaic corner of the social scene? Second, while what we call feudalism or the feudal order celebrated nobility in its ideological presentations, capitalism gave birth to another ideology which celebrated precisely the bourgeois. This new ideology has been dominant, at least in the centre of the capitalist world-economy, for at least 150–200 years. Yet the *Buddenbrooks* phenomenon goes on apace. And in Britain, even today, a life peerage is taken to be an honour.

2. An important polemical concept in contemporary thought – familiar in, but by no means limited to, Marxist writings – is that of the 'betrayal by the bourgeoisie' of its historical role. In fact, this concept refers to the fact that in certain countries, those that are less 'developed', the local (national) bourgeoisie has turned away from its 'normal' or expected economic role in order to become landowners or rentiers, that is, 'aristocrats'. But it is more than their aristocratization in terms of personal biography; it is their collective aristocratization in terms of collective biography. That is to say, it is a question of the timing of this shift in terms of a sort of national calendar. Given an implicit theory of stages of development, at a certain point the bourgeoisie should take over the state apparatus, create a so-called 'bourgeois state', industrialize the country, and thereby collectively accumulate significant amounts of capital – in short follow the presumed historical path of Britain. After that moment, perhaps it would be less important if individual bourgeois 'aristocratized' themselves. But before that moment, such individual shifts render more difficult (even make impossible) the national collective transformation. In the twentieth century, this kind of analysis has been the underpinning of a major political strategy. It has

been used as the justification, in Third International parties and their successors, of the so-called 'two-stage theory of national revolution', wherein socialist parties have the responsibility not only to carry out the proletarian (or second-stage) revolution but also to play a very large role in carrying out the bourgeois (or first-stage) revolution. The argument is that the first stage is historically 'necessary' and that, since the national bourgeoisie in question has 'betrayed' its historic role, it becomes incumbent on the proletariat to play this role for it.

Now, the whole concept is doubly curious. It is curious that one thinks that one social class, the proletariat, has both the obligation and the social possibility of performing the historical tasks (whatever that means) of another social class, the bourgeoisie. (I note in passing that, although the strategy was in fact launched by Lenin or at least with his benediction, it smacks very much of the moralism for which Marx and Engels denounced the Utopian Socialists.) But the idea of 'betrayal' is even more curious when looked at from the angle of the bourgeoisie itself. Why should a national bourgeoisie 'betray' its historic role? Presumably, it has everything to gain from performing this role. And since everyone – conservative, liberals, Marxists – agree that bourgeois capitalists always pursue their own interests, how is it that in this instance they appear not to have seen their own interests? It seems more than a conundrum; it seems to be a self-contradicting assertion. The strangeness of the very idea is accentuated by the fact that quantitatively the number of national bourgeoisies that are said to have 'betrayed' their historic roles turns out not to be small but very large – indeed, the vast majority.

Ownership and Control

3. The language of 'aristocratization of the bourgeoisie' has tended to be applied to situations in European countries primarily in the sixteenth to the eighteenth centuries, and the language of 'betrayal of the bourgeoisie' has tended to be applied to situations in non-European zones in the twentieth century. There is a third language, however, which has been applied primarily to situations in North America and Western Europe in the late nineteenth and twentieth centuries. In 1932, Berle and Means wrote a famous book in which they pointed out a trend in the structural history of the modern business enterprise, a trend they called the 'separation of ownership and control'.[5] By this they meant the shift from a situation in which the legal owner of a business was also its manager to one (i.e., the modern corporation) in which the legal owners were many, dispersed and virtually reduced to being merely investors of

money capital, while the managers, with all the real economic decision-making power, were not necessarily even partial owners and were in formal terms salaried employees. As everyone now recognizes, this twentieth-century reality does not match the nineteenth-century description, by either liberals or Marxists, of the economic role of the bourgeois.

The rise of this corporate form of enterprise did more than change the structures at the top of the enterprises. It also begat a whole new social stratum. In the nineteenth century, Marx had forecast that, as capital centralized, there would over time occur a growing polarization of classes, such that eventually only a bourgeoisie (very tiny) and a proletariat (very numerous) would remain. By that he meant in practice that in the course of capitalist development two large social groupings, the independent small agricultural producers and the independent small urban artisans, would disappear via a double process: a few would become large-scale entrepreneurs (that is, bourgeois), and most would become wage workers (that is, proletarians). While liberals were not making for the most part parallel predictions, nothing in Marx's own prediction in so far as it was merely a social description was incompatible with liberal theses. Conservatives, such as Carlyle, thought the Marxist prediction essentially correct, and they shivered at the thought.

In fact, Marx was right, and the membership of these two social categories has indeed diminished dramatically world-wide in the last 150 years. But in the period since the Second World War, sociologists have been noticing, until it has become a veritable commonplace, that the disappearance of these two strata has gone hand in hand with the emergence of new strata. The language that began to be used was that as the 'old middle class' was disappearing, a 'new middle class' was coming into existence.[6] By the new middle class was meant the growing stratum of largely salaried professionals who occupied managerial or quasi-managerial positions in corporate structures by virtue of the skills in which they had been trained at universities – originally, primarily the 'engineers', then later the legal and health professionals, the specialists in marketing, the computer analysts and so on.

Two things should be noted here. First of all, a linguistic confusion. These 'new middle classes' are presumed to be an 'intermediate stratum' (as in the eleventh century), but now one located between the 'bourgeoisie' or the 'capitalists' or 'top management' and the 'proletariat' or the 'workers'. The bourgeoisie of the eleventh century was the *middle* stratum, but in the terminology of the twentieth century, the term is used to describe the top stratum, in a situation in which many still refer to three identifiable strata. This confusion was compounded in the 1960s by attempts to rebaptize the 'new middle classes' as the 'new working classes', thereby seeking to reduce three strata to two.[7] This change in name was fostered largely for its political implications, but it did point to another changing reality: the differences in style of life and income level between skilled workers and these salaried professionals were narrowing.

Second, these 'new middle classes' were very difficult to describe in the nineteenth-century categories of analysis. They met some of the criteria of being 'bourgeois'. They were 'well-to-do'; they had some money to invest (but not too much, and that mainly in stocks and bonds); they certainly pursued their own interests, economically and politically. But they tended to be comparable to wage-workers, in so far as they lived primarily on current payments for work (rather than on returns from property); to that extent, they were 'proletarian'. And their often quite hedonistic style of life de-emphasized the puritanical strain associated with bourgeois culture; to that extent they were 'aristocratic'.

4. There was a Third World analogue to the 'new middle classes'. As one country after another became independent after the Second World War, analysts began to take note of the rise of a very significant stratum – educated cadres employed by the government, whose income levels made them quite well-to-do in comparison with most of their compatriots. In Africa, where those cadres stood out most sharply in the virtual absence of other varieties of 'well-to-do' people, a new concept was created to designate them, the 'administrative bourgeoisie'. The administrative bourgeoisie was quite traditionally 'bourgeois' in style of life and social values. It represented the social underpinning of most regimes, to the point that Fanon argued that African one-party states were 'dictatorships of the bourgeoisie', of precisely this bourgeoisie.[8] And yet of course these civil servants were not bourgeois at all in the sense of playing any of the traditional economic roles of the bourgeois as entrepreneur, employer of wage labour, innovator, risk taker, profit maximizer. Well, that is not quite correct. Administrative bourgeois often played these classic economic roles, but when they did, they were not celebrated for it, but rather denounced for 'corruption'.

5. There is a final arena in which the concept of the bourgeoisie and/or the middle classes has come to play a confusing but central role – namely, in the analysis of the structure of the state in the modern world. Once again, whether we look at conservative, liberal or Marxist doctrine, the advent of capitalism was presumed to be in some way correlated and closely linked with political control of the state machinery. Marxists said that a capitalist economy implied a bourgeois state, a view most succinctly summarized in the aphorism that 'the state is the executive committee of the ruling class'.[9] The heart of the Whig interpretation of history was that the drive towards human freedom

proceeded in parallel fashion in the economic and political arenas. *Laissez-faire* implied representative democracy or at least parliamentary rule. And what were conservatives complaining about, if not the profound link between the cash nexus and the decline of traditional institutions (first of all, at the level of the state structures)? When conservatives talked of Restoration, it was the monarchy and aristocratic privilege they were intent on restoring.

And yet note some persistently dissenting voices. In that heartland of bourgeois triumph, Victorian Britain, at the very moment of the triumph, Walter Bagehot examined the continuing essential role of the monarchy in maintaining the conditions which permit a modern state, a capitalist system, to survive and to thrive.[10] Max Weber insisted that the bureaucratization of the world, his choice of the key process of capitalist civilization, would never be feasible at the very top of the political system.[11] And Joseph Schumpeter, asserted that, since in effect the bourgeoisie was incapable of heeding the warnings of Bagehot, the edifice of rule must inevitably crumble. The bourgeoisie, by insisting on ruling, would bring about its own demise.[12] All three were arguing that the equation of bourgeois economy and bourgeois state was not as simple as it looked.

In the corner of the Marxists, the theory of the state, of the class basis of the (bourgeois) state, has been one of the most thorny issues of the last thirty years, most notably in the debates between Nicos Poulantzas and Ralph Miliband.[13] The phrase, the 'relative autonomy of the state', has become a cliché enjoying wide nominal support. What does it refer to, if not the fact that there now are acknowledged to be so many versions of 'bourgeoisie' or 'middle classes' that it is hard to argue that any one of them actually controls the state in the direct mode of the Marxist aphorism? Nor does the combination of them seem to add up to a single class or group.

The Concept Reconsidered

Thus the concept, bourgeois, as it has come down to us from its medieval beginnings through its avatars in the Europe of the *Ancien Régime* and then of nineteenth-century industrialism, seems to be difficult to use with clarity when talking about the twentieth-century world. It seems even harder to use it as an Ariadne's thread to interpret the historical development of the modern world. Yet no one seems ready to discard the concept entirely. I know of no serious historical interpretation of this modern world of ours in which the concept of the bourgeoisie, or alternatively of the middle classes, is absent. And for good reason. It is hard to tell a story without its main protagonist. Still, when a concept shows a persistent ill fit with reality – and in all the major competing ideological interpretations of this reality – it is perhaps time to review the concept and reassess what really are its essential features.

Let me begin by noting another curious piece of intellectual history. We are all very conscious that the proletariat, or, if you will, waged workers, have not simply been historically there; they have in fact been created over time. Once upon a time, most of the world's labour were rural agricultural producers, receiving income in many different forms but rarely in the form of wages. Today, a large (and ever larger) part of the world's work force is urban and much of it receives income in the form of wages. This shift is called by some 'proletarianization', by others the 'making of the working class'.[14] There are many theories about this process; it is the subject of much study.

We are also aware, but it is less salient to most of us, that the percentage of persons who might be called bourgeois (in one definition or another) is far greater today than previously, and has no doubt augmented steadily since perhaps the eleventh century, and certainly since the sixteenth. And yet, to my knowledge, virtually no one speaks of 'bourgeoisification' as a parallel process to 'proletarianization'. Nor does anyone write a book on the making of the bourgeoisie; rather they write books on *'les bourgeois conquérants'*.[15] It is as though the bourgeoisie were a given, and therefore acted upon others: upon the aristocracy, upon the state, upon the workers. It seems not to have origins, but to emerge full-grown out of the head of Zeus.

Our nostrils should flair at such an obvious *deus ex machina* – and a veritable *deus ex machina* it has been. For the single most important use of the concept, the bourgeoisie/the middle classes, has been in explaining the origins of the modern world. Once upon a time, so the myth is recited, there was feudalism, or a non-commercial, non-specialized economy. There were lords and there were peasants. There were also (but was it by chance alone?) a few urban burghers who produced and traded through the market. The middle classes rose, expanded the realm of monetary transaction and unleashed thereby the wonders of the modern world. Or, with slightly different wording but essentially the same idea, the bourgeoisie did not only rise (in the economic arena) but subsequently rose up (in the political arena) to overthrow the formerly dominant aristocracy. In this myth, the bourgeoisie/middle classes must be a given in order for the myth to make sense. An analysis of the historical formation of this bourgeoisie would inevitably place in doubt the explanatory coherence of the myth. And so it has not been done, or not been done very much.

The reification of an existential actor, the urban burgher of the late Middle Ages, into an unexamined essence, the bourgeois – that bourgeois who conquers the modern world – goes hand in hand with a mystification about his psychology or his ideology. This bourgeois is supposed to be an 'individualist'. Once again, notice the concordance of conservatives, liberals and Marxists. All three schools of thought have asserted that unlike in past epochs (and, for Marxists in particular, unlike in future ones) there exists a major social actor, the bourgeois entrepreneur, who looks out for himself and himself alone. He feels no social commitment, knows no (or few) social constraints, is always pursuing a Benthamite calculus of pleasure and pain. The nineteenth-century liberals defined this as the exercise of freedom and argued, a little mysteriously, that if everyone did this with full heart, it would work out to everyone's advantage. No losers, only gainers. The nineteenth-century conservatives and the Marxists joined together in being morally appalled at and sociologically sceptical of this liberal insouciance. What for liberals was the exercise of 'freedom' and the source of human progress was seen by them as leading to a state of 'anarchy', immediately undesirable in itself and tending in the long run to dissolve the social bonds that held society together.

I am not about to deny that there has been a strong 'individualist' strain in modern thought, reaching its acme of influence in the nineteenth century, nor that this strain of thought was reflected – as cause and consequence – in significant kinds of social behaviour by important social actors in the modern world. What I wish to caution against is the logical leap that has been made: from viewing individualism as *one* important social reality, to viewing it as *the* important social reality of the modern world, of bourgeois civilization, of the capitalist world-economy. It has simply not been so.

The basic problem resides in our imagery about how capitalism works. Because capitalism requires the free flow of the factors of production – of labour, capital and commodities – we assume that it requires, or at least that capitalists desire, a *completely* free flow, whereas in fact it requires and capitalists desire a *partially* free flow. Because capitalism operates via market mechanisms based on the 'law' of supply and demand, we assume that it requires, or capitalists desire, a perfectly competitive market, whereas it requires and capitalists desire markets that can both be utilized and circumvented at the same time, an economy that places competition and monopoly side by side in an appropriate mix. Because capitalism is a system that rewards individualist behaviour, we assume that it requires, or capitalists desire, that everyone act on individualist motivations, whereas in fact it requires and capitalists desire that both bourgeois and proletarians incorporate a heavy dosage of anti-individualist social orientation into their mentalities. Because capitalism is a system which has been built on the juridical foundation of property rights, we assume that it requires and capitalists desire that property be sacrosanct and that private property rights extend into ever more realms of social interaction, whereas in reality the whole history of capitalism has been one of a steady decline, not an extension, of property rights. Because capitalism is a system in which capitalists have always argued for the right to make economic decisions on purely economic grounds, we assume that this means they are in fact allergic to political interference in their decisions, whereas they have always and consistently sought to utilize the state machineries and welcomed the concept of political primacy.

Endless Accumulation

In short, what has been wrong with our concept of the bourgeois is our inverted (if not perverse) reading of the historical reality of capitalism. If capitalism is anything, it is a system based on the logic of the *endless* accumulation of capital. It is this endlessness that has been celebrated or chastised as its Promethean spirit.[16] It is this endlessness which, for Emile Durkheim, had anomie as its enduring counterpart.[17] It is from this endlessness that Erich Fromm insisted we all seek to escape.[18]

When Max Weber sought to analyse the necessary link between the Protestant ethic and the spirit of capitalism, he described the social implications of the Calvinist theology of predestination.[19] If God were omnipotent, and if only a minority could be saved, human beings could do nothing to ensure that they would be among this minority, since if they could, they would thereby determine God's will and he would not then be omnipotent. Weber pointed out, however, that this was all very well logically, but it was impossible psycho-logically. Psychologically, one might deduce from this logic that any behaviour is permissible, since it is all predestined. Or one might become totally depressed and hence inactive, since all behaviour is futile in terms of the only legitimate objective, salvation. Weber argued that a logic that is in conflict with a psycho-logic cannot survive, and must be bent. Thus it was with Calvinism. To the principle of predestination the Calvinists added the possibility of foreknowledge, or at least of negative foreknowledge. While we could not influence God's behaviour by our deed, certain kinds of negative or sinful behaviour served as signs of the absence of grace. Psychologically, now all was well. We were urged to behave in a proper manner since, if we did not, that was a sure sign that God had forsaken us.

I should like to make an analysis parallel to that of Weber, distinguishing between the logic and psycho-logic of the capitalist ethos. If the object of the exercise is the endless accumulation of capital, eternal hard work and self-denial are always logically *de rigueur*. There is an iron law of profits as well as an iron law of wages. A penny spent on self-indulgence is a penny removed from the process of investment and therefore of the further accumulation of capital. But although the iron law of profits is logically tight, it is psycho-logically impossible. What is the point of being a capitalist, an entrepreneur, a bourgeois if there is no personal reward whatsoever? Obviously, there would be no point, and no one would do it. Still, logically, this is what is demanded. Well, of course, then the logic has to be bent, or the system would never work. And it has clearly been working for some time now.

Just as the combination omnipotence–predestination was modified (and ultimately undermined) by foreknowledge, so the combination accumulation–savings was modified (and ultimately undermined) by rent. Rent, as we know, was presented by the classical economists (including Marx, the last of the classical economists) as the veritable antithesis of profit. It is no such thing; it is its avatar. The classical economists saw a historical evolution from rent towards profit, which translated into our historical myth that the bourgeoisie overthrew the aristocracy. In fact, however, this is wrong in two ways. The temporal sequence is short-run and not long-run, and it runs in the other direction. Every capitalist seeks to transform profit into rent. This translates into the following statement: the primary objective of every 'bourgeois' is to become an 'aristocrat'. This is a short-run sequence, not a statement about the *longue durée*.

What is 'rent'? In narrowly economic terms, rent is the income that derives from control of some concrete spatio-temporal reality which cannot be said to have been in some sense the creation of the owner or the result of his own work (even his work as an entrepreneur). If I am lucky enough to own land near a fording point in a river and I charge a toll to pass through my land, I am receiving a rent. If I allow others to work on my land for their own account or to live in my building, and I receive from them a payment, I am called a rentier. Indeed in eighteenth-century France, rentiers were defined in documents as 'bourgeois living nobly on their revenues', that is, avoiding business or the professions.[20]

Now, in each of these cases it is not quite true that I have done nothing to acquire the advantage that has led to the rent. I have had the foresight, or the luck, to have acquired property rights of some kind which is what permits me legally to obtain the rent. The 'work' that underlay the acquisition of these property rights has two features. It was done in the past, not the present. (Indeed it was often done in the distant past, that is, by an ancestor.) And it required the sanctification by political authority, in the absence of which it could earn no money in the present. Thus rent = the past, and rent = political power.

Rent serves the existing property owner. It does not serve the one who seeks, by dint of current work, to acquire property. Hence rent is always under challenge. And since rent is guaranteed politically, it is always under political challenge. The successful challenger, however, will as a consequence acquire property. As soon as he does, his interest dictates a defence of the legitimacy of rent.

Rent is a mechanism for increasing the rate of profit over the rate that one would obtain in a truly competitive market. Let us return to the example of the river crossing. Suppose we have a river such that there is only a single point narrow enough to permit the building of a bridge. There are various alternatives. The state could proclaim that all land is potentially private land and that the person who happens to own the two facing lots on the opposing shores at the narrowest point can build a private bridge and charge a private toll for crossing it. Given my premiss that there is only one feasible point of crossing, this person would have a monopoly and could charge a heavy toll as a way of extracting a considerable portion of the surplus-value from all the commodity chains whose itinerary involved crossing the river. Alternatively, the state could proclaim the opposing shores public land, in which case one of two further ideal-typical possibilities present themselves. One, the state builds a bridge with public funds, charging no toll or a cost-liquidating toll, in which case no surplus-value would have been extracted from those commodity chains. Or two, the state announces that the shores being public, they can be used by competing small boat owners to transport goods across the river. In this case, the acute competition would reduce the price of such services to one yielding a very low rate of profit to the boat owners, thus allowing a minimal extraction of surplus by them from the commodity chains traversing the river.

Rent and Monopoly

Note how in this example rent seems to be the same thing, or nearly the same thing, as monopoly profit. A monopoly, as we know, means a situation in which, because of the absence of competition, the transactor can obtain a high profit, or one could say a high proportion of the surplus-value generated in the entire commodity chain of which the monopolized segment is a part. It is quite clear, in fact self-evident, that the nearer an enterprise is to monopolizing a spatio-temporally specific type of economic transaction, the higher the rate of profit. And the more truly competitive the market situation, the lower the rate of profit. Indeed this link between true competitiveness and low rates of profit is itself one of the historic ideological justifications for a system of free enterprise. It is a pity capitalism has never known widespread free enterprise. And it has never known widespread free enterprise precisely because capitalists seek profits, maximal profits, in order to accumulate capital, as much capital as possible. They are thereby not merely motivated but structurally forced to seek monopoly positions, something which pushes them to seek profit-maximization via the principal agency that can make it enduringly possible, the state.

So, you see, the world I am presenting is topsy-turvy. Capitalists do not want competition, but monopoly. They seek to accumulate capital not via profit but via rent. They want not to be bourgeois but to be aristocrats. And since historically – that is, from the sixteenth century to the present – we have had a deepening and a widening of the capitalist logic in the capitalist world-economy, there is more not less monopoly, there is more rent and less profit, there is more aristocracy and less bourgeoisie.

Ah, you will say, too much! Too clever by half! It does not seem to be a recognizable picture of the world we know nor a plausible interpretation of the historical past we have studied. And you will be right, because I have left out half the story. Capitalism is not a stasis; it is a historical system. It has developed by its inner logic and its inner contradiction. In another language, it has secular trends as well as cyclical rhythms. Let us therefore look at these secular trends, particularly with respect to our subject of enquiry, the bourgeois; or rather let us look at the secular process to which we have given the label of bourgeoisification. The process, I believe, works something like this.

The logic of capitalism calls for the abstemious puritan, the Scrooge who begrudges even Christmas. The psycho-logic of capitalism, where money is the measure of grace more even than of power, calls for the display of wealth and thus for 'conspicuous consumption'. The way the system operates to contain this contradiction is to translate the two thrusts into a generational sequence, the *Buddenbrooks* phenomenon. Wherever we have a concentration of successful entrepreneurs we have a concentration of *Buddenbrooks* types. *Ergo*, the aristocratization of the bourgeoisie in late seventeenth-century Holland, for example. When this is repeated as farce, we call it the betrayal of the historic role of the bourgeoisie – in twentieth-century Egypt, for example.

Nor has this only been a question of the bourgeois as consumer. His penchant for the aristocratic style can also be found in his original mode of operation as an entrepreneur. Until well into the nineteenth century (with lingering survivals today), the capitalist enterprise was constructed, in terms of labour relations, on the model of the medieval manor. The owner presented himself as a paternal figure, caring for his employees, housing them, offering them a sort of social security programme, and concerning himself not merely with their work behaviour but with their total moral behaviour. Over time, however, capital has tended to concentrate. This is the consequence of the search for monopoly, the elimination of one's competitors. It is a slow process because of all the counter-currents which are constantly destroying quasi-monopolies. Yet enterprise structures have gradually become larger and involved the separation of ownership and control – the end of paternalism, the rise of the corporation, and the emergence therefore of new middle classes. Where the 'enterprises' are in fact state-owned rather than nominally private, as tends to be the case in weaker states in peripheral and especially semiperipheral zones, the new middle classes take the form, in large part, of an administrative bourgeoisie. As this process goes on, the role of the legal owner becomes less and less central, eventually vestigial.

How should we conceptualize these new middle classes, the salaried bourgeoisies? They are clearly bourgeois along the axis of life-style or consumption, or (if you will) the fact of being the receivers of surplus-value. They are not bourgeois, or much less so, along the axis of capital or property rights. That is to say, they are much less able than the 'classic' bourgeois to turn profit into rent, to aristocratize themselves. They live off their advantages attained in the present, and not off privileges they have inherited from the past. Furthermore, they cannot translate present income (profit) into future income (rent). That is to say, they cannot one day represent the past off which their children will live. Not only do they live in the present, but so must their children and their children's children. This is what bourgeoisification is all about – the end of the possibility of aristocratization (that fondest dream of every classical propertied bourgeois), the end of constructing a past for the future, a condemnation to living in the present.

Reflect upon how extraordinarily parallel this is to what we have traditionally meant by proletarianization – parallel, not identical. A proletarian by common convention is a worker who is no longer either a peasant (that is, a petty land-controller) or an artisan (that is, a petty machine-controller). A proletarian is someone who has only his labour-power to offer on the market, and no resources (that is, no past) on which to fall back. He lives off what he earns in the present. The bourgeois I am describing also no longer controls capital (has therefore no past) and lives off what he earns in the present. There is, however, one striking difference between them: the bourgeois lives much, much better. The difference seems to have nothing, or very little, to do any longer with control of the means of production. Yet somehow this bourgeois, product of bourgeoisification, obtains the surplus-value created by that proletarian, product of proletarianization. So if it is not control of the means of production, there must still be something this bourgeois controls which that proletarian does not.

'Human Capital'

Let us at this point note the recent emergence of another quasi-concept, that of human capital. Human capital is what these new-style bourgeois have in abundance, whereas our proletarian does not. And where do they acquire the human capital? The answer is well known: in the educational systems, whose primary and self-proclaimed function is to train people to become members of the new middle classes, that is, to be the professionals, the technicians, the administrators of the private and public enterprises which are the functional economic building-pieces of our system.

Do the educational systems of the world actually create human capital, that is, train persons in specific difficult skills which merit economically some higher reward? One might perhaps make a case that the highest parts of our educational systems do something along this line (and even then only in part), but most of our educational system serves rather the function of socialization, of babysitting and of filtering who will emerge as the new middle classes. How do they filter? Obviously, they filter by merit, in that no total idiot ever gets, say, the PhD (or at least it is said to be rare). But since too many (not too few) people have merit (at least enough merit to be a member of the new middle classes), the triage has to be, when all is said and done, a bit arbitrary.

No one likes the luck of the draw. It is far too chancy. Most people will do anything they can to avoid arbitrary triage. They will use their influence, such as they have, to ensure winning the draw, that is, to ensure access to privilege. And those who have more current advantage have more influence. The one thing the new middle classes can offer their children, now that they can no longer bequeath a past (or at least are finding it increasingly difficult to do so), is privileged access to the 'better' educational institutions.

It should come as no surprise that a key locus of political struggle is the rules of the educational game, defined in its broadest sense. For now we come back to the state. While it is true the state is increasingly barred from awarding pastness, encrusting privilege and legitimating rent – that is, property is becoming ever less important as capitalism proceeds on its historical trajectory – the state is by no means out of the picture. Instead of awarding pastness through honorifics, the state can award presentness through meritocracy. Finally, in our professional, salaried, non-propertied bourgeoisies we can have 'careers open to talent', providing we remember that, since there is too much talent around, someone must decide who is talented and who is not. And this decision, when it is made among narrow ranges of difference, is a political decision.

We can summarize thus our picture. Over time, there has indeed been the development of a bourgeoisie within the framework of capitalism. The current version, however, bears little resemblance to the medieval merchant whose description gave rise to the name, and little resemblance either to the nineteenth-century capitalist industrialist whose description gave rise to the concept as it is generally defined today by the historical social sciences. We have been bemused by the accidental and deliberately distracted by the ideologies at play. It is none the less true that the bourgeois as receiver of surplus-value is the central actor of the capitalist drama. He has, however, been always as much a political as an economic actor. That is to say, the argument that capitalism is a unique kind of historical system in that it alone has kept the economic realm autonomous from the political seems to me a gigantic misstatement of reality, albeit a highly protective one.

This brings me to my last point, about the twenty-first century. The problem with this final avatar of bourgeois privilege, the meritocratic system – the problem, that is, from the point of view of the bourgeoisie – is that it is the least (not the most) defensible, because its basis is the thinnest. The oppressed may swallow being ruled by and giving reward to those who are to the manner born. But being ruled by and giving reward to people whose only asserted claim (and that a dubious one) is that they are smarter, that is too much to swallow. The veil can more readily be pierced; the exploitation becomes more transparent. The workers, having neither tsar nor paternal industrialist to calm their angers, are more ready to elaborate on a narrowly interest-based explanation of their exploitation and such misfortunes as befall them. This is what Bagehot and Schumpeter were talking about. Bagehot still hoped that Queen Victoria would do the trick. Schumpeter, coming later, and from Vienna not from London, teaching at Harvard and thus having seen it all, was far more pessimistic. He knew it could not last too long, once it was no longer possible for bourgeois to become aristocrats.

Notes

1. G. Matoré, *Le Vocabulaire et la société médiévale*, Paris 1985, p. 292.
2. G. Duby, *Les Trois Ordres ou l'imaginaire du féodalisme*, Paris 1978.

3. M. Canard, 'Essai de sémantique: Le mot "bourgeois"', *Revue de philosophie française et de litterature*, XXVII, p. 33.

4. D. J. Roorda, 'The Ruling Classes in Holland in the Seventeenth Century', in J. S. Bromley and E. H. Kossman, eds, *Britain and the Netherlands*, II, Gröningen 1964, p. 119; and idem, 'Party and Faction', *Acta Historiae Nederlandica*, II, 1967, pp. 196–7.

5. A. Berle and G. Means, *The Modern Corporation and Private Property*, New York 1932.

6. See, for a notable example, C. Wright Mills, *White Collar*, New York 1951.

7. See, for example, A. Gorz, *Stratégie ouvrière et néocapitalisme*, Paris 1964.

8. F. Fanon, *The Wretched of the Earth*, New York, 1964, pp. 121–63.

9. K. Marx, F. Engels, *The Communist Manifesto* [1848], New York 1948.

10. W. Bagehot, *The English Constitution* [1867], London 1964.

11. M. Weber, *Economy and Society* [1922], III, New York 1968, e.g. pp. 1403–5.

12. J. Schumpeter, *Capitalism, Socialism and Democracy*, New York 1942, Ch. 12.

13. R. Miliband, *The State in Capitalist Society*, London 1969; N. Poulantzas, *Political Power and Social Classes* [1968], NLB, London 1973; and see the debate in *New Left Review* 58, 59, 82 and 95.

14. E. P. Thompson, *The Making of the English Working Class*, revised edn, London 1968.

15. C. Morazé, *Les Bourgeois Conquérants*, Paris 1957.

16. D. Landes, *Prometheus Unbound*, Cambridge 1969.

17. E. Durkheim, *Suicide* [1897], Glencoe 1951.

18. E. Fromm, *Escape from Freedom*, New York 1941.

19. M. Weber, *The Protestant Ethic and the Spirit of Capitalism* [1904–05], London 1930.

20. G. V. Taylor, 'The Paris Bourse on the Eve of the Revolution', *American Historical Review*, LXVII, 4, July 1961, p. 954. See also M. Vovelle and D. Roche, 'Bourgeois, Rentiers and Property Owners: Elements for Defining a Social Category at the End of the Eighteenth Century', in J. Kaplow, ed., *New Perspectives and the French Revolution: Readings in Historical Sociology*, New York 1965; and R. Forster, 'The Middle Class in Western Europe: An Essay', in J. Schneider, ed., *Wirtschaftskräften und Wirtschaftswege: Beitrage zur Wirtschaftsgeschichte*, 1978.

10

From Class Struggle
to Classless Struggle?

Etienne Balibar

Whither Marxism? Let me first of all examine the form of the question.[1]
It presupposes that there is some doubt concerning not only the present
direction of Marxism, but also its final destination, and whether it will in
fact ever get there. In 1913, in a famous article entitled 'The Historical
Destiny of the Doctrine of Karl Marx', Lenin put forward the idea that
the Paris Commune occupied a pivotal place within world history. From
the time of the Commune, he argued, can be dated the first visible, self-
evident manifestations of the 'law' which makes it possible to make
sense of the 'apparent chaos' of history, and get one's bearings within it:
the law of the class struggle, as formulated by Marx himself during the
selfsame period. And, in Lenin's view, the correspondence between the
two was so close that he was able to declare that 'the dialectic of history
was such that the theoretical victory of Marxism compelled its enemies
to *disguise themselves* as Marxists'.[2] In other words, Marxism was in the
process of becoming the dominant 'world view'. Over several decades,
socialist revolutions only reinforced the certainty that this was so in the
eyes of millions of people, not all of them idiots or careerists. But
paradoxically, and if one excepts an imposing body of ideological
functionaries in those states where Marxism is official doctrine (though
one may question whether in fact they seriously believe in it themselves),
that kind of statement is probably only to be found today on the lips of a
few theorists of neo-liberalism for whom the slightest hint of a social
policy in the most limited of welfare states is already enough to constitute an outbreak of 'Marxism'. In the eyes of everybody else, what
seems to be more in evidence is rather the decline of Marxism, indeed,

the withering away of Marxism! But as certainties go, what value should we place upon this new orthodoxy?

I do not intend to offer a direct answer, since the question itself is badly framed. What is more important, it seems to me, is for us to underline and develop the contradictions covered over by what one may call, using Lacan's words, these successive 'assertions of anticipated certainty'.[3] At best we can hope to shift the ground of the debate. But first a few observations on method are in order.

First, it is a point of elementary logic that, to the question 'Whither Marxism?', *Marxism itself, as a theory, cannot offer any positive response.* This is true even if we simply ask Marxism to determine the general drift of its own development. That would suppose Marxism could have knowledge of its own 'meaning'. What it is fair to expect of Marxism – this is something it is far from having achieved – is that it should study the effects on its own theoretical history of its 'importation' into social movements and, in return, the effects of the historical situations in which it has been invested as a 'material force'. But it is out of the question for it to master the results of its own conceptual dialectic itself, or those of the 'real' dialectic of its 'worldly realization'. On such questions as these it is possible only to reflect, in the philosophical sense of the term, without pre-existing rules (Lyotard). No reflection, however, is adequate to its own object, 'immanent' in the investigation it intends to carry out.

Second, there is a dialectical thesis of great generality, but difficult to challenge, which can immediately be applied to Marxism, in so far as it *exists* (as a theory, an ideology, a form of organization, or an object of controversy . . .): 'All that comes to exist deserves to perish' (the quote is from Goethe's *Faust* and is used by Engels to describe the workings of the 'Hegelian system').[4] Marxism, therefore, in each of its existing forms, is inevitably bound to perish, sooner or later, and this applies, too, to its form as *theory.* If Marxism *is going* somewhere, it can only be towards its own destruction. Let me now add another thesis, this time from Spinoza:* there is more than one way to perish. Some of these ways represent a dissolution pure and simple, without residue. Others take the shape of a recasting, a replacement or revolution: here something subsists, even though it may be disguised as its own opposite. In retrospect (and only in retrospect), it will be possible to say, from the manner of its perishing, what kind of stuff Marxism was made of. But if we advance the hypothesis that the process of 'perishing' is already underway, and has even reached quite an advanced stage (there are several clues that suggest this may be the case), then the conjuncture and

---

* Balibar is referring here to Proposition XXXIX of Spinoza's *Ethics – Transl.*

intellectual intervention once more come into their own, and it becomes possible to risk identifying the core of meaning, on the practico-theoretical level (on which the outcome of the process depends) and developing it in a certain direction.

There is a third point. The historical impact of Marxism, as it appears to us now, as it completes its cycle of elaboration, practical deployment, institutionalization and 'crisis', has an astonishingly contradictory, even doubly contradictory aspect.

On the one hand, without it being possible to say precisely at what point this took place (perhaps at that moment – which was too late in one sense, too early in another – when in some Communist parties the 'dictatorship of the proletariat' was abandoned as an objective), it became clear that the 'predictions' and revolutionary 'programme' of Marxism would never be realized as such, for the simple reason that the 'conditions' on which they were founded – a certain configuration of the class struggle and capitalism – no longer existed, since capitalism had moved 'beyond' those conditions, and thus beyond Marxism itself. But no serious analysis of the modalities of this superseding [*dépassement*] of Marxism can ignore the fact that to some extent (and arguably to a vital degree) it was itself an indirect result of Marxism's own success: particularly to the extent that the 'rationalizations' of capitalism in the twentieth century have been a response or riposte to the 'challenge' of the Soviet revolution (the legitimate offspring – or considered as such – of Marxism) and especially its repercussions within the various labour movements and in national liberation struggles. Marxism has thus been party to the superseding [*dépassement*] of its own future prospects.

On the other hand, Marxism (or a certain brand of Marxism, though the derivation of one from the other cannot be rejected a priori) took itself to be *realized* – and proclaimed itself as such – in various 'socialist revolutions' and by the 'construction of socialism'. Whatever the trans-formations already undergone or still being undergone by the theory and prospect of 'transition' in those countries where socialism is said to have been 'realized', those societies themselves have used Marxism in order to think of themselves officially as 'classless' societies, or at least as societies 'without class struggle'. And it is for the most part in this normative form that something of Marxism has passed, irreversibly, into actual institutions. However, while such societies, since the end of the Second World War, are far from having become politically static or societies without history, this has been due in particular to the acute form periodically taken by class struggles of the most classic sort (workers' struggles), and even revolutionary class struggles (as in China and Poland) closely identified with democratic campaigns directed against the monopolistic party–state. Here, by another paradox,

Marxism, as a theory of social conflicts, appears to be ever *in advance* of its own 'completion'.

This is the reason for the extraordinary way in which Marxism is intertwined with the divisions and social formations of the present; it seems that the relation to Marxism still divides the contemporary world, but it would seem, too, that class struggles, the 'law' – or principle of intelligibility – of which it aims to set out, are never where they ought to be ...

I must move on now to this central theme. Let me formulate it as succinctly as possible: it is fairly clear that the identity of Marxism depends entirely on the definition, import and validity of its analysis of class and class struggle. Without this analysis, there is no Marxism – neither as a specific theorization of the social, nor as the articulation of political 'strategy' and history. Conversely, *something* of Marxism can be considered inescapable as long as class struggle remains a principle of intelligibility of social transformation – that is, if not as the sole 'fundamental determination' or 'motor' of historical movement, at least as a universal, irreconcilable antagonism from which no politics can abstract itself. And this would still be the case no matter what adjustments it might be appropriate to make to the description of those struggles and the 'laws' governing their general tendency.

But it is precisely on this point that there is controversy and it is here that the factual evidence of Marxism has become unclear. A number of the notions it originally developed as part of a seemingly coherent whole – terms like 'revolution', or, more especially, 'crisis' – have become trivialized in the extreme. On the other hand, class struggle, at least in the 'capitalist' world, has disappeared from the scene, either because those who lay claim to it seem to have less and less purchase on the complexity of the social, or, at the same time, because, in the practice of the majority of people and in the most significant political arenas, classes themselves have lost their *visible* identity. Their identity, then, has come more and more to seem like a myth. It is a myth, one might say, that has been fabricated by theory, and projected on to real history by the ideology of organizations (primarily workers' parties) and more or less completely 'internalized' by heterogeneous social groups, who saw in it a way of having their claims to certain rights and demands acknowledged in conditions that are today largely outdated. Yet if classes have only mythical status, how can the idea of class struggle itself not become totally divorced from reality?

It is true that there are a number of different ways in which this verdict can be formulated. The crudest version is to rewrite the history of the last two hundred years in such a way as to show that the polarization of society into two (or three) antagonistic classes was *always* a myth, in which case its relevance would extend no further than the history and psychology of political imagery and thought.

But it may be conceded also that the scheme of class antagonism *did* correspond once, at least in some approximate fashion, to the reality of 'industrial societies' at the end of the nineteenth century. Now, one could argue simply that this is no longer the case, or is increasingly less so, as a result of a whole series of changes including, on the one hand, the spread of salaried working conditions, the intellectualization of labour and the development of tertiary activities – with the end result that the 'proletariat' no longer exists. On the other hand, these changes also include the completion of the dissociation of the functions of ownership from those of management and the extension of social control (of the state, in other words) over the economy – with the consequence that there is no 'bourgeoisie' any more. Once the 'middle classes', or the 'petty bourgeoisie', or 'bureaucracy', or 'new social strata', and all those other endless theoretical and political conundrums over which Marxism has repeatedly stumbled, begin to invade the landscape and squeeze out the typical figures of the worker and the capitalist boss (even if exploited labour and finance capital are still with us), classes and class struggle *turn into* political myth, and Marxism itself into a mythology.

Nevertheless, there will be critics who will question whether there is not some gigantic fraud involved in proclaiming the disappearance of classes at a moment (the 1970s and 1980s) when, against a background of world economic crisis, compared by economists to the slump of the 1930s, a whole series of social phenomena which, for Marxism, are an effect of exploitation and class struggle are plain for all to see, ranging from massive pauperization and unemployment to the accelerated rundown of the former bastions of capitalist industrial production, that is, the destruction of capital in conjunction with a sharp rise in financial and monetary speculation. At the same time, government policies are being introduced which, even from a perspective which scarcely qualifies as Marxist, have to be seen as corresponding to 'class' politics, and have as their objective, not the general interest (in the sense of the collective interest or even the interest of society), but rather the economic health of companies, economic warfare, the profitable use of 'human capital', the free movement of workers and so on. Are these policy objectives not the class struggle made flesh?

But what is lacking, as Suzanne de Brunhoff rightly argues, is any articulation between the social, the political and the theoretical. As a result, the visibility of class antagonisms turns into opaqueness. No doubt neo-liberal and neo-conservative policies have tended to get bogged down in problems of inability to govern, the lack of security in international relations, and the contradictions within their own populism (and moralism), but they have had undeniable *negative* successes in terms of the break-up and delegitimation of the institutional forms of the labour movement or the organized class struggle. The fact that attempts to undermine these have had to be deliberate and persistent would tend to suggest that the myth is putting up some resistance. But these successes have come at a time when, in most capitalist centres, the labour movement has had decades of organization, experience and theoretical debate behind it. Many of the hardest and most important of the typical workers' struggles of the last few years, like the British miners' strike, or the action of steelworkers or railway workers in France, have taken the shape of isolated trade disputes (which could even be described as 'corporatist' in nature), thus as honourable but defensive last-ditch stands without significance for the collective future. And, at the same time, social conflict has assumed a series of different forms, some of which, in spite of – or because of – their lack of institutional stability, seem to be of much greater significance. This applies to conflicts between generations, conflicts linked with the threat to the environment from technology, as well as other so-called 'ethnic' or 'religious' conflicts, and endemic forms of war and transnational terrorism.

This last case, then, would be perhaps the most radical version of the 'disappearance of classes': that is to say, instead of a fading-away pure and simple of socioeconomic struggles and the interests they represent, what would happen is that class would cease to be politically central; class, the argument would run, would be reabsorbed into the multiform conflictual fabric of society, and the ubiquity of conflict would be accompanied by no hierarchization, no visible division of society into 'two camps', no 'last instance' determining either the conjuncture or its evolution, no other vector of transformation except the random outcome of technological constraints, ideological passions and interests of state. In short, the situation would owe more to Hobbes than to Marxism – and one can argue that this is reflected in recent developments in political philosophy.

Thinking about a situation like this demands, it seems to me, not so much a suspension of judgement regarding the validity of the theoretical postulates of Marxism, but rather that one should dissociate clearly the moment for analysing concepts and historical forms from the moment for devising programmes or slogans. There are good reasons to think that the confusion between the two has regularly affected Marxism's perception of the universality and objectivity of its own arguments, by giving them in advance the status of practical truths. To dissipate this confusion is therefore not a way of escaping into 'pure' theory, but rather a necessary, if insufficient, condition for developing an articulation between theory and practice which operates as a mode of strategic invention, not as a case of speculative empiricism.

What I propose to do now is to formulate some elements towards such an analysis by undertaking a critical examination of the concept of class struggle. First, I isolate certain ambivalent features of the conception of class as set out by Marx, the influence of which persists throughout all its later developments. Second, I look at the possibility of incorporating into that theory some aspects of the class struggle which indeed contradict the simple version of it that might be advanced. It would also be appropriate – but this is something I shall have to do elsewhere – to consider in what ways, from a Marxist viewpoint, it might be possible to characterize social processes and relations which prove *irreducible* to theorization, or even incompatible with it, and consequently define its real internal limits (or, if you will, the internal limits of the anthropology underlying Marxism: I am referring, for instance, to what is known as the 'mechanization of intelligence', or relations of sexual oppression, or specific aspects of nationalism and racism).

The 'Marxist Theory' of Class

I do not intend to summarize, yet again, the fundamental concepts of 'historical materialism', but to underline what, in Marx's own work, if one takes it at its word (that is, as a theoretical experience rather than a system), confers on the analysis of class struggle a certain ambivalence, the effect of which, one can also argue, was to give it the 'free play' that was needed for it to be applied to practical situations. I shall not spend too long on arguments that are well known or have been put forward by me elsewhere.

One initial circumstance needs our attention: the extreme disparity in the treatment of class struggle in Marx's 'historico-political' writings on the one hand, and in *Capital* on the other.

Naturally enough, the former, more than any of Marx's other texts, suffer indirectly from the circumstances of their writing. The pictures they paint are like an adaptation of a basic historical scheme to the peripeteia of empirical history (for the most part European history), and they oscillate constantly between a posteriori rectification and anticipation. At time, these adaptations call for the production of conceptual artefacts, such as the notorious theme of the 'labour aristocracy'. At others, they point to serious logical difficulties, like the idea, inspired by Bonapartism, that the bourgeoisie cannot exercise political power itself, as a class. But at other moments they develop a much more subtle dialectic of the 'concrete', as with the idea that revolutionary and counter-revolutionary crises condense into a single dramatic sequence various phenomena that display both the break-up of class represen- tation and the polarization of society into antagonistic camps. At bottom, these analyses never seriously call into doubt a representation of history that may be characterized as strategic, consisting of the consti- tution and confrontation of collective forces having their own particular identity and social function and their own exclusive political interests. This is what the *Communist Manifesto* means by 'an uninterrupted, now hidden, now open fight'.[5] As a result, it becomes possible to personify the classes, and treat them as the material or ideological agents in history. Personification of this type implies of course a fundamental *symmetry* in the terms that it sets up one against the other.

This, however, is precisely what is missing from the analyses in *Cap- ital* (and is profoundly incompatible with its 'logic'). *Capital* sets out a process which is, admittedly, entirely attributable to the class struggle but it comprises a fundamental *dissymmetry*, to the extent that one could go as far as to say that, from the point of view of *Capital,* the anta- gonistic classes actually never come 'face to face'. In fact, the bourgeois or capitalists (I shall return to the problems posed by this dual desig- nation later) never figure in *Capital* as *one social group*, but only as the 'personification', the 'masks' and the 'bearers' of capital and its various functions. Only when these functions are in conflict with one another do capitalist 'class fractions' (entrepreneurs and financiers, or merchants) begin to take on some sociological consistency; or again, when they come up against the interests of landed property and pre-capitalist classes, considered as 'outside' the system. Conversely, when in the process of production and reproduction the proletariat takes shape as a concrete, tangible reality (as the 'collective labourer', or 'labour- power'), it does so from the outset. It can be said that in the strong sense of the word there is in *Capital* not two, three or four classes, but *only one*, the proletarian working class, whose existence is at one and the same time the condition of the valorization of capital, the result of its accumulation, and the obstacle which the automatic nature of its move- ment constantly encounters.

Consequently, not only does the dissymmetry of the two 'funda- mental classes' (the personal absence of the one corresponding to the presence of the other, and vice versa) not contradict the idea of class struggle, it appears to be the direct expression of the underlying structure of that struggle (as Marx argued, all science would be unneces- sary if the essence of things was identical with their appearance), to the extent that the struggle is always already engaged *within* the production and reproduction of the conditions of exploitation, and not simply superimposed upon the latter.

The fact remains that 'Marxism' is the unity of these two points of view (or, as I hope to make clearer later, the unity of a definition and an economic personification, and a political definition of class, within a single historical drama). To be schematic, the unity of the different points of view of *Capital* and the *Communist Manifesto* is guaranteed, it would seem, by a series of relations of expression and representation, linking the question of labour to that of power, and by the logic of the development of these contradictions.

At this point, it is necessary to examine closely the way in which Marx – the Marx of *Capital* – understands the origin of the contradictions in the very conditions of existence of the proletariat, and he does this in the form of a 'concrete' historical situation in which, at a certain moment, there is an inextricable link between the intolerable character of *one* form of life entirely dictated by productive wage labour and the *absolute* limits of an economic form relying entirely on the increasing exploitation of that labour.

Let me give a brief summary. The analysis in *Capital* articulates a 'form' and a 'content' or, to put it another way, a moment of universality and a moment of particularity. The form (the universal) is the *self-movement of capital*, the indefinite process of its metamorphoses and accumulation. The particular content is represented by a series of inter-linked moments in the transformation of 'human material' into wage labour-power (bought and sold as a commodity), its use in a process of production of surplus-value and its reproduction on the scale of society at large. Considered in its historical dimensions (or as a tendency which is unavoidable in any society to the degree that it falls subject to the 'logic' of capitalism), one may say that this interlinking is the *proletarianization* of the workers. But while, in spite of its own crises, the self-movement of capital apparently derives an immediate unity from its own continuous movement, proletarianization cannot be theorized in terms of a single concept except if one combines together at least three types of outwardly distinct social phenomena (or, to put this another way, three types of history). These are as follows:

1. The moment of *exploitation* proper, in its commodity form, as the exaction and appropriation of surplus-value by capital: the quantitative difference between *necessary labour*, equivalent to the reproduction of labour-power in given historical conditions, and *surplus labour* convertible into means of production consistent with technological development. For this difference and this productive appropriation to take place, what is necessary at one and the same time is a stable legal form (the wage contract) and a constant balance of forces (involving technical constraints, workers' or employers' coalitions, the regulatory inter-

vention of the state imposing a 'wage norm').

2. The moment for which the best term is *domination*: this is the social relation instituted within production itself, and penetrating into the tiniest 'pores' of the worker's working time, initially by means of the simple formal subsumption of labour under the control of capital, leading – via the division of labour, mechanization, intensive working methods and the breakdown of production into separate operations – to the real subsumption of labour under the demands of valorization. Here, in particular, is where a decisive role is played by the division between manual and intellectual labour, that is, the expropriation of working skills and their incorporation within scientific knowledge, by which time they can be turned against the worker to undermine the worker's own autonomy. In conjunction with this, it is also important to look at the development of the 'intellectual capacities' in production (technology, planning, programming) and the reciprocal effects of the capitalist form upon labour-power itself, which must be conditioned and periodically reshaped (by family, school, factory or community medical care) as to its physical, moral and intellectual habits, none of which happens, of course, without resistance.

3. The moment corresponding to *lack of security* and *competition* between workers, as reflected in the cyclical nature, like a process of attraction and repulsion, says Marx, of work and unemployment (which is, in all its different forms, a 'specifically proletarian risk', as Suzanne de Brunhoff puts it). Marx views competition as a necessity of capitalist social relations, one which can be thwarted by workers organizing in trade unions, and by the interest of capital itself in maintaining stability in one section of the working class, but which can never be completely eradicated and always ends up reasserting itself (notably in crises and in capitalist strategies for the resolution of crises). Here he makes a direct connection with the different forms of the 'industrial reserve army' and 'relative surplus population' (lumping together colonization, the competitive employment of men, women and children, and immigration and so on), that is, those 'laws of population' which, throughout the history of capitalism, have perpetuated the initial violence of proletarianization.

Here, then, are three aspects of proletarianization that are also three phases in the reproduction of the proletariat. As I have suggested elsewhere,[6] they contain an implicit dialectic of 'mass' and 'class', by which I mean the continuous transformation of historically heterogeneous masses or populations (marked with various particular characteristics) into a working class, or successive avatars of *the* working class, together with a corresponding development in the forms of 'massification' specific to class situation ('mass working', 'mass culture', 'mass movements').

Marx's reasoning is characterized by the unification of these three moments into a single ideal type that is both logically coherent and empirically identifiable, except for variations according to circumstances ('De te fabula narratur', he said to his German readers in the preface to *Capital*). This unification is the counterpart of the movement of capital, it represents its other side. It is thus a necessary condition for theorizing the 'logic of capital' in concrete terms as the universal expansion of the value form. Only when labour-power is fully a commodity does the commodity form hold sway over the whole of production and social circulation. But only when the different aspects of proletarianization are unified in a single process (as a product, Marx says, of the same 'double mill' [*Zwickmühle*] as material production itself) is labour-power fully a commodity.*

But this leads immediately to historical difficulties, which can be resolved only by questionable empirico-speculative assumptions, like, for instance, the claim that, with few exceptions, the tendency of the division of labour in production is towards the deskilling and levelling out of workers, resulting in a generalization of 'simple labour', undifferentiated and interchangeable, and causing 'abstract' labour, the substance of value, to exist, so to speak, in the real world. And this leads in turn to a deep-seated ambiguity as to the very meaning of the 'historical laws' of capitalism (and the contradictions of this particular mode of production). As we shall see, this ambiguity is at the very heart of Marxist representations of class.

But I want to linger a moment longer on Marx's description of proletarianization. What I should like to do, in a few words, is to convey the ambivalence of this description with regard to the classic categories of the *economic* and the *political*. The ambivalence exists not only for us, but also for Marx. Indeed, two different readings of the analyses of *Capital* are constantly possible, according to whether one gives priority, using the terms I introduced earlier, to 'form' or, alternatively, to 'content'. Either an 'economic theory of class' or a 'political theory of class' is possible on the basis of the same text.

---

*This is a reference to Chapter 23 (Simple Reproduction) of *Capital* vol. 1. The original text reads, 'Es ist die Zwickmühle des Prozesses selbst, die den einen stets als Verkäufer seiner Arbeitskraft auf den Warenmarkt zurückschleudert und sein eigenes Produkt stets in das Kaufmittel des anderen verwandelt', which Ben Fowkes translates as follows: 'It is the alternating rhythm of the process itself which throws the worker back onto the market again and again as a seller of his labour power and continually transforms his own product into a means by which another man can purchase him.' (Marx, *Capital* vol. 1, New Left Review/Penguin, Harmondsworth 1976, p. 723) – *Transl.*

From the first point of view, each of the moments in the process of proletarianization (and the moments of these moments, right down into the detailed social history of the eighteenth and nineteenth centuries, particularly in England) are predetermined by the cycle of value, valorization and capital accumulation, and this constitutes not only a social *constraint*, but the hidden *essence* of the practices assigned to the working class. No doubt, from what Marx says, this essence is a 'fetish', a projection of historical social relations into the illusory space of objectivity, and in the last resort an alienated form of the true essence, that 'ultimate' reality, human labour. But the recourse to this foundation, far from making it impossible to devise an economistic interpretation of the process of development of these 'forms', on the contrary, makes it an unavoidable horizon beyond which it is impossible to go. For the correlation between the categories of labour in general and of commodity (or value) lies at the heart of classical economics. The idea of political conflict, then, ever present in the description of the methods used to extract value and of the resistance they provoke (ranging from strikes and riots protesting against mechanization or the forced settlement of the town, to workplace legislation, state social policies and working-class organization), cannot stand on its own, but is only an expression of contradictions in economic logic (or the logic of alienated labour in its 'economic' form).

However, this interpretation is reversible, if the primacy of form is replaced by the primacy of content, from the perspective of which form is only a contingent, 'tendential' outcome. Instead of class struggle being the *expression* of economic forms, it now becomes the *cause* (necessarily a changing one, subject to all the randomness of the conjuncture and the state of relations of force) of their relative coherence. All that is needed is for the same term 'labour' to be taken to refer, not to an anthropological essence, but rather to a complex set of social and material practices, the unity of which is only the result of their having been brought together in some institutional place (production, business or factory) and at some period in the history of Western societies (for example, the period of dissolution of craftwork by the industrial revolution, or the period of urbanization).

What seems very clear, then, if one looks at the actual text of Marx's analysis, is not that there is a predetermined linking of forms, but rather *an interplay of antagonistic strategies*, strategies of exploitation, domination and resistance constantly being displaced and renewed as a consequence of their own effects. (Notably the institutional effects, which is why it is of crucial importance to study the legislation on the length of the working day, for this was the first manifestation of the 'welfare state', and it was a pivotal moment historically in the passage from the formal to the real subsumption of work under capital, from absolute to relative surplus-value, or alternatively from extensive to intensive exploitation.) In this context, class struggle becomes, as it were, the *political basis* (an 'unstable' basis, in Negri's terms, just as 'non-identical with itself' as labour) against the background of which it is possible to make out different variations in the economy which in themselves, however, have no autonomy.

Nevertheless, as I have said, these two interpretations are finally reversible, in the same way as form and content in general. And this conveys quite clearly the ambiguity of Marx's position. His enterprise is both a 'critique of political economy' by virtue of its demonstration of the antagonisms in production and the omnipresent nature of politics and of relations of force (whereas the ideology of the free market cuts its losses by confining conflict to the involvement of the state and government, believing itself to have ushered in the reign of rational calculation and of general interest vouchsafed by an invisible hand) and, at the same time, a demonstration or denunciation of the *limits of politics* as a pure sphere of law, sovereignty and contract (these limits are not so much external as *internal* ones, since political forces reveal themselves internally as economic forces, expressing 'material' interests).

Because they are reversible, these two interpretations are unstable. This can be seen here and there within Marx's own writings in a number of vanishing points in his analysis (particularly, at the end of the manuscript of *Capital*, the economistic pseudo-definition of social class in terms of the distribution of income, inspired by Ricardo; or the apocalyptic prospect of the collapse of capital once it reaches its 'absolute historical limits'). All in all, the oscillation between economism and politicism constantly affects the understanding of contradictions in the capitalist mode of production. Two views of these contradictions are possible: either they refer to the way in which, after a certain stage is reached, the economic effects of capitalist relations of production cannot but *be transformed into their opposite* (and turn from being 'conditions of development' into 'obstacles', resulting in crisis and revolution), or else they refer to an unchanging reality, present from the very outset – that is to say, human labour-power is *irreducible to the state of a commodity* and will continue resisting in ever stronger and better-organized ways till the system itself is overthrown (which, properly speaking, is what is meant by the class struggle). It is striking that Marx's notorious statement about the 'expropriation of the expropriators' being the 'negation of a negation' can be read in both these two ways.

But this oscillation cannot be preserved as such. For the theory to be intelligible and applicable, it must be fixed at one point or another. In

Marx, but more so in the work of his successors, this is the function of the idea of dialectics as a general idea of the immanence of politics in economics and the historicity of economics. But most of all, this is where the idea of the revolutionary proletariat comes in, as a unity of contraries, replete with meaning for theory *and* practice, and representing the long sought-after correspondence between economic objectivity and political subjectivity. The premises of the idea are clearly present in Marx's work itself (this is what I mean by his speculative empiricism). Another way of putting it would be to say that what it expresses is the ideal identity of the *working class* as an 'economic' class and the *proletariat* as a 'political subject'. It is worth asking whether, in the strategic representation of class struggle, this identity is not the same for all classes, but one would have to acknowledge that only the working class enjoys it as of right, which is why it can be thought of as the 'universal class' (whereas the other classes are always rough approximations, as may be seen, once more, from the revealing idea that 'the bourgeoisie cannot rule in its own name', while the proletariat can – and necessarily must – be revolutionary in its own name).

Of course, much time could be spent observing the slippages and obstacles that affect this theoretical unity and in reality postpone the moment of identity through time, whether it be due to a 'lagging behind of consciousness', or professional or national 'divisions' in the working class, or 'crumbs from the imperialist table' and so on. At a pinch, one could consider, as Rosa Luxemburg did, that the class identity of the proletariat exists really only in the revolutionary *act* itself. But these details only confirm the idea that this identity is already contained in potential form in the correlation between the objective unity of the working class, as produced by the development of capitalism, and its subjective unity, as inscribed in principle, at any rate, in the radical negativity of its situation, that is, the incompatibility between its very interests and existence and the development of which it is in fact the product. In other words, there is incompatibility between, on the one hand, the objective *individuality* of the working class, in which partake all those individuals who 'belong' to it as a consequence of their place within the social division of labour, and the *autonomous project* for the transformation of society, which is the only thing that makes it possible to theorize and organize the defence of their immediate interests and bring about an end to exploitation (create the 'classless society', socialism or communism, that is).

In this way, then, it emerges that there is a relationship of mutual presupposition between the way in which Marxism understands the historically determining character of class struggle and the way it understands the dual identity, subjective and objective, of the classes themselves, and primarily the proletariat. And a similar relationship obtains between the way it understands the meaning of historical trans-formations and the way it understands the continuity of existence, the continued identity of classes as they appear on the stage of history as actors in the drama.

The premises for this circularity, as I mentioned above, are to be found in Marx's own work. They are present in the idea that revolu-tionary subjectivity is a simple awakening to the radical negativity that is implicit in the situation of exploitation, and they are present, too, in the idea that this situation, though it may be by degrees and in stages, expresses a unified process of proletarianization corresponding through and through to a single logic. It comes as no surprise that, in these conditions, the structural idea of an *irreconcilable antagonism* never ceases being projected into the historical fiction of a *simplification of class relations*, at the end of which the vital issues of the human enter-prise (that is, exploitation or emancipation) ought to be displayed 'in broad daylight', on a 'global' scale.

But all that is needed for this circularity to become unravelled, or for the elements of theoretical analysis and Messianic ideology that are fused together in the contradictory unity of Marxism to become divorced from one another, is for the empirical discontinuities that may be observed between the different aspects of proletarianization to be seen as structural discontinuities, that is, discontinuities that are not transitional, but implicit in the concrete conditions of 'historical capital-ism' (in Wallerstein's term). The social function of the bourgeoisie (which, contrary to what Engels and Kautsky imagined, cannot be understood as a 'superfluous class') cannot be reduced to that of a 'bearer' of the economic functions of capital. Moreover, 'bourgeoisie' and 'capitalist class', even as far as the dominant fraction is concerned, are not interchangeable designations. Finally, and this is not the least of the snags we have to face up to, revolutionary (or counter-revolution-ary) ideology is not, historically, just another name for a univocal and universal self-consciousness, but the active product of particular circum-stances, cultural forms and institutions.

Each of these rectifications and distortions has come to light through historical experience as well as the work of historians or sociologists, and they have resulted in a deconstruction of early Marxist theory. Do they entail the abolition pure and simple of its principles of analysis? One may wonder, with good reason, whether they do not rather open the possibility of a recasting of that theory, to the extent that, if one under-takes a radical critique of those ideological presuppositions which support the belief in the development of capitalism as a 'simplification of class antagonisms' (containing 'in itself' the necessity of a classless society), it then becomes possible to take the concepts of class and class struggle as referring to a *process of transformation without pre-established end*, in other words an endless transformation of the identity of social classes. In that case, a Marxist could with total seriousness take up – in order to return it to its sender – the idea of a dissolution of class in the sense of a cast of players invested with mythic identity and continuity. In a word, what is at issue is the need to advance both the historical and structural hypothesis of a 'class struggle without class'.

Marx Beyond Marx

Let me return for a moment to the oscillation within Marxism between the 'economic' interpretation and the 'political' interpretation of class struggle. In their approach to historical complexity, both are reductive, and their character is well known today, each having made it possible, at least in part, to see the true characteristics of its fellow.

What the Communist tradition (from Lenin to Gramsci, Mao Zedong and Althusser) lays bare in the economistic evolutionism of 'orthodox' Marxism is its ignorance of the role of the state in the reproduction of relations of exploitation, linked with the integration of the representative organizations of the working class into the system of the state apparatus (or, in Gramsci's terms, their subordination to bourgeois hegemony). In addition, in its analysis of imperialism, it attributes this integration to the isolation of exploited workers resulting from the international division of labour. But this critique, through its voluntaristic emphasis on the 'overthrow of power' and on the 'primacy of politics', ends up resurrecting a *less* democratic state apparatus than in those countries where the social-democratic workers' movement had its beginnings, state apparatuses in which the monopoly exercised by a leading party, substituting for the working class, has been seen to make common cause with productivism and nationalism.

I do not deduce any pre-existing logic from these observations (unlike theorists of so-called 'totalitarianism'), but I should like to draw some conclusions from a comparison between them and the difficulties in Marx's theory. Borrowing Negri's phrase for my own purposes, I shall attempt to show how this comparison can enable us to take Marx's concepts 'beyond Marx'.

The ambiguity in the representations of the economic and the political in Marx's work ought not to blind us to the break it makes with previous conceptions. In one sense, the ambiguity that is found is really nothing more than the price paid for that break. By discovering that the sphere of labour relations is not a 'private' sphere, but one that is immediately constitutive of political forms in modern society, Marx did not simply make a decisive break with the liberal representation of political space as a sphere of 'public' law, power and opinion. He anticipated a social transformation of the state that has proved irreversible. Simultaneously, by showing that it is impossible politically, by authoritarian or contractual means, to get rid of the antagonism in the sphere of production or to achieve under capitalism a stable balance of interests or a 'sharing of power' between social forces, he exposed as a sham the state's claim to constitute a community of essentially 'free and equal' individuals. And in particular to constitute the community of the national state. It is worth noting in this connection that every 'social state' in the nineteenth and twentieth century, including the *socialist* state, has been not only a national state, but a *nationalist* state also.

In this sense, Marx provided a historical basis for the puzzling idea that what *binds* social groups and individuals together is not a higher common good, or a state of law, but a perpetually evolving conflict. This is why, even – or particularly – though 'economic' concepts, class struggle and class itself have always been eminently *political* concepts, indicative of a potential recasting of the concept of official politics. This break and recasting are what are obscured, and more or less completely negated, both by 'orthodox' economism and evolutionism and by revolutionary statism, where the notion of class struggle finishes up by becoming a stereotypical front for organizational techniques and state dictatorship. For this reason, it is imperative to examine more closely the historical relationship between class identities, organizational phenomena and transformations of the state.

I want to suggest, to begin with, that what showed itself in the nineteenth and twentieth century as a relatively autonomous 'proletarian identity' needs to be understood as an objective *ideological effect*. An ideological effect is not a 'myth', or at least it cannot be reduced to one (all the more so since it does not imply that the 'truth of the myth' lies in individualism, since individualism is itself, *par excellence*, an ideological effect linked to the market economy and the modern state). In the same way, it is not possible to reduce to a myth the presence on the political stage of a force that identifies itself and is acknowledged as the 'working class', however intermittent its direct political acts may be, however variable its unity and divisions. Without its presence, the persistence of the social question and its role in the transformation of the state would remain unintelligible.

But what the work of historians does force us to register is that there is nothing spontaneous, automatic or invariable about this ideological effect. It is the result of a permanent dialectic of working-class practice and organizational forms in which the forces in play include not only 'living conditions', 'working conditions' and 'economic conjunctures', but also the forms taken by national politics in the framework of the state (for instance, the questions of universal suffrage, national unity, wars, secular versus religious education and so on). In short, it is a constantly overdetermined dialectic in which a relatively individualized class is formed only through the relations it maintains with all the other classes within a network of institutions.

This inversion of perspective comes down to an admission, in accordance with what is historically observable on the surface, that there is no such thing as the 'working class' solely on the basis of some more or less homogeneous sociological situation, but that it exists only where there is a labour movement. In the same way, it is a realization that the labour movement exists only where there are workers' organizations (parties, trade unions, stock exchanges or co-operatives).

This is where things become complicated and more interesting. We must be careful not to identify, step by step, the labour movement with workers' organizations, or the (relative) unity of class with the labour movement. This would be a kind of reductionism in reverse, the same indeed as that underpinning the idealized representation of class as 'subject'. There have always been, necessarily, considerable discontinuities between the three terms involved (the labour movement, workers' organizations and class), and this has been what has generated the contradictions which make up the real history, social and political, of class struggle. In this way, not only have workers' organizations (notably class-based political parties) never 'represented' the totality of the labour movement, but they have periodically been forced into conflict with it, partly because their representativity was founded on the idealization of certain fractions of the 'collective labourer' that occupied a central position at a given stage in the industrial revolution, and partly because it corresponded to a form of political compromise with the state. As a result, there has always been a moment when the labour movement has needed to reconstitute itself *in opposition* to existing practices and forms of organization. This is why splits, ideological conflicts (between reformism or revolutionary radicalism) and the classic and recurring dilemmas of 'spontaneity' versus 'discipline' are no accidents but represent the very substance of this relation.

In the same way, the labour movement has never expressed or embodied the totality of class practices, what one might call the forms of worker sociability, that are linked to the living and working conditions that prevail in the working-class space of the factory, the family, the environment or ethnic solidarity. This is not because of some lagging behind of consciousness, but because of the irreducible diversity of the interests, life-forms and discourses which characterize proletarianized individuals, however violent the constraints imposed upon them by exploitation not to mention the many different forms taken by exploitation. In return, these class practices (that is to say, trade-based traditions, collective strategies for resistance, particular cultural symbols) have, on every occasion, given the movement and its organizations the benefit of their unifying potential (in strikes and revolts as well as the formulation of demands).

But there is more. Not only is there constant discontinuity between the practices, movements and organizations that make up a 'class' in its relative historical continuity, there is an essential impurity in each of these terms. No class organization (particularly no mass party), even when it developed a *workerist* ideology, was ever *purely working class*. On the contrary, it was constituted by the more or less conflictual coming together or fusion of certain 'avant-garde' workers' fractions and groups of intellectuals, who either came to it from the outside, or in part joined from the inside, as 'organic intellectuals'. Similarly, no significant social movement, even when it took on a definite proletarian character, was ever founded on purely anti-capitalist demands and objectives, but always on a combination of anti-capitalist objectives and democratic, or national, or anti-militaristic objectives, or cultural ones (in the widest sense of the term). In the same way, the elementary solidarity linked with class practices, resistance and the quest for social utopia was always, though varying with each place and historical moment, both a professional solidarity and a solidarity based on generation, gender, nationality, common urban or agrarian location, or military action (indeed the forms of the workers' movement in Europe after 1914 would be unintelligible without the experience of life in the trenches in the First World War).

In this sense, what history shows is that social relations are not established *between* hermetically closed classes, but that they are formed *across* classes – including the working class – or alternatively that *class struggle takes place within classes themselves*. But it shows too that the state, by means of its institutions, its mediating or administrative functions, its ideals and discourse, is always already present in the constitution of class.

This is true, first and foremost, of the 'bourgeoisie', and this in particular is where classical Marxism has fallen down. Its conception of the state apparatus as an organism or 'machine' outside 'civil society', sometimes as a neutral tool in the service of the ruling class, or else as a parasitic bureaucracy, is something it inherited from liberal ideology and simply inverted to challenge the idea of the general interest; but it is a conception that prevented it from properly articulating the constitutive role of the state.

It can be argued, it seems to me, that any 'bourgeoisie' is, in fact, in the strong sense of the term, a *state bourgeoisie*. This means that the bourgeois class does not take over state power *after* being constituted as the economically dominant class but, on the contrary, that it becomes economically dominant (as well as socially and culturally) to the extent that it develops, utilizes and controls the state apparatus, and undergoes a process of transformation and diversification in order to achieve this (or it merges with the social groups responsible for the functioning of the state: the army and intelligentsia). This is one of the possible meanings of Gramsci's idea of hegemony taken to its logical conclusion. In the strict sense, then, there is no such thing as the 'capitalist class'; only capitalists of different types (industrialists, traders, financiers, share-holders) who form a class only on condition that, to an ever increasing extent, they unite with *other* social groups who are apparently outside the 'basic social relation': intellectuals, civil servants, managers, landowners. A significant amount of modern political history reflects the vicissitudes of this 'union'. This does not imply of course that the bour-geoisie is constituted independently of the existence of capital or capital-ist entrepreneurs; rather it suggests that the unity of capitalists themselves, the settling of their own conflicts of interest, the perform-ance of those 'social' functions that need to be carried out for there to be an exploitable work force at their disposal, would all be impossible without the constant mediation of the state (and thus if they were unable – as sometimes happens – to transform themselves into 'managers' of the state and enter into association with the non-capitalist members of the bourgeoisie in order to manage and utilize the state).

At the extreme, a historical bourgeoisie is a bourgeoisie that period-ically invents new forms of the state, at the cost of its own transform-ation, which may be violent. Thus, for instance, the contradictions between financial profit and the entrepreneurial function were regulated only by means of the 'Keynesian' state, which also provided the 'struc-tural forms', as Aglietta puts it, that enabled bourgeois hegemony over the reproduction of labour-power to move on from nineteenth-century paternalism to twentieth-century social policies. This, in turn, is a more satisfactory explanation as to why the enormous disparities in income, life-style, power and prestige that exist within the bourgeois class, or the split between ownership of financial wealth and economic and technical management (in what is sometimes known as the 'techno-structure'), or the fluctuations in private and public property, sometimes lead to second-ary contradictions within the ruling class, but seldom jeopardize its very constitution, as long as the political sphere fulfils its regulatory functions effectively.

But what is the case for the bourgeoisie is also true of the exploited class, though in a different and – in the light of Marxist orthodoxy – a more paradoxical way. It too is 'within the state', unless one prefers to think of the state being 'within it'. The three aspects of proletarianization analysed by Marx can always be considered to be tendentially present within a capitalist formation but, since the beginnings of the modern era (in the period of 'primary accumulation'), it has never been possible to articulate them without the mediation of the state. I do not mean this simply in the sense that there was a need for some external safeguard, outside the social order, which could be met by the 'repressive apparatus' of the state, but also in the sense that there was a need for mediation in internal conflicts as well. In reality, mediation is necessary for each of the moments of proletarianization (in fixing wage norms and labour rights, in deciding policies for the import and export of the workforce, hence policies affecting the territorialization and mobilization of the working class) and, in particular, it is required at a given point to coordinate their respective evolution (in order to manage the labour market, unemployment, social security, health, schooling and training, for without these things there would be no 'labour-power commodity' constantly being reproduced and supplied to the market). *Without the state, labour-power would not be a commodity.* And at the same time, the *irreducibility* of labour-power to the status of a commodity, whether it shows itself in revolt or crisis or by a combination of the two, puts constant pressure on the state to transform itself.

With the development of the social state, these interventions, that were there from the outset, have taken on merely a more organic, bureaucratic form within an economic plan intended to co-ordinate, at least on a national level, the movements of finance and commodities. But by the same token, the social state, and the system of social relations it implies, have become an immediate arena of contention for class struggle and the combined economic and political effects of 'crisis'. This is all the more the case since state control over the relations of production, what Henri Lefebvre went so far as to call the 'state mode of production', has expanded in tandem with other transformations in the wage relation, including the formal generalization of salaried working to the overwhelming majority of social functions, the ever greater direct dependence of the choice of profession on schooling (and consequently the fact that school no longer just *reproduces* class inequalities, but *produces* them in the first place), the tendency for direct wages (which are paid out to the individual, according to 'labour' and 'skills/qualifications') to be transformed into indirect wages (which are paid out on a collective basis, or rather determined on a collective basis, according to 'need' and 'status'), finally the breaking up into a series of discrete tasks and mechanization of unproductive work (services, commerce, scientific research, in-service training, communications and so on) which in turn makes it possible for it to be transformed into a process of valorization of state or private capital investment, within the context of a generalized economy. All these transformations mark the end of free-market liberalism, or rather its second demise, its transformation into a political myth, since state control and commodification have now become rigorously inseparable.

This account, to which more detail could be added, has, however, one obvious failing. It leaves out something that is far from incidental and which, if the description were to be left as it is, would skew the analysis and, more importantly, the attempt to draw political conclusions from it. My account is situated implicitly (as is almost always the case with Marx's own, when he is dealing with a 'social formation') within a national framework; I have assumed that the space in which class struggle takes place and class is constituted is a national space. More specifically, my analysis neutralizes the fact that capitalist social relations develop simultaneously in a national framework (belonging to the nation-state) and a global framework.

How is it possible to make up for this? It is not enough to refer to 'international' relations of production and communication here. What is needed is a concept that expresses more clearly the *originally transnational* character of the economico-political processes on which the class struggle depends for its particular configurations. To this end, I want to borrow the concept of a capitalist 'world-economy' from Braudel and Wallerstein, without however prejudging the issue as to whether national formations are determined unilaterally by the structure of the world-economy or vice versa. On this basis, to keep to what is essential, let me add two correctives to my earlier account which will enable me to describe certain contradictions that are constitutive of class anatagonisms and which classical Marxism has more or less neglected (even when it has raised the problem of imperialism).

Once capitalism is viewed as a 'world-economy', the question arises as to whether it is possible to speak of the existence of a *world bourgeoisie*. This constitutes an initial difficulty, not only in the sense that the bourgeoisie, on a global scale, will be riven by conflicts of interest more or less coinciding with national allegiances (since after all there are also permanent conflicts of interest within the national bourgeoisie) but also in a much stronger sense.

From the very origins of modern capitalism, the space of the accumulation of value has always been global. Braudel has shown how an economy based on monetary profit presupposes the circulation of money and commodities between nations, or rather between civilizations and different modes of production, not only in the phase of its 'pre-history' or 'primary accumulation' (as Marx argued), but throughout the whole of its development. Becoming gradually more dense, and carried forward by specific social groups, it in turn determines the specialization of centres of production, corresponding to ever more numerous 'products' and 'needs.' Wallerstein has begun to produce a detailed history of the way in which this circulation progressively absorbs all branches of production either into *wage* relations at the core, or *capitalist non-wage* relations on the periphery. This process implies the violent domination of non-market economies by market economies, that is, of the periphery by the core. It was within this framework that nation-states became stable individualized units and the better established among them hampered the emergence of new politico-economic cores. In this sense, it may indeed be said that imperialism is contemporary with capitalism itself, though it was only after the industrial revolution that the *whole* of production became organized for the world market.

What then happens is a gradual reversal in the social function of capitalists. In the beginning, they constituted a 'transnational' group (this is what financial capitalists or the middlemen between dominant and dominated nations have remained). It is possible to suggest that the ones who were the most successful on the world scale were the ones who managed, over a long period of time, to gather other 'bourgeois' groups around them, to control state power and to develop nationalism (unless the sequence happened in reverse, with the state favouring the constitution of a capitalist bourgeoisie to enable it to keep its place in the arena of world political struggle). The internal social functions of the bourgeoisie and its involvement in external competition were mutually complementary. But at the (provisional) other end of the process, one contradiction present from the outset may be seen to have got much worse. As large firms turn into multinationals, and basic industrial processes are dispersed throughout the world, and as labour-force migrations become more intense, not only is circulating capital moving on a world scale, but so too is productive capital. Correlatively, financial circulation and monetary production take place immediately on the world scale (and before long this will be happening in 'real time', even in 'anticipated time' as a result of computerization and the installation of direct links between stock markets and the main banks).

But *there can be no world state or single international currency.* The internationalization of capital does not lead to unified social and political 'hegemony', but at best to the traditional attempt on the part of certain national bourgeoisies to exert world domination by subordinating capitalists, states, economic policies and communication networks to their own strategies, increasingly integrating the economic and military functions of the state with each other (the process is sometimes referred to as the emergence of the 'superpowers'; I have tried to describe it elsewhere, in response to E.P. Thompson, as a super-imperialism).[7] These strategies remain purely national ones, even when they are part of a contradictory attempt to re-create certain of the characteristics of the nation-state on a wider scale (the virtually sole example of this is Europe). They are not to be confused with the emergence, typical of the present era, though still at an embryonic stage, of *political forms* that increasingly fall more or less completely outside the monopoly of the nation-state.

In their present form at any rate, the social (or 'hegemonic') functions of the bourgeoisie are tied to national or quasi-national institutions. The modern equivalents of the old structures of paternalism (for instance, the activity of public or private international humanitarian organizations) are not able to carry out the tasks of regulating social conflict previously assumed by the welfare state, except to a very limited extent. The same applies to the planning of monetary and demographic flows that, in spite of the ever increasing number of 'supranational' institutions, cannot be organized and carried out on a global scale. It seems therefore, in terms of the general tendency at any rate, that the internationalization of capital does not lead to integration at a higher level, but rather to the relative *dissolution* of the bourgeoisie. The capitalist classes in the underdeveloped countries or 'new industrial countries' can no longer organize themselves as 'social' or 'hegemonic' bourgeoisies in the shelter of their home markets and a colonialist, protectionist state. The capitalist classes in the 'old industrial countries', even in the most powerful among them, cannot regulate social conflict on the world scale. As for the state bourgeoisies in the socialist countries, they are being forced by the gradual integration of the economy within the world market and by the dynamic of super-imperialism to 'modernize', to transform themselves, that is, into capitalist classes in the proper sense of the term, but as a result their hegemony (whether this is repressive or ideological: in practice it is a combination of the two, according to the degree of legitimacy derived from the type of revolution that brought it to power), as well as their unity, is put in jeopardy.

This is where a second corrective must be introduced. The internationalization of capital has co-existed from the beginning with an irreducible plurality of strategies of exploitation and domination. The forms of hegemony are directly dependent on these. To adopt Sartre's terms, one might say that any historical bourgeoisie is made by the strategies of exploitation it develops just as much as – if not more than – it makes them. For any strategy of exploitation represents the articulation of an economic policy, linked with a certain productive combination of technology, finance and incitements to surplus labour, together with a social policy for the management and institutional control of the population. But the development of capitalism does not do away with the original diversity of exploitation; on the contrary, it increases it, so to speak, by constantly adding new technological superstructures and new-style enterprises to it. As I have suggested elsewhere in the wake of others such as Robert Linhart, what characterizes the capitalist process of production is not simple exploitation but the constant tendency to super-exploitation, without which there would be no means of counteracting the tendency of the rate of profit to fall (or the 'diminishing returns' of a given productive combination, that is, the increasing costs of exploitation). But super-exploitation is not universally compatible with the rational organization of exploitation itself, if it implies, for instance, maintaining a mass of workers at a very low level of subsistence and training, or the absence of welfare legislation and democratic rights which, elsewhere, have become an integral part of the conditions of reproduction and use of labour-power (not to mention, as with apartheid, the denial of citizenship pure and simple).

For this reason, the (shifting) distinction between the core and the periphery of the world-economy corresponds also to the geographical and politico-cultural distribution of strategies of exploitation. Contrary to the illusions of development, which suppose that inequalities represent merely a lagging behind that will gradually be made up, the valorization of capital in the world-economy implies that practically *all historical forms of exploitation should be used simultaneously*, from the most 'archaic' (including unpaid child labour as in Moroccan or Turkish carpet factories) to the most 'up-to-date' (including job 'restructuring' in the latest computerized industries), the most violent (including agricultural serfdom in Brazilian sugar plantations), or the most civilized (including collective bargaining, profit-sharing, state unionization). These forms, which are broadly speaking *mutually incompatible* (for cultural, political or technical reasons) must remain separate from one another. Or rather it is important for them to remain so, as far as is possible, to avoid the formation of 'dual societies' in which social blocs that are *at different stages of development* come into conflict in explosive ways. Using the term in a rather different sense than is intended, one can suggest that Wallerstein's 'semiperiphery' exactly corresponds to the coming together at one specific conjuncture, within the same state-organized space, of forms of exploitation that are not at the same stage of development. A conjuncture of this sort can last for a long time (even centuries), but it is always unstable, which is perhaps why the semi-periphery is the privileged place for what we traditionally call 'politics').

But is this situation not becoming more general, in the 'old' nation-states as well, now that they have become national social states, under the impact of labour-force migration, capital transfers and policies for exporting unemployment? Dual societies also have 'dual' proletariats, which means that they have no single proletariat in the classical sense. Whether or not one shares the view of writers like Claude Meillassoux, who argue that apartheid in South Africa is a paradigm for the overall situation, one must agree that the multiplicity of strategies and modes of exploitation coincides, at least in principle, with the major world division between two modes of reproduction of labour-power. One is integrated within the capitalist mode of production, and involves mass consumption, general access to schooling, various forms of indirect wages and unemployment benefit, even if this is often inadequate and precarious (in fact all these characteristics depend on an institutional but not immutable balance of forces). The other, however, leaves all or a part of reproduction (in particular 'generational reproduction') up to pre-capitalist modes of production, or, more accurately, *unwaged* modes of production that are dominated and destructured by capitalism; here there is an immediate relationship with the phenomena of 'absolute surplus population', the *destructive* exploitation of labour-power and racial discrimination.

To a large degree, these two modes are present today in the same national formations. The dividing line is not fixed once and for all. On the one hand the 'new poverty' is growing, while on the other there are increasing demands for 'equal rights'. Nevertheless, the tendency is for one of these proletariats to be reproduced by the exploitation of the other (which does not prevent it from being dominated itself). Far from bringing about a unification of the working class, the phase of economic crisis (though it is important to ask exactly *for whom* and *in what sense* there is a crisis) is leading to an increasingly radical separation between the different aspects of proletarianization by the erection of geographical – and also ethnic, generational and sexual – barriers. Thus, though the world-economy is the real battleground of the class struggle, there is no such thing as a world proletariat (except 'as an idea'), indeed, it exists even less than does a world bourgeoisie.

Let me try to draw these threads together and sketch out a provisional conclusion. The account I have just outlined is more complex than the one that Marxists have, over a lengthy period, defended against all comers. To the extent that the programme of simplification was inherent in the Marxist conception of history (its teleology), it is fair to say this account is not a Marxist one, and even that it marks an abandonment of Marxism. It is, however, clear that that programme represents only one aspect of the situation, even though it is found throughout the work of Marx, who never renounced it. To those who recall the fierce debates of the 1960s and 1970s between 'historicist' and 'structuralist' interpretations of Marxism I should like to suggest that the crucial alternative is not the choice between structure and history, but between teleology (whether subjectivist or objectivist) and structural history. This is the reason that, in order to have greater purchase on history, I have endeavoured to elaborate at least some of the structural concepts of original Marxism and to set out their implications.

In my account, classical Marxism has been recitified in respect of one key point. There is *no fixed separation, even in terms of tendency, between social classes.* The idea of antagonism must be set free from the military and religious metaphor of the 'two camps' (and thus the alternative of 'civil war' versus 'consensus'). Only exceptionally does the class struggle take the form of civil war, whether on the level of representation or physical reality, and that is mainly when it is over-determined by religious or ethnic conflict, or when it is combined with war between states. But it does take on many other forms, the multiplicity of which cannot be circumscribed a priori, and which are no more 'inessential' than civil war, for the obvious reason, as I have been arguing, that there is no single 'essence' of class struggle (which is why, among other things, I find rather unsatisfactory the Gramscian distinction between war of movement and war of position, which still remains caught within the same metaphor). Let us accept once and for all that classes are not social super-individualities, neither as objects nor as subjects; in other words, they are not castes. Both structurally and historically, classes overlap and become meshed together, at least in part. In the same way that there are necessarily bourgeoisified proletarians, there are proletarianized bourgeois. This overlap never occurs without there being material divisions. In other words, 'class identities', which are relatively homogeneous, are not a result of predestination but of conjuncture.

Nevertheless, relating the individualization of class back to the conjuncture, and thus to the contingencies of politics, does not at all imply eliminating antagonism. Abandoning the metaphor of the 'two camps' (to the extent that it is manifestly tied to the idea that the state and civil society are separate spheres, and in other words to the vestiges of liberalism in Marx's thinking, in spite of the revolutionary short-circuit he effects between the economic and the political) does not mean exchanging it for a metaphor of a social continuum characterized by simple 'stratification' and 'general mobility'. The break-up of proletarianization into a number of partly independent and partly contradictory processes does not abolish proletarianization. Less than ever are citizens in modern society equal in respect of the arduous nature of their everyday lives, their own autonomy or dependency, the security they enjoy in their lifetime or the dignity they have in death, or the consumption and education, or information, to which they have access. And more than ever these different 'social' dimensions of citizenship are coupled with collective inequality with regard to political power and decision-making, whether in the areas of administration, the economic system, international relations or peace and war. All these inequalities are linked, in mediated ways, to the expansion of the value-form and the 'infinite' process of accumulation, just as they are linked to the reproduction of political alienation and the way in which the forms of class struggle can be turned into mass impotence in a framework of regulation of social conflict by the state.

Here, so to speak, is the double bind within which the production of commodities by commodities (including 'immaterial' commodities) and state-based socialization imprison individual and collective practice: resistance to exploitation enables exploitation to be extended, calls for security and autonomy fuel domination and collective insecurity (at any rate in a period of 'crisis'). But one must not forget that the cycle does not unfold on the same spot: on the contrary, it is constantly moving, subject to unpredictable movements, irreducible to the logic of the generalized economy, disruptive of national and international order, which it produces itself. It is therefore not a determinism. It does not exclude either mass confrontation or revolution, whatever its political form.

All in all, the 'disappearance of classes', their loss of identity or substance, is both a reality and an illusion. It is a reality because in effect the universalization of antagonism brings about a dissolution of the myth of a universal class by destroying the local institutional forms in which, for roughly a hundred years, the labour movement, on the one hand, and the bourgeois state, on the other, had, relatively speaking, unified a national bourgeoisie and proletariat. But it is an illusion because the 'substantial' identity of the classes was only ever a secondary effect of the practice of classes as social actors and, seen from this angle, nothing very new has occurred: by losing 'classes' in this sense, we have in fact lost nothing. The present 'crisis' is a crisis of the specific forms of representation and determinate practices of class struggle, and as such it may have considerable historical implications. But it does not represent a disappearance of antagonism itself, or, put another way, an end to the series of antagonistic forms of class struggle.

The theoretical fruits of this crisis are that we are now able, at last, to dissociate the question of the transition towards a society without exploitation, or the *break* with capitalism, from that of the *limits* of the capitalist mode of production. If these 'limits' exist (which is doubtful, since, as we have seen, there is no end to the dialectic of the forms of social integration of the workers, proletarianization, technological innovation and the intensification of surplus labour), they are not directly related to revolutionary change, which can only come from the political opportunities offered by the destabilization of the relations between classes – from the economy–state complex, that is. Again, what needs to be asked is *for whom* and *in what respect* is there a 'crisis'.

Revolutions in the past were always closely dependent *at one and the same time* on social inequalities, the demand for civic rights and the historical vicissitudes of the nation-state. They were sparked off by the contradiction between the claim on the part of the modern state to constitute a 'community', and the reality of different forms of exclusion. One of the most profound and subversive aspects of Marx's critique of the economy and politics, as we have seen, is the fact that it does not view human societies as being based on general interest, but on the regulation of antagonisms. It is true, as I have noted, that Marx's anthropology takes *labour* as the 'essence' of humankind and of social relations, the fundamental practice that alone determines antagonism. Without this reduction, liberal ideology, which identifies freedom with private property, could not have been radically challenged. The question that we now face is whether it is possible today for us to move beyond it, yet to do so without imagining that labour and the division of labour have disappeared, since, on the contrary, they are constantly becoming more extensive and diverse and are encroaching on new activities (such as those which, traditionally, were part not of 'production' but consumption). One thing, however, is certain: without ever merging with them, the division of labour necessarily cuts across other divisions from which its own effects can be isolated in only an abstract way. 'Ethnic' conflicts, or more precisely the effects of racism, are also universal. The same is true, at least in some civilizations, of antagonisms based on sexual difference, which itself is implicit in any organization or institution belonging to a social group (including of course the working class, if one follows Françoise Duroux on this point). The class struggle can and must be understood as *a* determining structure affecting *all* social practices, without however being the *only one*. Or, to put it more clearly, it is precisely to the extent that it affects all practices that it necessarily interferes with the universality of other structures. Universality here is not synonymous with unicity, any more than overdetermination is the same as indeterminacy.

At this point we are perhaps beginning to drift more and more from what can still be called Marxism. But by formulating the thesis of the universality of antagonisms in these terms, what is clear is the importance of those elements in the Marxist problematic that are more inescapable than ever. Nothing demonstrates this better, it seems to me, than the re-emergence of the way in which the problem of class is articulated with nationalism. In its liberal-democratic as well as its populist-authoritarian forms, nationalism has proved entirely compatible with both economic individualism and state planning or, rather, with various combinations of the two. It has been the key to the synthesis of particular modes of life and ideologies within a single dominant ideology, one which was capable of lasting and of being imposed on 'dominated' groups, and which politically could neutralize the radical effects of economic 'laws'. Without it the bourgeoisie could not have been constituted in either the economy or the state. It might be said as a result, in the terminology of systems analysis, that the national and nationalist state has become the major 'complexity reducer' in modern history. This is why nationalism tends to be constituted as a 'total' world-view (and why it is always to be found, even in the form of a denial, wherever such world-views are made official). But I suggested earlier that it was unlikely that those supranational nationalisms which one sees beginning to form here and there (by reference to 'Europe', the 'West', the 'socialist community', the 'Third World' and so on) might ever achieve the same totalization. Conversely, we must admit that the socialist ideology of class and class struggle, which did develop in constant confrontation with nationalism, has ended up copying it, by a kind of historical mimicry. It in turn became a 'complexity reducer', simply by substituting the criterion of class (even the criterion of class *origin*) for that of the state, with all its ethnic presuppositions, in the synthesis of multiple social practices (pending their merger within the prospect of a 'class state'). This is the uncertainty that faces us at present; namely, that to prevent the crisis of nationalism from ending in an excess of nationalism and its extended reproduction, what is needed is that the example of class struggle becomes visible in the representation of the social – but as its irreducible *other*. The ideology of class and class struggle, therefore, under whatever name is appropriate, must rediscover its autonomy while liberating itself from mimicry. To the question 'whither Marxism?', the answer, then, is: nowhere, unless this paradox is confronted in all its implications.

Notes

1. This chapter first appeared as a paper delivered at the 'Hannah Arendt Memorial Symposium in Political Philosophy', New School for Social Research, New York, 15–16 April 1987.

2. V. I. Lenin, *Collected Works*, Progress Publishers, Moscow 1963, vol. 18, p. 584 (*Translator's note*).

3. Cf. Jacques Lacan, *Ecrits*, Editions du Seuil, Paris 1966, pp. 197–213 (*Translator's note*).

4. *Faust I*, 11, 1339-40: '*alles, was entsteht,/Ist wert, daß es zugrunde geht*'. The phrase is quoted by Engels towards the beginning of his famous essay, 'Ludwig Feuerbach and the End of Classical German Philosophy' (*Translator's note*).

5. Marx, *The Communist Manifesto*, in *The Revolutions of 1848*, NLR/Penguin, Harmondsworth 1973, p. 68.

6. Cf. Etienne Balibar, 'L'Idée d'une politique de classe chez Marx', in B. Chavance, ed., *Marx en perspective*, Paris 1985.

7. See Etienne Balibar, 'The Long March for Peace', in E.P. Thompson *et al.*, eds, *Exterminism and Cold War*, Verso, London 1982.

Bibliography

Aglietta, Michel, *The Theory of Capitalist Regulation: The U.S. Experience*, transl. D. Fernbach, Verso, London 1979.

Althusser, Louis, 'Reply to John Lewis (Self Criticism)', in *Essays in Self-Criticism*, transl. G. Lock, New Left Books, London 1976.

—— *Lenin and Philosophy, and Other Essays*, transl. B. Brewster, New Left Books, London 1971, 1977.

Balibar, Etienne, *Cinq études du matérialisme historique*, Maspero, Paris 1974.

—— (with A. Tosel and C. Luporini), *Marx et sa critique de la politique*, Maspero, Paris 1979.

—— 'Classe' and 'Lutte des classes', in G. Labica, ed., *Dictionnaire critique du marxisme*, PUF, Paris 1982.

—— 'Sur le concept de la division du travail manuel et intellectuel', in J. Belkhir *et al.*, eds, *L'Intellectuel, l'intelligentsia et les manuels*, Anthropos, Paris 1983.

—— 'L'Idée d'une politique de classe chez Marx', in B. Chavance, ed., *Marx en perspective*, Editions de L'EHESS, Paris 1985.

—— 'Après l'autre Mai', in *La Gauche, le pouvoir, le socialisme: hommage à Nicos Poulantzas*, ed. C. Buci-Glucksmann, PUF, Paris 1983.

—— 'The long march for peace', in E.P. Thompson *et al.*, eds, *Exterminism and Cold War*, Verso, London 1982.

Baudelot, Christian, and Roger Establet, *L'Ecole capitaliste en France*, Maspero, Paris 1971.

Baudelot, Christian, Roger Establet and Jacques Toiser, *Qui travaille pour qui?*, Maspero, Paris 1979.

Bertaux, Daniel, *Destins personnels et structure de classe*, PUF, Paris 1977.

Bidet, Jacques, *Que faire du capital? Matériaux pour une refondation*, Meridiens-Klincksieck, Paris 1985.

Bourdieu, Pierre, and Jean-Claude Passeron, *Reproduction in Education, Society and Culture*, transl. R. Nice, Sage, London 1977.

Braudel, Fernand, *Civilization and Capitalism, 15th-18th Century* (3 vols), Collins, London 1981-84.

Brunhoff Suzanne de, *The State, Capital and Economic Policy*, transl. M. Sonenscher, Pluto, London 1978.

—— *L'Heure du marché, critique du liberalisme*, PUF, Paris 1986.

Biagio, Giovanni de, *La teoria politica delle classi nel 'Capitale'*, De Donato, Bari 1976.

Drach, Marcel, *La Crise dans les pays de l'Est*, La Découverte, Paris 1984.

Duroux, Françoise, 'La Famille des ouvriers: mythe ou politique?', unpublished doctoral thesis, University of Paris-VII, 1982.

Engels, Friedrich, with Karl Kautsky, 'Notwendige und überflüssige Gesellschaftsklassen', (1881), *M.E.W.*, vol. 19, p. 287.

Establet, Roger, *L'Ecole est-elle rentable?*, PUF, Paris 1987.

Ewald, François, *L'Etat-providence*, Grasset, Paris 1986.

Foster, John, *Class Struggle and the Industrial Revolution*, Methuen, London 1977.

Foucault, Michel, *Discipline and Punish: Birth of the Prison*, transl. A. Sheridan, Penguin, Harmondsworth 1979.
Freyssenet, Michel, *La Division capitaliste du travail*, Savelli, Paris 1977.
Gaudemar, Jean-Paul de, *La Mobilisation générale*, Champ Urbain, Paris 1979.
Gilroy, Paul, *There Ain't No Black in the Union Jack*, Hutchinson, London 1987.
Hobsbawm, Eric, *Industry and Empire*, Penguin, Harmondsworth 1968.
Laclau, Ernesto, and Chantal Mouffe, *Hegemony and Socialist Stategy. Towards a Radical Democratic Politics*, Verso, London 1985.
Lefebvre, Henri, *De l'Etat*, vol. 3, 'Le Mode de production étatique', UGE, Paris 1977.
Le Goff, Jacques, *Du silence à la parole. Droit du travail, société, état (1830–1985)*, Calligrammes, Quimper 1985.
Linhart, Robert, *Le Sucre et la faim*, Minuit, Paris 1980.
Lyotard, Jean-François, *The Differend: Phrases in Dispute*, Manchester University Press, Manchester 1989.
Meillassoux, Claude, *Maidens, Meal and Money: Capitalism and the Domestic Community*, Cambridge University Press, Cambridge 1981.
Moore, Stanley, *Three Tactics. The Background in Marx*, Monthly Review Press, New York 1963.
Moynot, Jean-Louis, *Au milieu du gué, CGT, syndicalisme et démocratie de masse*, PUF, Paris 1982.
Negri, Antonio, *La Classe ouvrière contre l'Etat*, Galilée, Paris 1978.
Noiriel, Gérard, *Longwy: Immigrés et prolétaires 1880–1980*, PUF, Paris 1984.
—— *Workers in French Society in the Nineteenth and Twentieth Century*, Berg, Oxford 1989.
Poulantzas, Nicos, *Classes in Contemporary Capitalism*, Verso, London 1978.
Przeworski, Adam, 'Proletariat into Class: The Process of Class Formation from Karl Kautsky's *The Class Struggle* to Recent Controversies', *Politics and Society*, vol. 7, no. 4, 1977.
Schöttler, Peter, *Naissance des bourses du travail. Un appareil idéologique d'Etat à la fin du XIXᵉ siècle*, PUF, Paris 1985.
Stedman Jones, Gareth, *Languages of Class*, Cambridge University Press, Cambridge 1983.
Therborn, Göran, 'L'Analisi di classe nel mondo attuale: il marxismo come scienza sociale', *Storia del Marxismo*, vol. IV, Einaudi, Milan 1982.
Thompson, E. P. 'Eighteenth-Century English Society: Class Struggle without Classes?', *Social History*, vol. 3, no. 2, 1978.
—— *The Making of the English Working Class*, Penguin, Harmondsworth 1968.
Touraine, Alain and Michel Wieviorka, *The Workers' Movement*, Cambridge University Press, Cambridge 1987.
Travail, Journal of the AEROT, edited by Robert Linhart (64 rue de la Folie-Méricourt, 75011 Paris).
Trentin, Bruno, *Da sfruttati a produttori. Lotte operaie e sviluppo capitalistico dal miracolo economico alla crisi*, De Donato, Bari 1977.
Verret, Michel, *L'Ouvrier français* I: l'éspace ouvrier, Armand Colin, Paris 1979.
Vincent, Jean-Marie, *Critique du travail. Le faire et l'agir*, PUF, Paris 1987.
Wallerstein, Immanuel, *The Modern World-System* (3 vols), Academic Press, New York, 1974–89.
—— *The Capitalist World-Economy*, Cambridge University Press, Cambridge 1979.
—— *Historical Capitalism*, Verso, London 1983.

PART IV

Displacements of
Social Conflict?

11

Social Conflict in Post-Independence Black Africa: The Concepts of Race and Status-Group Reconsidered

Immanuel Wallerstein

The Theoretical Confusion

Everyone 'knows' that something called 'racial tensions' exists in South Africa, in the United States, in Great Britain. Some people think it exists in parts of Latin America, in the Caribbean, in various countries of south and southeast Asia. But is there such a thing as 'racial tension' to be found in the independent states of Black Africa? Conversely, everyone 'knows' that 'tribalism' exists in Black Africa. Is 'tribalism' a phenomenon only of Africa or is it also known in industrialized, capitalist states?

The problem arises from some conceptual difficulties. The categories of social strata or social groupings in everyday scientific use are many, overlapping and unclear. One can find such terms as class, caste, nationality, citizenship, ethnic group, tribe, religion, party, generation, estate and race. There are no standard definitions – quite the contrary. Few authors even try to put the terms into relation with each other.

One famous attempt was that of Max Weber who distinguished three basic categories: class, status-group [*Stand*], and party (see Weber, 1968, pp. 302–7, 385–98, 926–40). One trouble with Weber's categorization is that it is not logically rigorous, but is in many ways constructed out of examples. And he draws these examples largely from nineteenth-century Europe, the European Middle Ages and Classical Antiquity. Fair enough for Weber, but for those who deal with the empirical reality of the twentieth-century non-European world, it may be difficult to find an appropriate reflection in Weber's distinctions. Weber defines class more or less in the Marxist tradition, as a group of persons who relate in similar ways to the economic system. He defines party as a group who are associated together within a corporate group to affect the allocation and exercise of power. Status group, however, is in many ways a residual category. There seem to be positive criteria, to be sure. Status groups are primordial[1] groups into which persons are born, fictitious families presumably tied together by loyalties which are not based on calculated goal-orientated associations, groups encrusted with traditional privileges or lack of them, groups which share honour, prestige rank and, above all, style of life (often including a common occupation) but which do not necessarily share a common income level or class membership.[2]

Does not the nation, the nation towards which we have 'nationalist' sentiments, fit this definition very closely? It would seem so. Yet it is not national affiliation which is usually first thought of when use is made of the concept of status group. Weber's concept was inspired primarily by medieval estates, a category of rather limited applicability to contemporary Africa. Much of the literature of modern Africa, rather, talks of a 'tribe' and/or 'ethnic group'. Most writers would take 'ethnic group' as the most meaningful empirical referent of status group, and there is no doubt it fits the spirit of Weber's concept. The term *race* is often used, though its relation, in the spirit of most authors, to status group is left inexplicit. *Race* is used in studies of Africa primarily with reference to conflicts between White persons of European descent and Black persons indigenous to the continent (a third category in some areas being persons coming from or descended from immigrants from the Indian subcontinent). But the term is seldom used to distinguish varieties among the indigenous Black population.

Are *race* and *ethnic group* then two different phenomena, or two variations of the same theme? Given the terminological confusion,[3] it might be best to describe first the empirical reality and see what might follow theoretically rather than to lay out in advance a theoretical framework within which to explain the empirical reality.

The Empirical Data: How Many Kinds of Status-Groups?

Pre-colonial Africa included many societies that were complex and hierarchical. No one has ever estimated what percentage of Africa's land area or population was in such groups, as opposed to segmentary societies, but surely at least two-thirds of it was. Some of these states had 'estates' – that is, categories of people with hereditary status: nobles, commoners, artisans, slaves, etc. Some of these states had 'ethnic groups' – categories of people with separate designations indicating presumed separate ancestry. These were usually the outcome of conquest situations.[4] Many states had, in addition, a recognized category of 'non-citizens' or 'strangers' (see Skinner, 1963). Finally, even the non-hierarchical societies usually had a division of persons according to some specified principle of classification which created a fictitious descent group, often called a 'clan' by anthropologists, or according to generation, that is, an 'age set'.[5]

The establishment of colonial rule changed none of these categorizations immediately. It did, however, impose at least one new one – that of colonial nationality, which was double or even triple (for example, Nigerian, British West African, British imperial).

In addition, in many instances, religious categories took on a new salience under colonial rule. Christians emerged as a significant subgroup, both within the 'tribe'[6] and within the 'territory'.[7] Although Islam predates European colonial rule almost everywhere, it is probable that Moslems became in many areas a more self-conscious category in counterpoise to Christians. The sudden spread of Islam in some areas seems to indicate this (see Hodgkin, 1962; also Froelich, 1962, ch. 3). And everywhere, new 'ethnic groups' came into existence.[8] Finally, *race* was a primary category of the colonial world, accounting for political rights, occupational allocation and income.[9]

The rise of the nationalist movements and the coming of independence created still more categories. Territorial identification – that is, nationalism – became widespread and important. Along with such territorial identification came a new devotion to ethnic identification, often called tribalism. As Elizabeth Colson (1967, p. 205) said:

> Probably many youths found their explicit allegiance to particular ethnic traditions at the same time that they made their commitment to African independence ... in Africa it has been the school man, the intellectual, who has been most eager to advance his own language and culture and who has seen himself as vulnerable to any advantages given to the language and culture of any other groups within the country.

The economic dilemmas of the educated classes in the post-Independence era exacerbated this tendency to 'tribalism' (see Wallerstein, 1971). Finally, nationalism also involved Pan-Africanism. That is, there came to be a category of 'Africans' corresponding to its opposite, the 'Europeans'. At first, this dichotomy seemed to correlate with skin colour. In 1958, however, Africa as a concept began to include, for many, northern (Arab) Africa (but still did not include White settlers in North, East or southern Africa).[10]

Independence also intruded one other significant variable: a rather

Several factors in addition to tribal insularity reinforce the division of Africa's indigenous population into subgroups. A continuous imaginary line drawn through Mauritania, Mali, Niger, Chad and Sudan indicates for the Sudanic belt a general dividing
point. Peoples to the north of the line are lighter skinned, Arabized, and Moslem;
peoples to the south are generally darker skinned and Christian/animist. A similar line,
running from the West Coast into Central Africa through the Ivory Coast, Ghana,
Togo, Dahomey, Nigeria, Cameroon and the Central African Republic, indicates the
same sort of division: peoples to the north and south of the line tend toward the opposite in mode of life, culture-family, religion and education.

rigid juridical definition of first-class membership in the larger moral community, that of citizenship. The lines drawn by this concept were different not only from those of pre-colonial Africa but also from those of the colonial era. During the colonial era, for example, a Nigerian could vote in a Gold Coast election, if he had transferred residence, since both territories were part of British West Africa, and the individual was a British subject. After Independence, however, although colonial era federal administrative units often survived as units of national aspiration, membership in them no longer conferred rights of equal participation in each territorial subunit, now a sovereign nation-state, as many a politician and civil servant came to learn in the early post-Independence years.

It is clear from even the briefest glance at the literature that there is no independent country in Africa in which the indigenous population is not divided into subgroups which emerge as significant elements in the political divisions of the country. That is to say, 'tribal' or ethnic affili-ations are linked to political groupings or factions or positions, are often linked to occupational categories, and are surely linked to job allocation. When foreign journalists comment on this, African politicians often deny the truth of such analysis. Such denials, however, as well as the contradictory assertions by outside observers, serve ideological rather than analytic ends. Thus, there are a long list of well-known ethno-political rivalries in African states (for example, Kikuyu versus Luo in Kenya; Bemba versus Lozi in Zambia; Sab versus Samaale in Somalia). In each of these cases, often despite presumed efforts of the government or a nationalist political movement to prevent it, individuals have been aligned and/or mobilized on 'tribal' lines for political ends (cf. Rothschild, 1969; Rotberg, 1967; Lewis, 1958).

In some countries, these so-called tribal divisions have been re-inforced by some additional factors. In Ethiopia, for example, the divisions between the Amhara or Amhara-Tigre and the Eritreans co-incides more or less with a religious division between Christians and Moslems, of which the participants are fully conscious, all the more since such a conflict has a long historical tradition behind it (see Jesman, 1963).

Along the West African coast and into central Africa, there are seven contiguous states (the Ivory Coast, Ghana, Togo, Dahomey, Nigeria, Cameroon, and Central African Republic) through which a continuous horizontal line could be drawn. The peoples to the north and south of this line tend to be opposite in a series of features: savannah versus forest in soil conditions and corresponding large culture-family; Moslem/animist versus Christian/animist in religion; less modern edu-cation versus more modern education (largely the result of more

Christian missionaries in the southern halves during the colonial era (see Milcent, 1967; also Schwartz, 1968). A similar line might be drawn in Uganda between the non-Bantu, less educated north and the Bantu, more educated (and more Christianized) south (see Hopkins, 1967; also Edel, 1965).

Further to the north, in the so-called Sudanic belt, an analogous line might be drawn through Mauritania, Mali, Niger, Chad and Sudan. In the north of Mauritania, Chad and Sudan, the people are lighter skinned, Arabized and Moslem. To the south, they are darker skinned and Christian/animist. In Mali and Niger, however, those to the south are Moslem, as well. In all these states except the Sudan, those to the north are more likely to be nomadic and less educated. In Mauritania and the Sudan, those to the north are in the majority and in power. In Mali, Niger and Chad, the reverse is true (see Watson, 1963; Paques, 1967; Shepherd, 1966). Because these cultural distinctions in the Sudanic belt countries correlate with skin-colour differences, these divisions are sometimes spoken of as 'racial'.

There is a further group of countries interesting to note. These are states which existed as political entities in pre-colonial times and have survived as such through the colonial and post-Independence era, and in which there were clear pre-colonial 'tribal' stratifications. These are Zanzibar (Arabs and Afro-Shirazis), Rwanda (Tutsi and Hutu), Burundi (Tutsi and Hutu), Madagascar (Merina and others). In all these cases (except Burundi) the pre-colonial majoritarian lower stratum has now achieved political top status (see Lofchie, 1963; Kuper, 1970; Ziegler, 1967; Kent, 1962). Where similar pre-colonial stratification systems existed within larger colonial and post-colonial units, the political outcome has been far more ambiguous (Fulani sultanates in Nigeria and Cameroon, Hima kingdoms in Uganda and Tanganyika).

Since self-rule and Independence, there have been a large number of 'repatriations' of Africans to their 'home' countries. Empires are notoriously liberal in the movement of peoples. It serves the purpose of optimal utilization of personnel. Nation-states, on the other hand, are trying precisely to demonstrate that privileges accrue to the status of citizen.

The first group to feel this pressure were politicians. As independence approached, the category of French West African or British East African tended to disappear. Malians who had made their political career in Upper Volta, or Ugandans who had made theirs in Kenya, found it prudent to go back to their home base. In addition to these discrete recognitions of a new political reality, there were the public and semi-public expulsions of large categories of persons: Dahomeans (and Togolese) from the Ivory Coast, Niger and elsewhere; Nigerians and

Togolese from Ghana; Malians from Zaïre. In each of these cases, those expelled had occupied positions in the money economy at a time of growing unemployment. The groups in question found themselves suddenly defined as non-nationals rather than as Africans. This was *a fortiori* true of categories of non-Africans, even where they had in some cases taken out formal citizenship: Arabs in Zanzibar, Asians in Kenya, sporadic expulsions of Lebanese in Ghana. Thus far, no major wholesale expulsion of Europeans has taken place in Black Africa, although there was an exodus of Belgians from Zaïre at one point.

This rapid sketch of the African scene is meant to underline one point: there is no useful distinction among the presumed varieties of status groups, such as ethnic groups, religious groups, races, castes. They are all variations of a single theme: grouping people by an affinity that mythically predates the current economic and political scene and which is a claim to a solidarity overriding those defined in class or ideological terms. As such, they appear, as Akiwowo (1964, p. 162) says of tribalism, as 'a set of patterned responses, adaptive adjustments if you will, to the unanticipated consequences of the processes of nation-building'. Or, in the more blunt words of Skinner (1967, p. 173), their central function is 'to permit people to organize into social, cultural or political entities able to compete with others for whatever goods and service [are] viewed as valuable in their environment'.

In so far as this function is inherent in the concept, then by definition status groups cannot exist prior to some larger society of which they are a part, even when groups claim to be organized or to exist in more than one societal system.[11] What Fried (1967, p. 15) states cautiously of 'tribes' is true of all status-groups:

> Most tribes seem to be secondary phenomena in a very specific sense: they may well be the product of processes stimulated by the appearance of relatively highly organized societies amidst other societies which are organized much more simply. If this can be demonstrated, tribalism can be viewed as a reaction to the creation of complex political structure rather than as a necessary preliminary stage in its evolution.

In the modern world situation, a status-group is a collective claim to power and allocation of goods and services within a nation-state on grounds that are formally illegitimate.

The Relationship of Class and Status-Group

How then do such claims stand in relation to the claims of class solidarity? Marx, in using the concept of class, distinguished between classes *an sich* and *für sich.* Weber (1968, p. 930) repeated this distinction when he said: 'Thus every class may be the carrier of any one of the innumerable possible forms of class action, but this is not necessarily so. In any case, a class does not in itself constitute a group (*Gemeinschaft*).'

Why is it that classes are not always *für sich*? Indeed, why is it they are so seldom *für sich*? Or to put the question another way: how do we explain that status-group consciousness is so pervasive and powerful a political force in Africa and throughout the world, today and throughout history? To answer that it is false consciousness is simply to push the question one step logically back, for then we should have to ask how it is that most people most of the time exhibit false consciousness.

Weber (1968, p. 938) has a theory to account for this. He states:

> As to the general economic conditions making for the predominance of stratification by status, only the following can be said. When the bases of the acquisition and distribution of goods are relatively stable, stratification by status is favored. Every technological repercussion and economic transformation threatens stratification by status and pushes the class situation into the foreground. Epochs and countries in which the naked class situation is of predominant significance are regularly the periods of technical and economic transformations. And every slowing down of the change in economic stratification leads, in due course, to the growth of status structure and makes for a resuscitation of the important role of social honor.

Weber's explanation seems very simple and makes class consciousness the correlate of progress and social change, stratification by status the expression of retrograde forces – a sort of vulgar Marxism. While one may agree with the moral thrust of the theorem, it is not very predictive of the smaller shifts in historical reality nor does it explain why one can find modern economic thrusts in status-group garb (see Favret, 1967), as well as mechanisms of the preservation of traditional privilege in class consciousness (see Geertz, 1967).

Favret (1967, p. 73) gives us a clue in her discussion of a Berber rebellion in Algeria:

> [In Algeria] primordial groups do not exist substantively, unaware of their archaism, but reactively. The anthropologist tempted by collecting traditional political phenomena is in danger therefore of a colossal misunderstanding in interpreting them naively, for their context is today inverted. The choice for the descendants of the segmentary tribes of the nineteenth century is no longer among ends – to co-operate with the central government or to institutionalize dissidence – for only the former choice is henceforth possible. The choice – or the fate – of the peasants of the underdeveloped agricultural sector is in the means of attaining this end; among which, paradoxically, is dissidence.

Favret pushes us to look at claims based on status-group affiliation not in the intellectual terms of the actors in the situation, but in terms of the actual functions such claims perform in the social system. Moerman makes a similar appeal in an analysis of the Lue, a tribe in Thailand, about whom he asks three trenchant questions: What are the Lue? Why are the Lue? When are the Lue? He concludes (1967, p. 167):

> Ethnic identification devices – with their important potential of making each ethnic set of living persons a joint enterprise with countless generations of unexamined history – seem to be universal. Social scientists should therefore describe and analyse the ways in which they are used, and not merely – as natives do – use them as explanations.... It is quite possible that ethnic categories are rarely appropriate subjects for the interesting human predicates.

Perhaps then we could reconceive the Weberian trinity of class, status-group and party not as three different and cross-cutting groups but as three different existential forms of the same essential reality. In which case, the question shifts from Weber's one of the conditions under which stratification by status takes precedence over class consciousness to the conditions under which a stratum embodies itself as a class, as a status-group or as a party. For such a conceptualization, it would not be necessary to argue that the boundary lines of the group in its successive embodiments would be identical – quite the contrary, or there would be no function to having different outer clothing – but rather that there exist a limited set of groups in any social structure at any given time in relation to, in conflict with, each other.

One approach, suggested by Rodolfo Stavenhagen, is to see status-groups as 'fossils' of social classes. He argues (1962, pp. 99–101) that:

> Stratifications [i.e., status-groups] represent, in the majority of cases, what we call social *fixations*, frequently by juridical means, certainly subjectively, of specific social relations of production, represented by class relations. Into these social *fixations* intrude other secondary, accessory factors (for example, religious, ethnic) which reinforce the stratification and which have, at the same time, the function of 'liberating' it of its links with its economic base; in other words, of maintaining its strength even if its economic base changes. Consequently, stratifications can be thought of as jusifications or rationalizations of the established economic system, that is to say, as ideologies. Like all phenomena of the social superstructure, stratification has a quality of inertia which maintains it even when the conditions which gave it birth have changed. As the relations between classes are modified ... stratifications turn themselves into *fossils* of the class relations on which they were originally based.... [Furthermore], it seems that the two types of groupings (dominant class and higher stratum) can coexist for some time and be encrusted in the social structure, according to the particular historical circumstances. But sooner or

later a new stratification system arises which corresponds more exactly to the current class system.

In a later analysis, using Central American data, Stavenhagen spells out how, in a colonial situation, two caste-like lower status-groups (in that case, *indios* and *ladinos*) could emerge, become encrusted, and survive the various pressures at what he called class clarification. He argues that two forms of dependence (a colonial form, based on ethnic discrimination and political subordination) and a class form (based on work relations) grew up side by side and reflected a parallel ranking system. After Independence, and despite economic development, the dichotomy between *indios* and *ladinos*, 'profoundly ensconced in the values of the members of society', remained as 'an essentially conservative force' in the social structure. 'Reflecting a situation of the past ... [this dichotomy] acts as a constraint on the development of the new class relations' (1963, p. 94). In this version, present stratification is still a fossil of the past, but it is not so simply a fossil of class relations *per se.*

Another approach would be to see class or status affiliation as options open to various members of the society. This is the approach of Peter Carstens. In two recent papers, one by Carstens (1970) and one by Allen (1970), there is agreement that Africans working on the land in the rural areas should be thought of as 'peasants' who are members of the 'working class', that is, who sell their labour-power even when they are technically self-employed cash-crop farmers. But while Allen is concerned with emphasizing the pattern of tied alternation between cash-crop farming and wage-earning,[12] Carstens is more concerned with explaining the status-group apparatus of peasant class organization, or what he calls 'peasant status systems'.

Carstens (1970, p. 9) starts with the argument that 'the retention or revival of tenuous tribal loyalties are resources available to persons to establish prestige or esteem'. He reminds us (1970, p. 10) that 'the same institutions that effected the hidden force that produced a peasant *class*, also created peasant *status* systems. For example ... the surest way to achieve recognition, prestige, and esteem in the eyes of the ruling class as well as from the local peasants is to participate in the externally imposed educational and religious institutions.' It therefore follows that 'it is only by the manipulation of their internal status systems that they are able to gain access to other status systems which are located in the higher class. The strategy of status manipulation is best seen then as a means for crossing class boundaries' (1970, p. 8).

The strength of stratification by status can be seen in this light. Status honour is not only a mechanism for the achievers of yore to maintain their advantages in the contemporary market, the retrograde force described by Weber; it is also the mechanism whereby the upward strivers obtain their ends within the system (hence the correlation of high ethnic consciousness and education, to which Colson called attention). With support from two such important groups, the ideological primacy of status-group is easy to understand. It takes an unusual organizational situation to break through this combination of elements interested in preserving this veil (or this reality – it makes no difference).

Weber was wrong. Class consciousness does not come to the fore when technological change or social transformation is occurring. All modern history gives this the lie. Class consciousness only comes to the fore in a far rarer circumstance, in a 'revolutionary' situation, of which class consciousness is both the ideological expression and the ideological pillar. In this sense, the basic Marxian conceptual instinct was correct.

The African Data Reanalysed

Let us now return to the empirical reality of contemporary independent Africa in the light of this theoretical excursus. Independent Black Africa is today composed of a series of nation-states, members of the United Nations, almost none of which can be considered a national society, in the sense of having a relatively autonomous and centralized polity, economy and culture. All these states are part of the world-social-system, and most are all well integrated into particular imperial economic networks. Their economic outlines are basically similar. The majority of the population works on the land, producing both crops for a world market and food for their subsistence. Most are workers, either in the sense of receiving wages from the owner of the land or in the sense of being self-employed in a situation in which they are obliged to earn cash (and see farming as an economic alternative to other kinds of wage employment). There are others who work as labourers in urban areas, often as part of a pattern of circulatory migration.

In each country, working for the most part for the government, there is a bureaucratic class which is educated and seeking to transform some of their wealth into property. In every case, there are certain groups (one of several) who are disproportionately represented in the bureaucratic class, as there are other groups disproportionately represented among urban labourers. Almost everywhere there is a group of Whites holding high status and filling technical positions. Their prestige rank has scarcely changed since colonial rule. The local high rank of Whites reflects the position of these countries in the world-economic-system where they are 'proletarian' nations, suffering the effects of 'unequal exchange'.[13]

The degree of political autonomy represented by formal sovereignty enabled the local elites or elite groups to seek their upward mobility in the world-system by a rapid expansion of the educational system of their countries. What is individually functional in terms of the world-system is collectively dysfunctional. The workings of the world-system do not provide sufficient job outlets at the national level. This forces elite groups to find criteria by which to reward parts of themselves and to reject others. The particular lines of division are arbitrary and change-able in details. In some places, the division is along ethnic lines; in others, along religious; in others, along racial lines; in most, in some implicit combination of all these.

These status-group tensions are the inefficacious and self-defeating expression of class frustrations. They are the daily stuff of contemporary African politics and social life. The journalists, who are usually closer to popular perceptions than the social scientists, tend to call this phenom-enon 'tribalism' when they write of Black Africa. Tribal, or ethnic, conflicts are very real things, as the civil wars in the Sudan and Nigeria attest most eloquently. They are ethnic conflicts in the sense that persons involved in these conflicts are commonly motivated by analyses which use ethnic (or comparable status-group) categories; furthermore, they usually exhibit strong ethnic loyalties. None the less, behind the ethnic 'reality' lies a class conflict, not very far from the surface. By this I mean the following straightforward and empirically testable proposition (not one, however, that has been definitively so tested): were the class differences that correlate (or coincide) with the status-group differences to disappear, as a result of changing social circumstances, the status-group conflicts would eventually disappear (no doubt to be replaced by others). The status-group loyalties are binding and affective, in a way that it seems difficult for class loyalties to be other than in moments of crisis, but they are also more transient from the perspective of the analyst. If the society were to become ethnically 'integrated', class antagonisms would not abate; the opposite is true. One of the functions of the network of status-group affiliations is to conceal the realities of class differentials. To the extent, however, that particular class antagon-isms or differentials abate or disappear, status-group antagonisms (if not differentials, but even differentials) also abate and disappear.

The Usefulness of the Concept of Race

In Black Africa, one speaks of 'ethnic' conflict. In the United States or in South Africa, one speaks of 'racial' conflict. Is there any point in having a special word, *race*, to describe status groupings that are the most salient in some countries but not in others (like Black African states)? If we were to regard each national case as discrete and logically separate, there would not be, since stratification by status serves the same purpose in each.

But the national cases are not discrete and logically separate. They are part of a world-system. Status and prestige in the national system cannot be divorced from status and rank in the world-system, as we have already mentioned in discussing the role of expatriate White Europeans in Black Africa today. There are international status-groups as well as national ones. What we mean by race is essentially such an international status group. There is a basic division between Whites and non-Whites. (Of course, there are varieties of non-Whites, and the categorization differs according to time and place. One grouping is by skin colour but it is not in fact very prevalent. Another more common one is by continent, although the Arabs often lay claim to being counted separately.)

In terms of this international dichotomy, skin colour is irrelevant. 'White' and 'non-White' have very little to do with skin colour. 'What is a Black? And first of all, what colour is he?' asked Jean Genêt. When Africans deny, as most do deny, that the conflict between the lighter-skinned Arabs of northern Sudan and the dark-skinned Nilotes of southern Sudan is a racial conflict, they are not being hypocritical. They are reserving the term *race* for a particular international social tension. It is not that the conflict in the Sudan is not real and is not expressed in status-group terms. It is. But it is a conflict which, though formally similar to, is politically different from, that between Blacks and Whites in the United States, or Africans and Europeans in South Africa. The political difference lies in its meaning in and for the world-system.

Race is, in the contemporary world, the only international status-group category. It has replaced religion, which played that role since at least the eighth century AD. Rank in this system, rather than colour, determines membership in the status group. Thus, in Trinidad, there can be a 'Black Power' movement, directed against an all-Black government, on the grounds that this government functions as an ally of North American imperialism. Thus, Quebec separatists can call themselves the 'White Niggers' of North America. Thus, Pan-Africanism can include white-skinned Arabs of North Africa, but exclude white-skinned Afrikaners of South Africa. Thus, Cyprus and Yugoslavia can be invited to tricontinental conferences (Asia, Africa and Latin America) but Israel and Japan are excluded. As a status-group category, race is a blurred collective representation for an international class category, that of the proletarian nations. Racism, therefore, is simply the act of maintaining the existing international social structure, and is not a neologism for racial discrimination. It is not that they are separate phenomena.

Racism obviously utilizes discrimination as part of its armoury of tactics, a central weapon, to be sure. But there are many possible situations in which there can be racism without discrimination, in any immediate sense. Perhaps there can even be discrimination without racism, though this seems harder. What is important to see is that these concepts refer to actions at different levels of social organization: racism refers to action within the world arena; discrimination refers to actions within relatively small-scale social organizations.

Summary

In summary, my main point is that status-groups (as well as parties) are blurred collective representation of classes. The blurred (and hence incorrect) lines serve the interests of many different elements in most social situations. As social conflict becomes more acute, status-group lines approach class lines asymptotically, at which point we may see the phenomenon of 'class consciousness'. But the asymptote is never reached. Indeed, it is almost as though there were a magnetic field around the asymptote which pushed the approaching curve away. Race, finally, is a particular form of status-group in the contemporary world, the one which indicates rank in the world social system. In this sense, there are no racial tensions today within independent Black African states. One of the expressions of national identity, however, as it will be achieved, will be increasing international status-group consciousness, or racial identification, which would then only be overcome or surpassed as one approached the asymptote of international class consciousness.

Notes

1. To use the term added by Shils (cf. Shils, 1957, pp. 130–45). For Shils, primordial qualities are 'significant relational' ones, more than just a 'function of interaction'. Their significance (p. 142) is 'ineffable' (cf. Geertz, 1963).
    2. Weber's (1968, p. 932) definition emphasizes honour:

In contrast to classes, *Stände* (status-groups) are normally groups. They are, however, often of an amorphous kind. In contrast to the purely economically determined 'class situation', we wish to designate as *status situation* every typical component of the life of man that is determined by a specific, positive or negative, social estimation of *honor*....
    Both propertied and propertyless people can belong to the same status-group, and frequently they do with very tangible consequences....
    In content, status honor is normally expressed by the fact that above all else a specific *style of life* is expected from all those who wish to belong to the circle.

3. The French-language literature is even more confusing, since the French word *race* is used by many writers where English writers would use 'tribe'.

4. Jean Suret-Canale (1969, p. 112) argues that both phenomena derive from conquest situations, but that for some unexplained reason assimilation proceeds faster in some areas than in others:

> As long as class antagonisms remained almost non-existent within a tribe ... no state superstructure emerged.... Where class antagonisms developed with the extension of slavery and the creation of a tribal aristocracy, various kinds of states ... emerged....
> When the creation of these states involved the domination and incorporation of other tribal groups, and the creation within the framework of the state of a new cultural and linguistic unity, the vestiges of tribal organization more or less disappeared ... for example, in Zululand.... It could happen that the division into classes retained the appearance of a tribal conflict: this was the case in the monarchies of the interlacustrian zone of eastern Africa (Rwanda, Burundi, etc.) where the conquerors, the pastoral Tutsi, constituted the aristocracy, dominating the indigenous peasants, the Hutu.

5. See the excellent discussion of the social organization of such non-hierarchical societies in Horton (1971).
6. See Busia (1951). Busia describes in some detail the causes and consequences of a Christian–non-Christian split among the Ashanti.
7. Uganda is a prime case, where politics crystallized to some extent along a religious trichotomy: Protestants, Catholics and Moslems.
8. I have argued this in Wallerstein (1960).
9. This point is argued throughout the works of George Balandier and Frantz Fanon.
10. Why this came to be so, and what were the consequences of this non-skin-colour definition of 'African-ness', I have discussed in Wallerstein (1967).
11. Cf. Weber (1968, p. 939):

> We should add one more general observation about classes, status-groups and parties: the fact that they presuppose a larger association, especially the framework of a polity, does not mean that they are confined to it. On the contrary, at all times it has been the order of the day that such association ... reaches beyond the state boundaries.... But their aim is not necessarily the establishment of a new territorial dominion. In the main they aim to influence the existing polity.

Except, I should add, in so far as one considers loyalty to a nation-state in a world-system as an expression of status-group consciousness.
12. 'Wage-earners experience fluctuations in their living standards and employment whereas the peasant producers experience fluctuations in their living standards and the intensity of work. A depression in the living standards of wage-earners or in increase in unemployment, however, produces a movement of labour back to peasant production or is borne because the resources of peasant production exist as an insurance cover' (Allen, 1970). Cf. a similar argument made by Arrighi (1969). There is an English version under the title 'Labour Supplies in Historical Perspective: A Study of the Proletarianization of the African Peasantry in Rhodesia' in Giovanni Arrighi and John S. Saul, *Essays on the Political Economy of Africa* (Monthly Review Press, New York 1973), pp. 180–234.
13. For an elaboration of the concept and an explanation of its social consequences, see Emanuel (1969).

References

Akiwowo, Akinsola A., 1964, 'The Sociology of Nigerian Tribalism', *Phylon*, vol. 251, no. 2, pp. 155–63.
Allen, V.L., 1970, 'The Meaning and Differentiation of the Working Class in Tropical

Africa', paper presented at the Seventh World Congress of Sociology, Varna, Bulgaria (13–19 September).

Arrighi, Giovanni, 1969, 'L'offertà di lavoro in una perspettiva storica', in *Sviluppo economico e sovrastrutture in Africa*, pp. 89–162, Einaudi, Turin.

Arrighi, Giovanni and John S. Saul, 1973, *Essays on the Political Economy of Africa*, Monthly Review Press, New York.

Busia, K. A., 1951, *The Position of the Chief in the Modern Political System of Ashanti*, Oxford University Press, London.

Carstens, Peter, 1970, 'Problems of Peasantry and Social Class in Southern Africa', paper presented at the Seventh World Congress of Sociology, Varna, Bulgaria (13–19 September).

Colson, Elizabeth, 1967, 'Contemporary Tribes and the Development of Nationalism', in June Helm, ed., *Essays on the Problem of Tribe*, pp. 201–6. Proceedings of the 1967 Annual Spring Meeting of the American Ethnological Society.

Edel, May, 1965. 'African Tribalism: Some Reflections on Uganda', *Political Science Quarterly*, vol. 80, no. 3, pp. 357–72.

Emanuel, Arghiri, 1969, *L'Echange inégal*. Maspero, Paris.

Favret, Jeanne, 1967, 'Le Traditionalisme par excès de modernité', *Archives européennes de sociologie*, vol. 8, no. 1, pp. 71–93.

Fried, Morton H., 1967, 'On the Concept of "Tribe" and "Tribal Society".' in June Helm ed., *Essays on the Problem of Tribe*, pp. 3–20. Proceedings of 1967 Annual Spring Meeting of the American Ethnological Society.

Froelich, J.-C., 1962. *Les Musulmans d'Afrique Noire*, Editions de l'Orante, Paris.

Geertz, Clifford, 1963, 'The Integrative Revolution, Primordial Sentiments and Civil Politics in the New States', in C. Geertz, ed., *Old Societies and New States*, pp. 105–57, Free Press, Glencoe.

—— 1967, 'Politics Past, Politics Present', *Archives européennes de sociologie*, vol. 8, no. 1, pp. 1–14.

Hodgkin, Thomas, 1962, 'Islam and National Movements in West Africa', *Journal of African History*, vol. 3, no. 1, pp. 323–7.

Hopkins, Terence K., 1967, 'Politics in Uganda: the Buganda Question', in J. Butler and A. A. Castagno, Jr, eds, *Transition in African Politics*, Boston University Papers on Africa, pp. 251–90, Praeger, New York.

Horton, Robin, 1971, 'Stateless Societies in the History of West Africa', in J. F. A. Ajayi and M. Crowder, eds, *A History of West Africa* (2 vols), vol. 1, Longmans, London.

Jesman, Czeslaw, 1963, *The Ethiopian Paradox*, Oxford University Press, London.

Kent, Raymond K., 1962 *From Madagascar to the Malagasy Republic*, Praeger, New York.

Kuper, Leo, 1970, 'Continuities and Discontinuities in Race Relations: Evolutionary or Revolutionary Change', *Cahiers d'études africaines*, vol. 10, no. 3 (39), pp. 361–83.

Lewis, I. M., 1958, 'Modern Political Movements in Somaliland', *Africa*, vol. 28, no. 3, pp. 244–61; vol. 28, no. 4, pp. 344–63.

Lofchie, Michael, 1963, 'Party Conflict in Zanzibar', *Journal of Modern African Studies*, vol. 1, no. 2, pp. 185–207.

Milcent, Ernest, 1967, 'Tribalisme et vie politique dans les Etats du Bénin', *Revue française d'études politiques africaines*, vol. 18, pp. 37–53.

Moerman, Michael, 1967, 'Being Lue: Uses and Abuses of Ethnic Identification', in June Helm, ed., *Essays on the Problem of Tribe*, pp. 153–69. Proceedings of 1967 Annual Spring Meeting of the American Ethnological Society.

Paques, Viviana, 1967, 'Alcuni problemi umani posti dallo sviluppo economico e sociale: il case della Repubblica del Ciad', *Il nuovo osservatore*, vol. 8, no. 63, pp. 580–4.

Rotberg, Robert I., 1967, 'Tribalism and Politics in Zambia', *Africa Report*, vol. 121, no. 9, pp. 29–35.

Rothschild, Donald, 1969, 'Ethnic Inequalities in Kenya', *Journal of Modern African Studies*, vol. 7, no. 4, pp. 689–711.

Schwarz, Walter, 1968, *Nigeria*, Pall Mall Press, London.

Shepherd, George W., Jr, 1966, 'National Integration and the Southern Sudan', *Journal of*

Modern African Studies, vol. 4, no. 2, pp. 193–212.

Shils, Edward, 1957, 'Primordial, Personal, Sacred and Civil Ties', *British Journal of Sociology*, vol. 8, no. 2, pp. 130–45.

Skinner, Elliott P., 1963, 'Strangers in West African Societies', *Africa*, vol. 33, no. 4, pp. 307–20.

—— 1967, 'Group Dynamics in the Politics of Changing Societies: The Problem of "Tribal" Politics in Africa', in June Helm, ed., *Essays on the Problem of Tribe*, pp. 170–85. Proceedings of 1967 Annual Spring Meeting of the American Ethnological Society.

Stavenhagen, Rodolfo, 1962, 'Estratificación social y estructura de clases (un ensayo de interpretación)', *Ciencias políticas y sociales*, vol. 8, no. 27, pp. 73–102.

—— 1963, 'Clases, colonialismo y aculturación: ensayo sobre un sistema de relaciones interétnicas en Mesoamérica'. *América Latina*, vol. 6, no. 4, pp. 103–63.

Suret-Canale, Jean, 1969, 'Tribus, classes, nations', *La nouvelle revue internationale*, vol. 130, pp. 110–24.

Wallerstein, Immanuel, 1960, 'Ethnicity and National Integration in West Africa', *Cahiers d'études africaines*, vol. 3, pp. 129–39.

—— 1967, *Africa: The Politics of Unity*, Random House, New York.

—— 1971, 'The Range of Choice: Constraints on the Politics of Governments of Contemporary African Independent States', in Michael F. Lochie, ed., *The State of the Nations*, pp. 19–33, University of California Press, Berkeley.

Waston, J. H. A., 1963, 'Mauritania: Problems and Prospects', *Africa Report*, vol. 8, no. 2, pp. 3–6.

Weber, Max, 1968, *Economy and Society* (3 vols), Bedminster Press, New York.

Ziegler, Jean, 1967, 'Structures ethniques et partis politiques au Burundi', *Revue française d'études politiques africaines*, no. 18, pp. 54–68.

12

'Class Racism'

Etienne Balibar

Academic analyses of racism, though according chief importance to the study of racist theories, none the less argue that 'sociological' racism is a popular phenomenon. Given this supposition, the development of racism within the working class (which, to committed socialists and communists, seems counter to the natural order of things) comes to be seen as the effect of a tendency allegedly inherent in the masses. Institutional racism finds itself projected into the very construction of that psycho-sociological category that is 'the masses'. We must therefore attempt to analyse the process of displacement which, moving from classes to masses, presents these latter both as the privileged *subjects* of racism and its favoured *objects*.

Can one say that a social class, by its situation and its ideology (not to mention its identity), is predisposed to racist attidues and behaviour? This question has mainly been debated in connection with the rise of Nazism, first speculatively and then later by taking various empirical indicators.[1] The result is quite paradoxical since there is hardly a social class on which suspicion has not fallen, though a marked predilection has been shown for the 'petty bourgeoisie'. But this is a notoriously ambiguous concept, which is more an expression of the aporias of a class analysis conceived as a dividing up of the population into mutually exclusive slices. As with every question of origins in which a political charge is concealed, it makes sense to turn the question around: not to look for the foundations of the racism which invades everyday life (or the movement which provides the vehicle for it) in the nature of the petty bourgeoisie, but to attempt to understand how the development of

204

racism causes a 'petty bourgeois' mass to emerge out of a diversity of material situations. For the misconceived question of the class bases of racism, we shall thus substitute a more crucial and complex question, which that former question is in part intended to mask: that of the relations between racism, as a supplement to nationalism, and the irreducibility of class conflict in society. We shall find it necessary to ask how the development of racism displaces class conflict or, rather, in what way class conflict is always already transformed by a social relation in which there is an inbuilt tendency to racism; and also, conversely, how the fact that the nationalist alternative to the class struggle specifically takes the form of racism may be considered as the index of the irreconcilable character of that struggle. This does not of course mean that it is not crucial to examine how, in a given conjuncture, the class conditions [*la condition de classe*] (made up of the material conditions of existence and labour, though also of ideological traditions and practical relationships to politics) determine the effects of racism in society: the frequency and forms of the 'acting out' of racism, the discourse which expresses it and the membership of organized racist movements.

The traces of a constant overdetermination of racism by the class struggle are as universally detectable in its history as the nationalist determination, and everywhere they are connected with the core of meaning of its phantasies and practices. This suffices to demonstrate that we are dealing here with a determination that is much more concrete and decisive than the generalities dear to the sociologists of 'modernity'. It is wholly inadequate to see racism (or the nationalism–racism dyad) either as one of the paradoxical expressions of the individualism or egalitarianism which are supposed to characterize modern societies (following the old dichotomy of 'closed', 'hierarchical' societies and 'open,' 'mobile' societies) or a defensive reaction against that individualism, seen as expressing nostalgia for a social order based on the existence of a 'community'.[2] Individualism only exists in the concrete forms of market competition (including the competition between labour powers) in unstable equilibrium with association between individuals under the constraints of the class struggle. Egalitarianism only exists in the contradictory forms of political democracy (where that democracy exists), the 'welfare state' (where that exists), the polarization of conditions of existence, cultural segregation and reformist or revolutionary utopias. It is these determinations, and not mere anthropological figures, which confer an 'economic' dimension upon racism.

Nevertheless, the *heterogeneity* of the historical forms of the relationship between racism and the class struggle poses a problem. This ranges from the way in which anti-Semitism developed into a bogus 'anti-capitalism' around the theme of 'Jewish money' to the way in which racial stigma and class hatred are combined today in the category of immigration. Each of these configurations is irreducible (as are the corresponding conjunctures), which make it impossible to define any simple relationship of 'expression' (or, equally, of substitution) between racism and class struggle.

In the manipulation of anti-Semitism as an anti-capitalist delusion, which chiefly occurred between 1870 and 1945 (which is, we should note, the key period of confrontation between the European bourgeois states and organized proletarian internationalism), we find not only the designation of a scapegoat as an object of proletarian revolt, the exploitation of divisions within the proletariat and the projective representation of the ills of an abstract social system through the imaginary personification of those who control it (even though this mechanism is essential to the functioning of racism).[3] We also find the 'fusion' of the two historical narratives which are capable of acting as metaphors for each other: on the one hand, the narrative of the formation of nations at the expense of the lost unity of 'Christian Europe' and, on the other, that of the conflict between national independence and the internationalization of capitalist economic relations, which brought with it the attendant threat of an internationalization of the class struggle. This is why the Jew, as an internally excluded element common to all nations but also, negatively, by virtue of the theological hatred to which he is subject, as witness to the love that is supposed to unite the 'Christian peoples', may, in the imaginary, be identified with the 'cosmopolitanism of capital' which threatens the national independence of every country while at the same time re-activating the trace of the lost unity.[4]

The figure is quite different when anti-immigrant racism achieves a maximum of identification between class situation and ethnic origin (the real bases for which have always existed in the inter-regional, international or intercontinental mobility of the working class; this has at times been a mass phenomenon, at times residual, but it has never been eliminated and is one of the specifically proletarian characteristics of its condition). Racism combines this identification with a deliberate confusion of antagonistic social functions: thus the themes of the 'invasion' of French society by North Africans or of immigration being responsible for unemployment are connected with that of the money of the oil sheikhs who are buying up 'our' businesses, 'our' housing stock or 'our' seaside resorts. And this partly explains why the Algerians, Tunisians or Moroccans have to be referred to generically as 'Arab' (not to mention the fact that this signifier, which functions as a veritable 'switch word', also connects together these themes and those of terrorism, Islam and so on). Other configurations should not, however, be forgotten, including those which are the product of an inversion of terms: for example, the theme of the 'proletarian nation', which was perhaps invented in the 1920s by Japanese nationalism[5] and was destined to play a crucial role in the crystallization of Nazism, which cannot be left out of consideration when one looks at the ways in which it has recently reappeared.

The complexity of these configurations also explains why it is impossible to hold purely and simply to the idea of racism *being used* against 'class consciousness' (as though this latter would necessarily emerge naturally from the class condition, *unless* it were blocked, misappropriated or de-natured by racism), whereas we accept as an indispensable working hypothesis that 'class' and 'race' constitute the two antinomic poles of a permanent dialectic, which is at the heart of modern representations of history. Morever, we suspect that the instrumentalist, conspiracy-theory visions of racism within the labour movement or among its theorists (we know what high price was to be paid for these: it is tremendously to the credit of Wilhelm Reich that he was one of the first to foresee this), along with the mechanistic visions which see in racism the 'reflection' of a particular class condition, have also largely the function of denying the presence of nationalism in the working class and its organizations or, in other words, denying the internal conflict between nationalism and class ideology on which the mass struggle against racism (as well as the revolutionary struggle against capitalism) depends. It is the evolution of this internal conflict I should like to illustrate by discussing here some historical aspects of 'class racism'.

Several historians of racism (Léon Poliakov, Michèle Duchet and Madeleine Rebérioux, Colette Guillaumin, Eric Williams on modern slavery, and others) have laid emphasis upon the fact that the modern notion of race, in so far as it is invested in a discourse of contempt and discrimination and serves to split humanity up into a 'super-humanity' and a 'sub-humanity', did not initially have a national (or ethnic), but a class signification or rather (since the point is to represent the inequality of social classes as inequalities of nature) a caste signification.[6] From this point of view, it has a twofold origin: first, in the aristocratic representation of the hereditary nobility as a superior 'race' (that is, in fact, the mythic narrative by which an aristocracy, whose domination is already coming under threat, assures itself of the legitimacy of its political privileges and idealizes the dubious continuity of its genealogy); and second, in the slave owners' representation of those populations subject to the slave trade as inferior 'races', ever predestined for servitude and incapable of producing an autonomous civilization. Hence the discourse of blood, skin colour and cross-breeding. It is only retrospectively that the notion of race was 'ethnicized', so that it could be integrated into the nationalist complex, the jumping-off point for its successive subsequent

metamorphoses. Thus it is clear that, from the very outset, racist representations of history stand in relation to the class struggle. But this fact
only takes on its full significance if we examine the way in which the
notion of race has evolved, and the impact of nationalism upon it from
the earliest figures of 'class racism' onwards – in other words, if we
examine its political determination.

The aristocracy did not initially conceive and present itself in terms of
the category of 'race': this is a discourse which developed at a late
stage,[7] the function of which is clearly defensive (as can be seen from the
example of France with the myth of 'blue blood' and the 'Frankish' or
'Germanic' origin of the hereditary nobility), and which developed when
the absolute monarchy centralized the state at the expense of the feudal
lords and began to 'create' within its bosom a new administrative and
financial aristocracy which was bourgeois in origin, thus marking a
decisive step in the formation of the nation-state. Even more interesting
is the case of Spain in the Classical Age, as analysed by Poliakov: the
persecution of the Jews after the *Reconquista*, one of the indispensable
mechanisms in the establishment of Catholicism as state religion, is also
the trace of the 'multinational' culture against which Hispanization (or
rather Castilianization) was carried out. It is therefore intimately linked
to the formation of this prototype of European nationalism. Yet it took
on an even more ambivalent meaning when it gave rise to the 'statutes of
the purity of the blood' (*limpieza de sangre*) which the whole discourse
of European and American racism was to inherit: a product of the
disavowal of the original interbreeding with the Moors and the Jews, the
hereditary definition of the *raza* (and the corresponding procedures for
establishing who could be accorded a certificate of purity) serves in
effect both to isolate an internal aristocracy and to confer upon the
whole of the 'Spanish people' a fictive nobility, to make it a 'people of
masters' at the point when, by terror, genocide, slavery and enforced
Christianization, it was conquering and dominating the largest of the
colonial empires. In this exemplary line of development, class racism
was already transformed into nationalist racism, though it did not, in the
process, disappear.[8]

What is, however, much more decisive for the matter in hand is the
overturning of values we see occurring from the first half of the nineteenth century onwards. Aristocratic racism (the prototype of what
analysts today call 'self-referential racism', which begins by elevating the
group which controls the discourse to the status of a 'race' – hence the
importance of its imperialist legacy in the colonial context: however
lowly their origins and no matter how vulgar their interests or their
manners, the British in India and the French in Africa would all see
themselves as members of a modern nobility) is already indirectly

related to the primitive accumulation of capital, if only by its function in the colonizing nations. The industrial revolution, at the same time as it creates specifically capitalist relations of production, gives rise to the *new racism* of the bourgeois era (historically speaking, the first 'neo-racism'): the one which has as its target the *proletariat* in its dual status as exploited population (one might even say super-exploited, before the beginnings of the social state) and politically threatening population.

Louis Chevalier has described the relevant network of significations in detail.[9] It is at this point, with regard to the 'race of labourers' that the notion of race becomes detached from its historico-theological connotations to enter the field of equivalences between sociology, psychology, imaginary biology and the pathology of the 'social body'. The reader will recognize here the obsessive themes of police/detective, medical and philanthropic literature, and hence of literature in general (of which it is one of the fundamental dramatic mechanisms and one of the political keys of social 'realism'). For the first time those aspects typical of every procedure of racialization of a social group right down to our own day are condensed in a single discourse: material and spiritual poverty, criminality, congenital vice (alcoholism, drugs), physical and moral defects, dirtiness, sexual promiscuity and the specific diseases which threaten humanity with 'degeneracy'. And there is a characteristic oscillation in the presentation of these themes: either the workers themselves constitute a degenerate race or it is their presence and contact with them or indeed their condition itself which constitute a crucible of degeneracy for the 'race' of citizens and nationals. Through these themes, there forms the phantasmatic equation of 'labouring classes' with 'dangerous classes', the fusion of a socioeconomic category with an anthropological and moral category, which will serve to underpin all the variants of sociobiological (and also psychiatric) determinism, by taking psuedo-scientific credentials from the Darwinian theory of evolution, comparative anatomy and crowd psychology, but particularly by becoming invested in a tightly knit network of institutions of social surveillance and control.[10]

Now this class racism is indissociable from fundamental historical processes which have developed unequally right down to the present day. I can only mention these briefly here. First, class racism is connected with a political problem that is crucial for the constitution of the nation-state. The 'bourgeois revolutions' – and in particular the French Revolution, by its radical juridical egalitarianism – had raised the question of the political rights of the masses in an irreversible manner. This was to be the object of one and a half centuries of social struggles. The idea of a *difference in nature* between individuals had become juridically and morally contradictory, if not inconceivable. It was, however, politically indispensable, so long as the 'dangerous classes' (who posed a threat to the established social order, property and the power of the 'elites') had to be excluded by force and by legal means from political 'competence' and confined to the margins of the polity – as long, that is, as it was important to *deny them citizenship* by showing, and by being oneself persuaded, that they constitutionally 'lacked' the qualities of fully fledged or normal humanity. Two anthropologies clashed here: that of equality of birth and that of a hereditary inequality which made it possible to re-naturalize social antagonisms.

Now, this operation was overdetermined from the start by national ideology. Disraeli[11] (who showed himself, elsewhere, to be a surprising imperialist theorist of the 'superiority of the Jews' over the Anglo-Saxon 'superior race' itself) admirably summed this up when he explained that the problem of contemporary states was the tendency for a single social formation to split into 'two nations'. In so doing, he indicated the path which might be taken by the dominant classes when confronted with the progressive organization of the class struggle: first divide the mass of the 'poor' (in particular by according the qualities of national authenticity, sound health, morality and racial integrity, which were precisely the opposite of the industrial pathology, to the peasants and the 'traditional' artisans); then progressively displace the markers of dangerousness and heredity from the 'labouring classes' as a whole on to foreigners, and in particular immigrants and colonial subjects, at the same time as the introduction of universal suffrage is moving the boundary line between 'citizens' and 'subjects' to the frontiers of nationality. In this process, however, there was always a characteristic lag between what was supposed to happen and the actual situation (even in countries like France, where the national population was not institutionally segregated and was subject to no original apartheid, except if one extends one's purview to take in the whole of the imperial territory): class racism against the popular classes continued to exist (and, at the same time, these classes remained particularly susceptible to racial stigmatization, and remained extremely ambivalent in their attitude towards racism). Which brings us to another permanent aspect of class racism.

I am referring to what must properly be called the *institutional racialization of manual labour*. It would be easy to find distant origins for this, origins as old as class society itself. In this regard, there is no significant difference between the way contempt for work and the manual worker was expressed among the philosophical elites of slave-owning Greece and the way a man like Taylor could, in 1909, describe the natural predisposition of certain individuals for the exhausting, dirty, repetitive tasks which required physical strength, but no intelligence or initiative (the 'man of the type of the ox' of the *Principles of Scientific*

Management: paradoxically, an inveterate propensity for 'systematic soldiering' is also attributed to this same man: this is why he needs a 'man to stand over him' before he can work in conformity with his nature).[12] However, the industrial revolution and capitalist wage labour here effect a displacement. What is now the object of contempt – and in turn fuels fears – is no longer manual labour pure and simple (we shall, by contrast, see this theoretically idealized – in the context of paternalistic, archaizing ideologies – in the form of 'craft work'), but *mechanized* physical work, which has become 'the appendage of the machine' and therefore subject to a violence that is both physical and symbolic without immediate precedent (which we know, moreover, does not disappear with the new phases of the industrial revolution, but is rather perpetuated both in 'modernized' and 'intellectualized' forms – as well as in 'archaic' forms in a great many sectors of production).

This process modifies the status of the human body (the human status of the body): it creates *body-men*, men whose body is a machine-body, that is fragmented and dominated, and used to perform one isolable function or gesture, being both destroyed in its integrity *and* fetishized, atrophied *and* hypertrophied in its 'useful' organs. Like all violence, this is inseparable from a resistance and also from a sense of guilt. The quantity of 'normal' work can only be recognized and extracted from the worker's body retrospectively, once its limits have been fixed by struggle: the rule is overexploitation, the tendential destruction of the organism (which will be metaphorized as 'degeneracy') and, at the very least, excess in the repression of the intellectual functions involved in work. This is an unbearable process for the worker, but one which is no more 'acceptable', without ideological and phantasmatic elaboration, for the worker's masters: the fact that there are body-men means that there are *men without bodies*. That the body-men are men with fragmented and mutilated bodies (if only by their 'separation' from intelligence) means that the individuals of each of these types have to be equipped with a *superbody*, and that sport and ostentatious virility have to be developed, if the threat hanging over the human race if to be fended off ...[13]

Only this historical situation, these specific social relations make it possible fully to understand the process of aestheticization (and therefore of sexualization, in fetishist mode) of the body which characterizes all the variants of modern racism, by giving rise either to the stigmatization of the 'physical marks' of racial inferiority or to the idealization of the 'human type' of the superior race. They cast light upon the true meaning of the recourse to biology in the history of racist theories, which has nothing whatever to do with the influence of scientific discoveries, but is, rather, a metaphor for – and an idealization of – the somatic phantasm. Academic biology, and many other theoretical discourses, can fulfil this function, provided they are articulated to the visibility of the body, its ways of being and behaving, its limbs and its emblematic organs. We should here, in accordance with the hypotheses formulated elsewhere regarding neo-racism and its link with the recent ways in which intellectual labour has been broken down into isolated operations, extend the investigation by describing the 'somatization' of intellectual capacities, and hence their racialization, a process visible everywhere – from the instrumentalization of IQ to the aestheticization of the executive as decision maker, intellectual and athlete.[14]

But there is yet another determining aspect in the constitution of class racism. The working class is a population that is both heterogeneous and fluctuating, its 'boundaries' being by definition imprecise, since they depend on ceaseless transformations of the labour process and movements of capital. Unlike aristocratic castes, or even the leading fractions of the bourgeoisie, it is not a social caste. What class racism (and, *a fortiori*, nationalist class racism, as in the case of immigrants) tends to produce is, however, the equivalent of a caste closure at least for one part of the working class. More precisely, it is maximum possible closure where social mobility is concerned, combined with maximum possible openness as regards the flows of proletarianization.

Let us put things another way. The logic of capitalist accumulation involves *two* contradictory aspects here: on the one hand, mobilizing or permanently de-stabilizing the conditions of life and work, in such a way as to ensure competition on the labour market, draw new labour power continually from the 'industrial reserve army' and maintain a relative over-population; on the other hand, stabilizing collectivities of workers over long periods (over several generations), to 'educate' them for work and 'bond' them to companies (and also to bring into play the mechanism of correspondence between a 'paternalist' political hegemony and a worker 'familialism'). On the one hand, class condition, which relates purely to the wage relation, has nothing to do with antecedents or descendants; ultimately, even the notion of 'class belonging' is devoid of any practical meaning; all that counts is class situation, *hic et nunc*. On the other hand, at least a section of the workers have to be the sons of workers, a *social heredity* has to be created.[15] But with this, in practice, the capacities for resistance and organization also increase.

It was in response to these contradictory demands that the demographic and immigration policies and policies of urban segregation, which were set in place both by employers and the state from the middle of the nineteenth century onwards – policies which D. Bertaux has termed *anthroponomic* practices[16] – were born. These have two sides to them: a paternalistic aspect (itself closely connected to nationalist propaganda) and a disciplinary aspect, an aspect of 'social warfare' against the savage masses and an aspect of 'civilizing' (in all senses of the term) these same masses. This dual nature we can still see perfectly illustrated today in the combined social and police approach to the 'suburbs' and 'ghettos'. It is not by chance that the current racist complex grafts itself on to the 'population problem' (with its series of connotations: birth rate, depopulation and over-population, 'interbreeding', urbanization, social housing, public health, unemployment) and focuses preferentially on the question of the *second generation* of what are here improperly called 'immigrants' with the object of finding out whether they will carry on as the previous generation (the 'immigrant workers' properly so-called) – the danger being that they will develop a much greater degree of social combativeness, combining class demands with cultural demands; or whether they will add to the number of 'declassed' individuals, occupying an unstable position between subproletarianization and 'exit' from the working class. This is the main issue for class racism, both for the dominant class and for the popular classes themselves: to mark with generic signs populations which are collectively destined for capitalist exploitation – or which have to be held in reserve for it – at the very moment when the economic process is tearing them away from the direct control of the system (or, quite simply, by mass unemployment, is rendering the previous controls inoperative). The problem is to keep 'in their place', from generation to generation, those who have no fixed place; and for this, it is necessary that they have a genealogy. And also to unify in the imaginary the contradictory imperatives of nomadism and social heredity, the domestication of generations and the disqualification of resistances.

If these remarks are well founded, then they may throw some light on what are themselves the contradictory aspects of what I shall not hesitate to call the 'self-racialization' of the working class. There is here a whole spectrum of social experiences and ideological forms we might mention: from the organization of collectivities of workers around symbols of ethnic or national origin to the way in which a certain workerism, centred on criteria of class origins (and, consequently, on the institution of the working-class family, on the bond which only the family establishes between the 'individual' and 'his class') and the over-valorization of work (and, consequently, the virility which it alone confers), reproduces, within the ambit of 'class consciousness', some part of the set of representations of the 'race of workers'.[17] Admittedly, the radical forms of workerism, at least in France, were produced more by intellectuals and political apparatuses aiming to 'represent' the working class (from Proudhon down to the Communist Party) than by the workers themselves. The fact remains that they correspond to a tendency on the part of the working class to form itself into a closed 'body', to preserve gains that have been made and traditions of struggle and to turn back against bourgeois society the signifiers of class racism. It is from this reactive origin that the ambivalence characterizing workerism derives: the desire to escape from the condition of exploitation and the rejection of the contempt to which it is subject. Absolutely nowhere is this ambivalence more evident than in its relation to nationalism and to xenophobia. To the extent that in practice they reject official nationalism (when they do reject it), the workers produce in outline a political alternative to the perversion of class struggles. To the extent, however, that they project on to foreigners their fears and resentment, despair and defiance, it is not only that they are *fighting competition*; in addition, and much more profoundly, they are trying to escape their own exploitation. It is a hatred of *themselves*, as proletarians – in so far as they are in danger of being drawn back into the mill of proletarianization – that they are showing.

To sum up, just as there is a constant relation of reciprocal determination between nationalism and racism, there is a relation of reciprocal determination between 'class racism' and 'ethnic racism' and *these two determinations are not independent.* Each produces its effects, to some extent, in the field of the other and under constraints imposed by the other. Have we, in retracing this overdetermination in its broad outline (and in trying to show how it illuminates the concrete manifestations of racism and the constitution of its theoretical discourse), answered the questions we posed at the beginning of this chapter? It would be more accurate to say that we have reformulated them. What has elsewhere been called the excess which, by comparison with nationalism, is constitutive of racism turns out at the same time to be a shortfall as far as the class struggle is concerned. But, though that excess is linked to the fact that nationalism is formed in opposition to the class struggle (even though it utilizes its dynamic), and that shortfall is linked to the fact that the class struggle finds itself repressed by nationalism, *the two do not compensate one another*; their effects tend, rather, to be combined. The important thing is not to decide whether nationalism is first and foremost a means of imagining and pursuing the unity of state and society, which then runs up against the contradications of the class struggle, or whether it is primarily a reaction to the obstacles which the class struggle puts in the way of national unity. By contrast, it is crucially important to note that, in the historical field where *both* an unbridgeable gap between state and nation and endlessly re-emerging class antagonisms are to be found, nationalism necessarily takes the form of racism, at times in competition with other forms (linguistic nationalism, for example) and at times in combination with them, and that it thus becomes engaged in a perpetual headlong flight forward. Even when racism remains latent, or present only in a minority of individual consciousnesses, it is already that internal excess of nationalism which betrays, in both senses of the word, its articulation to the class struggle. Hence the ever recurring paradox of nationalism: the regressive imagining of a nation-state where the individuals would by their nature be 'at home', because they would be 'among their own' (their own kind), and the rendering of that state uninhabitable; the endeavour to produce a unified community in the face of 'external' enemies and the endless rediscovery that the enemy is 'within', identifiable by signs which are merely the phantasmatic elaboration of *its* divisions. Such a society is in a real sense a politically alienated society. But are not all contemporary societies, to some degree, grappling with their own political alienation?

Notes

1. Pierre Ayçoberry, *The Nazi Question; An Essay on the Interpretation of National Socialism (1922–73)*, transl. R. Hurley, Routledge & Kegan Paul, London 1981.
2. See the theorizations of Karl Popper, *The Open Society and Its Enemies* (2 vols), 5th edn (revised), Routledge & Kegan Paul, London 1966; and, more recently, of Louis Dumont, *Essays on Individualism: Modern Ideology in Anthropological Perspective*, University of Chicago Press, Chicago 1986.
3. The personification of capital, a social relation, begins with the very figure of the *capitalist.* But this is never sufficient in itself for arousing an emotional reaction. This is why, following the logic of 'excess', other real–imaginary traits accumulate: life-style, lineage (the '200 families'*), foreign origins, secret strategies, racial plots (the Jewish plan for 'world domination'), etc. The fact that, specifically in the case of the Jews, this personification is worked up in combination with a process of fetishization of money is clearly not accidental.
4. Matters are further complicated by the fact that the lost unity of 'Christian' Europe, a mythic figuration of the 'origins of its civilization', is thus represented in the register of race at the point when that same Europe is embarking upon its mission of 'civilizing the world', i.e. submitting the world to its domination, by way of fierce competition between nations.
5. Cf. Benedict Anderson, *Imagined Communities*, Verso, London 1983, pp. 92–3.
6. L. Poliakov, *The History of Anti-semitism* (4 vols), transl. R. Howard, Routledge & Kegan Paul, London 1974; M. Duchet & M. Rebérioux, 'Préhistoire et histoire du racisme', in P. de Commarond and C. Duchet, eds, *Racisme et société*, Maspero, Paris 1969; C. Guillaumin, *L'idéologie raciste. Genèse et langage actuel*, Mouton, Paris–The Hague 1972; 'Caractères spécifiques de l'idéologie raciste', *Cahiers internationaux de sociologie*, vol. LIII, 1972; 'Les ambiguïtés de la catégorie taxinomique "race"', in L. Poliakov ed., *Hommes et bêtes: Entretiens sur le racisme (I)*, Mouton, Paris–The Hague 1975; Eric Williams, *Capitalism and Slavery*, University of North Carolina Press, Chapel Hill 1944.

---

*The idea that 200 families held most of the wealth of France and used it to exert political power was current in France in the 1930s, being quoted by Daladier at the Radical Congress of 1934. It seems probable that the figure 200 derived from the number of shareholders allowed to attend the annual meeting of the Bank of France.

7. And one which substitutes itself, in the French case, for the 'ideology of the three orders', a basically theological and juridical ideology, which is, by contrast, expressive of the organic place occupied by the nobility in the building of the State ('feudalism' properly so-called).

8. L. Poliakov, *History of Anti-Semitism*, vol. 2, pp. 222–32.

9. Louis Chevalier, *Labouring Classes and Dangerous Classes in Paris during the First Half of the Nineteenth Century*, transl. F. Jellinek, Routledge & Kegan Paul, London 1973.

10. Cf. G. Netchine, 'L'individuel et le collectif dans les représentations psychologiques de la diversité des êtres humains au XIXᵉ siècle', in L. Poliakov, ed., *Ni juif ni grec: Entretiens sur le racisme* (II), Mouton, Paris–The Hague 1978; L. Murard and P. Zylberman, *Le Petit Travailleur infatigable ou le prolétaire régénéré. Villes-usines, habitat et intimités au XIXᵉ siècle*, Editions Recherches, Fontenay-sous-Bois 1976.

11. Cf. H. Arendt, 'Antisemitism', Part One of *The Origins of Totalitarianism*, André Deutsch, London 1986, pp. 68–79; L. Poliakov, *History of Anti-semitism*, vol. 3, pp. 328–37; Karl Polanyi, 'Appendix 11: Disraeli's "Two Nations" and the problem of colored races', *The Great Transformation*, Beacon Press, Boston 1957, pp. 290–94.

12. Frederick Winslow Taylor, *Principles of Scientific Management*, 1911. See the commentaries by Robert Linhart, *Lénine, les paysans, Taylor*, Seuil, Paris 1976; and Benjamin Coriat, *L'Atelier et le chronomètre*, Christian Bourgeois, Paris 1979. See also my study, 'Sur le concept de la division du travail manuel et intellectuel' in Jean Belkhir *et al.*, *L'Intellectuel, l'intelligentsia et les manuels*, Anthropos, Paris 1983.

13. Clearly, the 'bestiality' of the slave has been a continual problem, from Aristotle and his contemporaries down to the modern slave trade (the hypersexualization to which it is subject is a sufficient indication of this); but the industrial revolution brought about a new paradox: the 'bestial' body of the worker is decreasingly *animal* and increasingly technicized and therefore humanized. It is the panic fear of a *super-humanization* of man (in his body and his intelligence which is 'objectivized' by cognitive sciences and the corresponding techniques of selection and training), rather than his *sub-humanization* – or, in any case, the reversibility of these two – which discharges itself in phantasies of animality and these are projected for preference on to the worker whose status as an 'outsider' [*étranger*] confers upon him at the same time the attributes of an 'other male', a 'rival'.

14. See chapters 1 and 3 above.

15. Not only in the sense of individual filiation, but in the sense of a 'population' tending towards the practice of endogamy; not only in the sense of a transmission of skills (mediated by schooling, apprenticeship and industrial discipline) but in the sense of a 'collective ethic', constructed in institutions and through subjective identification. Alongside the works already cited, see J.-P. de Gaudemar, *La Mobilisation générale*, Editions du Champ Urbain, Paris 1979.

16. Daniel Bertaux, *Destins personnels et structure de classe*, PUF, Paris 1977.

17. C. G. Noiriel, *Longwy: Immigrés et prolétaires, 1880–1980*, PUF, Paris 1985; J. Frémontier, *La Vie en bleu: Voyage en culture ouvrière*, Fayard, Paris 1980; Françoise Duroux, 'La Famille des ouvriers: mythe ou politique?', unpublished thesis, Université de Paris VII, 1982.

13

Racism and Crisis

Etienne Balibar

In France today, the development of racism is generally presented as a *crisis* phenomenon, the more or less inevitable, more or less resistible effect of an economic crisis, but also of a crisis that is political, moral or cultural. This assessment of the situation contains a mixture of incontrovertible factors, on the one hand, and of evasions and more or less deliberate obfuscations, on the other. The ambiguities of the notion of crisis itself are here working all out to obscure the debate.[1] What is striking is that we are once again confronted with a circle: the 'rise of racism', its 'sudden aggravation', its incorporation into the increasingly influential programme of the parties of the Right and, more generally, into the discourse of politics form a crucial part of the characteristics by which we believe we can recognize a crisis – at least a *major* crisis – which deeply affects social relations and shows the future course of history to be uncertain, as in the past the rise of Nazism or the great 'upsurges' of anti-Semitism and nationalism did. Once we have set aside mechanistic explanations (of the type which state that economic crisis *leads to* unemployment; unemployment *leads to* exacerbation of competition between workers, which *leads to* hostility, xenophobia and racism) and mystical explanations (of the type which state that crisis *leads to* anxiety over decadence and a fascination among the masses for the 'irrational', of which racism is seen as an expression), undeniable correlations remain. It is industrialization, the growth of urban poverty, the dismantling of the welfare state and imperial decline which, in Britain since the 1970s, have given rise to conflict between communities, fuelled nationalism, created favourable conditions for the recuperation of Powellism by Thatcherism and the adoption of repressive 'law and order' policies, accompanied by intense propaganda pointing to the populations of colour as hotbeds of criminality.[2] And it seems that, since the beginning of the 1980s, French society has, in its turn, been going down the same path; the increase in racist crimes and police 'stray bullets',[3] projects for restriction of access to citizenship and the rise of the *Front National* being the premonitory signs of this. Others might put it differently and say that French society was poised on the edge of the same precipice.

Above all, it is undeniable that the fact of racism, the acts of violence which give it its substance, are becoming an active component of the social crisis and, consequently, having an influence upon its development. Between the issues of unemployment, urban development, schooling and also the functioning of political institutions (the question of the right to vote, for example) and the complex formed by phobic fear of immigrants, their own defensive reactions (or their children's) and the increasing antagonism between antithetical conceptions of 'French identity', there is an increasingly close connection. This is ultimately coming to seem a necessary connection. And it is this which is opening up a career for the 'worst-case scenario' specialists or the politics of fear, and which, correlatively, is encouraging a whole section of the national collectivity to practise censorship and self-censorship on this question. From the point when it becomes clear we may have to fear the worst (and the historical examples are to hand to support this), would it not be better to keep quiet about racism for fear of aggravating it? Or would it not indeed be better to suppress the cause of racism, lest we prove unable to control its effects (for which, read: send home the 'foreign bodies' whose presence gives rise to 'reactions of rejection', while perhaps being prepared to 'assimilate' all those who are 'assimilable' by their nature or their aspirations)?

Rather than cause and effect, we should in reality be speaking of the reciprocal action of crisis and racism in a particular conjuncture: in other words, we should characterize and *specify* the social crisis as a racist crisis and also investigate the characteristics of the 'crisis racism' springing up at a given moment in a given social formation. It is in this way that we shall have a chance of avoiding what I referred to above as evasions and obfuscations. In reality, it does not follow from the fact that racism is becoming more *visible*, that it has arisen from nothing, or almost nothing. What would clearly be true for other societies, such as that of the US for example, is in fact also true for our own: racism is anchored in material structures (including psychical and sociopolitical structures) of very long standing, which are an integral part of what is called national identity. Though it experiences fluctuations, though the tendency comes and goes, it never disappears from the social scene, or at least it remains waiting in the wings.

And yet a break, and one that initially passed unnoticed, has occurred. The open racism which, taking into consideration the existence of a latent structure and the conflict between that structure and the censorship that is a part of the official humanism of the liberal state, I propose to term the '*acting out*' of racism (on a scale which runs from mere words to 'individual' violence and from this to the organized movement whose ultimate objectives are an institutionalization of exclusion or discrimination) is changing its bearers and its targets. And it is these displacements which are most important for the analysis of the present conjuncture. It is not insignificant, either as regards its language or its objectives or its powers of propagation, that it is primarily the doing of intellectuals or members of the popular strata, of petty bourgeois in the traditional sense of the term (small property owners) or workers (mainly manual workers), any more than it is insignificant that its primary targets are Jews, Arabs, 'foreigners' in general, that it concentrates upon the foreigner in the legal sense, or that it is developing a phantasy of a purification of the social body, an extirpation of the 'false French', of the foreign part that is allegedly encysted within the nation. Crisis racism is not, then, something absolutely new, without precedent or origins. But it represents a crossing of certain *thresholds of intolerance* (which are generally turned on the victims themselves and described as 'thresholds of tolerance'). And it is the entry upon the stage, the 'acting out' of new social strata and classes (or rather of increasingly large numbers of individuals from new social strata) adopting a 'racializing' posture in ever more varied situations: in urban neighbourhood issues, for example, but also in such fields as work, sexual and family relations and politics.

More precisely, if it is true, as is suggested by the Hitlerian example in its radical form and by the colonial example and that of American segregation with their 'poor Whites', that racist ideology is essentially *interclass* (not only in the sense of a transcending of class solidarities, but also of their active negation), crisis racism is characteristic of a conjuncture in which the divides between classes no longer determine a tendentially different attitude towards 'foreigners', but yield rather to a social 'consensus' based on exclusion and tacit complicity in hostility towards them. At least it becomes a determining factor of the consensus which makes the difference between classes seem only relative.

In this perspective, one may – without claiming any great originality – suggest some indices which reveal that in present-day French society certain thresholds have *already* been crossed.

Let us consider first of all the formation of an immigration complex.

What we mean by this is not the mere fact that the heterogeneous population referred to as immigrants is prey to rejection or acts of aggression, but the fact that utterances of the type, 'There is an immigrant problem', or, 'The presence of immigrants poses a problem' (no matter what 'solution' is being proposed), have recently gained currency and are in the process of becoming generally acceptable. It is, in effect, characteristic of these utterances that they induce a transformation of every social 'problem' into a problem which is regarded as being posed *by the fact of* the presence of 'immigrants' or, at least, as being aggravated by their presence, and this is so whether the problem in question is that of unemployment, accommodation, social security, schooling, public health, morals or criminality. As a consequence they further serve to spread the idea that the reduction – and if possible the ending – of immigration (in practice the expulsion of as many immigrants as possible, beginning of course with the most 'difficult', the least 'acceptable' or 'assimilable', the least 'useful') would enable us to resolve our social problems. Or, quite simply, would remove an obstacle to their solution. Without even entering upon the technical refutation of these theses,[4] we touch here on a first paradox of some substance: *the less the social problems of the 'immigrants', or the social problems which massively affect immigrants, are specific, the more their existence is made responsible for them*, even in indirect ways. And this paradox in its turn induces a new effect, which is truly lethal. This is the implication of immigrants in – and their presumed responsibility for – a whole series of different problems which makes it possible to imagine them as so many aspects of one and the same 'problem', of one and the same crisis. We touch here upon the concrete form in which one of the essential characteristics of racism reproduces itself today: its capacity to lump together all the dimensions of 'social pathology' as effects of a single cause, which is defined with the aid of a series of signifiers derived from race or its more recent equivalents.

Yet there is more. The very categories of immigrant and immigration conceal a second paradox. They are categories which are *simultaneously unifying and differentiating*. They ascribe to a single situation or type 'populations' whose geographical origins, specific histories (and consequently cultures and styles of life), conditions of entry into the national space and legal statuses are wholly heterogeneous. Thus, just as many North Americans are incapable of pointing out a Chinese, a Japanese or a Vietnamese, or indeed a Filipino, or telling them apart (they are all 'slants'), or, alternatively, a Puerto Rican and a Mexican (they are all '*chicanos*'), many French people are unable to distinguish between an Algerian, a Tunisian, a Moroccan and a Turk (they are all 'Arabs', a generic designation which already constitutes a racist stereotype, and which opens the way to the full-blown insults: 'wogs', 'A-rabs' and so on). More generally, the word 'immigrant' is a catch-all category, combining ethnic and class criteria, into which foreigners are dumped indiscriminately, though not *all* foreigners and *not only* foreigners.[5] In fact it is a category which precisely makes it possible to split up the apparently 'neutral' set of foreigners, though not without some ambiguities. A Portuguese, for example, will be more of an 'immigrant' than a Spaniard (in Paris), though less than an Arab or a Black; a Briton or a German certainly will not be an 'immigrant', though a Greek may perhaps be; a Spanish worker and, *a fortiori*, a Moroccan worker will be 'immigrants', but a Spanish capitalist, or even indeed an Algerian capitalist, will not be. We here touch upon the differentiating aspect of the category, which is indissociable in practice from the unifying aspect discussed above: there is external differentiation as we have just seen, but also internal differentiation since unity is posited only to be realized in an infinite variety of forms. There is a daily casuistics of 'immigration' which is formulated in discourse and develops in behaviours, that become a positive 'matter of honour' (one must not make a mistake or get mixed up). Someone who 'doesn't like Arabs' may pride himself on having 'Algerian friends'. Someone who thinks the Arabs 'cannot be assimilated' (citing Islam or the heritage of colonialism) may demonstrate that the Italians or the Blacks can be. And so on. And like all casuistry, this one has its aporias. Though by definition it generates hierarchies, it endlessly runs up against – and is fuelled by – the incoherence of its own criteria (whether 'religious', 'national', 'cultural', 'psychological' or 'biological'), in search of an unattainable scale of superiority or dangerousness in which Blacks, Jews, Arabs, Mediterraneans and Asians would have 'their' place – that is, the imaginary place which would enable us to know 'what we should do with them', 'how we should treat them', 'how we should behave' in their presence.

Thus the category of immigration structures discourses and behaviours, but also, and this is no less important, it provides the racist – the individual and the group as racists – with *the illusion of a style of thinking, an 'object' that is to be known* and explored, which is a fundamental factor of 'self-consciousness'. Having written this sentence, I realize that it is ambiguous. For what we have here is not the illusion of thinking, but rather *effective* thinking upon an *illusory* object. Whoever classifies thinks, and whoever thinks exists. As it happens here, whoever classifies exists collectively. Or rather – and here again we must make a correction – causes to exist in practice that illusion that is collectivity based on the similitude of its members. It is for want of taking full account of this double effectivity that anti-racism too often falls prey to the illusion that racism is an absence of thought, an oligophreny in the strict sense, and that it would simply be enough to make people think or reflect for it to subside. Whereas in fact it is a question of changing people's modes of thought, which is the most difficult thing in the world.

We thus discover, for our part, that in present-day France, 'immigration' has become, *par excellence*, the name of race, a new name, but one that is functionally equivalent to the old appellation, just as the term 'immigrant' is the chief characteristic which enables individuals to be classified in a racist typology. This is the point at which we should recall that colonial racism already, typically, conferred an essential function on the casuistry of unity and differentiation, not only in its spontaneous discourse, but in its institutions and its governmental practices: forging the amazing general category of 'native'[6] and, at the same time, multiplying 'ethnic' subdivisions (at the origin of the very notion of *ethnie* [ethnic group] in France) within this 'melting pot', by means of pseudo-historical criteria, which were allegedly unequivocal, enabling hierarchies to be established and discriminations made ('Tonkinese' and 'Annamites', 'Arabs' and 'Berbers' and so on). Nazism acted in the same way, dividing the subhumans into 'Jews' and 'Slavs' and indeed further subdividing these and carrying back into the German population itself the crazed pursuit of genealogical typologies.

The effects produced by the formation of a generic category of immigration do not end there. This category tends also to take in individuals of French nationality who then find themselves confined to or rejected into a more or less shameful outsider status, at the very moment when nationalist discourse proclaims the indivisible unity of the populations historically assembled within the framework of a single state: this is, in practice, the case of Black West Indians and, of course, of a number of French people 'of foreign extraction', in spite of naturalization or of birth on French soil conferring French nationality upon them. In this way, contradictions arise between practice and theory, some of which might be considered amusing. A Kanak campaigning for independence in New Caledonia is theoretically a French citizen who is committing a treasonable act against the integrity of 'his country', but a Kanak in 'the metropolis', whether he wants independence or not, is never anything but a Black immigrant. When a (Right-wing) Liberal deputy expressed the opinion that immigration was 'an opportunity for France',[7] he found himself dubbed with the intendedly insulting nickname 'Stasibaou'!* The most significant phenomenon in this respect is the obstinacy with which conservative opinion (it would be decidedly hazardous to try to assign limits to this) refers to the children of Algerians born in France as 'the second immigrant generation' or the 'immigrants of the second

---

*'Stasibaou' is an Arabization of Stasi's name – *Transl.*

generation' and endlessly poses the question of the 'possibility of their integration' into French society *of which they are already a part* (by systematically confusing the notion of integration, that is, of belonging to a *de facto* historical and social entity, with that of conformity to a mythical 'national type', which is supposed to be a guarantee against all possibility of conflict).

We thus arrive at the second paradox I spoke of above: the less the population designated by the category of immigration is effectively 'immigrant', that is, foreign, not only by its status and social function, but also in its customs and culture,[8] the more it is denounced as a foreign body. In this paradox we find of course a characteristic feature of racism, with or without explicit race theory, namely the application of the genealogical principle. We may also suspect that the obsessive fear of interbreeding, of the pluri-ethnic or multicultural nation, is merely a special case of the resistance of a part of French society to its own transformations, and even a case of the disavowal of the transformations that have already been accomplished – a disavowal of its own history, that is. The fact that this resistance and this disavowal is emerging in an ever wider range of social groups, belonging to *all* social classes, and, most notably, the one which only recently represented in large part a force for transformation, may indeed rightly be regarded as a symptom of a profound crisis.

This leads us to identify a second symptom. And, having regard to the political history of French society, it is one which I consider to be as important as the formation of the immigration complex or, more precisely, to be indissociable from that formation. Whoever believed they could deal with the two separately would merely be constructing a fictive history. I am referring now to the *spread of popular racism and, particularly, of working-class racism*, indices of which have been apparent in recent years not so much perhaps in terms of collective acts of violence as in electoral trends and the isolation of the workplace struggles of immigrant workers.

A number of precautionary remarks are called for at this point, though ultimately these merely serve to underline the gravity of the consequences which the phenomenon implies. First, to speak of the *racism of a class* in an all-embracing way is, as all the surveys show, a meaningless expression, whatever 'indicators' one chooses (and taking into account that these indicators tend to magnify popular racism, while letting pass the strategies of denial of 'cultivated' individuals, more skilled in the wiles of the political language-game). It is in fact a type of projective utterance which itself partakes of a tendentially racist logic. By contrast, what is meaningful is to inquire into the frequency of racist attitudes and behaviour in given *situations* which are characteristic of a class condition or position – work, leisure, relationships with neighbours, the establishment of relations of kinship, political activism – and, most importantly, to evaluate in actual historical time the progress – or regress – in organized practices which presuppose either a resisting of the tendency to racism or a giving in to it.

Second, the privileged status granted here to the question of popular racism (or the racism of the 'popular masses') over that of the racism of the 'elites' or the dominant classes or over intellectual racism does not mean that these can actually be isolated, nor that the popular version is in itself more virulent than the others. It does, however, mean that the popularization of racism, which goes together with the disorganization of institutional forms of anti-racism specific to the exploited classes and in particular to the working class, constitutes by itself *a threshold* in the course of racism's becoming 'hegemonic', which it is very difficult to get back beyond once it has been crossed. Historical experience (whether it be the experience of anti-fascism or resistance to colonial wars) has shown, in effect, that, though the working class can claim no privileged role in the invention of anti-racism, that class forms an irreplaceable base for its development and efficacity, whether by its resistance to racist propaganda or by its commitment to political programmes incompatible in practice with a racist politics.

Third, to speak of an extension of racism in the working class (or *to* the working class) must not lead us to underestimate once again the antecedents of the phenomenon and the depth of their roots. Merely to restrict ourselves to the French example, everyone knows that xeno-phobia among workers is not new, and that Italians, Poles, Jews, Arabs and so on have successively been on the receiving end of it. And it does not relate so much to the mere fact of structural immigration and competition on the labour market (France has, for centuries, been a country that imported labour) as to the way in which the employers and the state have organized the hierarchization of workers, reserving skilled and supervisory jobs for those who are 'French' of more or less recent date and unskilled jobs for the immigrant workers and, indeed, choosing models of industrialization which demanded a large unskilled labour force, which could be provided by resorting massively to immigration (a strategy which continues today: cf. the question of 'clandestine im-migration').[9] Thus the racism of French workers was organically linked to the relative privileges of skill, to the difference between exploitation and super-exploitation. There is no univocal causality here, as is shown by the key role played by the internationalism of immigrant activists in the history of the French labour movement. It can hardly be doubted, however, that the defence of these privileges, however tenuous and fragile they may have been, went hand in hand with the power of nationalism in the organizations of the working class (including the Communist party in its heyday, with its municipal, trade union and cultural 'transmission belts').

The question which then arises is twofold: when it comes about that the successive industrial revolutions – first of mass production, then of automation – lead to a massive deskilling of industrial work, bringing together immigrants and 'nationals' (especially women and the young unemployed) in a single form of exploitation and proletarianization, putting an abrupt end to the perspectives of collective 'upward mobility' for the national working class, will that destabilizaton express itself in a definitive splitting of the working class or in a radicalization of its struggles? The same question arises, but it is made the more acute, when the creeping economic crisis, with the phenomena of de-industrialization and decline of the old imperialist powers that accompany it, throws back into question the relative security of employment, standard of living and prestige which has been acquired in the course of class struggles and has become an integral part of the political 'compromise' and of the social 'balance'.

We here touch upon the heart of the dilemma: such a 'reproletarian- ization' necessarily overturns class practices and ideologies. But where does it lead? As historians of the working class have shown, that class becomes autonomous by constructing a tight network of ideals and forms of organization around a hegemonic social group (for example skilled workers in large-scale industry). At the same time that autonomy always remains ambivalent, since the hegemonic group is also the one which is able to gain recognition as a legitimate component part of the 'national collectivity', to win social advantages and civil rights.[10] It is particularly within the working class that the dilemma between the 'racialization' of modes of thinking and communication and a passing beyond latent racism in collective culture – which necessarily presup- poses a certain self-criticism – takes on the appearance of a real acid test, a question of political life or death. This is why the question of the fragility of the Left in the face of the rise of racism, the concessions it makes to it and the opportunities it offers it, is so decisive. In France at least the only politically powerful 'Left' there has been has been around the ideas of socialism and communism. Particularly decisive is the question of what will be the outcome of the crisis of ideologies and organizations which claim to be proletarian. The pretext of 'de- Stalinization' would lead to the most serious of political errors if it were to make us take lightly, or merely regard as a natural development, the racist meanderings of French communism, anchored as these are in the nationalist aspect of its political traditions, whether they lock it into populist competition with the political organizations that are more or less fascist or, more probably, contribute to its historical decline and the falling of a section of the popular classes under the sway of the *Front National*.[11]

These tendencies not only form part of the conditions leading to a worsening of the crisis, they contribute to every question of social rights and civil rights being perverted into a question of privileges that have to be protected or reserved for certain 'natural' beneficiaries. Rights are exercised in reality. Privileges may, in large part, be imaginary (indeed this is why they can generally be conferred upon exploited classes). Rights *grow* of themselves qualitatively through the extension of the number (and power) of those who enjoy and claim them. Privileges can only be guaranteed by the defence of an exclusiveness that is as restrictive as possible. It seems to me that we can in this way better understand why the crisis conjuncture combines within the popular classes an uncertainty (which at times leads to panic) as to the 'security' of existence and an uncertainty about collective 'identity'. The formation of the immigration complex I spoke of above is both a cause and an effect of that uncertainty, and the same is true of the tendential dissolution of the organized working class, around which a political tradition had formed which expressed the defence of economic and social interests in the language of rights and not in that of privileges. These two phenomena fuel one another. When they become politically inextricable, we have before us both a racist crisis and a crisis racism.

Notes

1. 'Crisis, what crisis?' some writers have justifiably inquired, thereby indicating that it is impossible to use this category to analyse historical conjunctures without immediately asking *for whom* there is a 'crisis', from the point of view of what 'system', of what tendency and in terms of what indicators (cf. S. Amin *et al.*, *Dynamics of Global Crisis*, Macmillan, London 1982, whose French title is *La Crise, quelle crise?*).

2. Cf. Kristin Couper and Ulysses Santamaria, 'Grande-Bretagne: la banlieue est au centre', *Cahiers de Banlieues 89: Citoyenneté et métissage*, supplement to *Murs, murs*, no. 11, 1985; and Paul Gilroy, *There Ain't No Black in the Union Jack. The Cultural Politics of Race and Nation*, Hutchinson, London 1987.

3. The increasing development of a symmetry between crimes and 'police stray bullets' (i.e. crimes committed by the police) is an important phenomenon, and one which has affinities with classic situations in the history of racism and in particular in the history of Nazism. It is also a confirmation, if any were needed, of the pertinence of the questions posed by Michel Foucault regarding 'illegalisms'. This whole question will have to be re-examined in another context, within the framework of an enquiry into the relations between racism and institutions, racism within 'society' and within the 'state'. Cf. K. Couper and U. Santamaria, 'Violence et légitimité dans la rue', *Le Genre humain*, no. 11, 'La Société face au racisme', Autumn–Winter, 1984–85.

4. Immigrants are not a drain on the resources of the welfare state; they add to its coffers: sending them away in large numbers would not create any jobs, but would actually destroy some by creating an imbalance in certain economic sectors; the participation of immigrants in criminal activity is not increasing any faster than that of the 'French'.

5. We shall here echo Jean Genêt's question on the Blacks, which is quoted by Wallerstein ('What is a Black? and, to begin with, what colour is he?') in asking, 'What is an immigrant, and, to begin with, where is he born?'

6. Astonishing since the native is, in theory, the person who is 'born in a place', meaning in this case *anywhere* in the colonial space: which means that an African from the colonies who has settled in France remains a 'native', but that a Frenchman in France clearly is not! On the construction of the notion of ethnic groups by colonial science, cf. J.-L. Amselle, E. M'Bokolo, *Au cœur de l'ethnie*, La Découvete, Paris 1985. The French prime minister (J. Chirac) declared recently 'The Kanaka people does not exist: it is a mosaic of ethnic groups'.

7. Bernard Stasi, *L'Immigration: une chance pour la France*, R. Laffont, Paris 1984.

8. Whatever hypotheses one may develop on the 'Franco-Algerian mix', to borrow R. Gallissot's expression (*Misère de l'antiracisme*, Editions de L'Arcantère, Paris 1985, pp. 93 *et seq.*). Cf. also Juliette Minces, *La Génération suivante*, Flammarion, Paris 1986.

9. See *inter alia* the dossier on 'Immigration' in the review *Travail* published by AEROT, no. 7, 1985; Albano Cordeiro, *L'Immigration*, La Découverte/Maspero, Paris 1983; Benjamin Coriot, *L'Atelier et le chronomètre*, Christian Bourgois, Paris 1979.

10. Cf. Gérard Noiriel, *Longwy. Immigrés et prolétaires*, PUF, Paris 1984 and *Workers in French Society in the Nineteenth and Twentieth Centuries*, Berg, Oxford 1989. Useful as they are, Zeev Sternhell's works (*La Droite révolutionnaire*, Seuil, Paris 1978, and *Ni droite ni gauche*, Seuil, Paris 1983) which stay within the sphere of the pure history of ideas, obscure the fundamental fact that, though it did not prevent xenophobia from existing within the working class, the part played by the organized labour movement in Dreyfusism (the victory of the Jaurès 'line' over the Guesde 'line') at least posed an obstacle, for three-quarters of a century, to its being theorized as a substitute for anti-capitalism.

11. Cf. E. Balibar, 'De Charonne à Vitry', *Le Nouvel Observateur*, 9 April 1981.

Postscript

Immanuel Wallerstein

In the Preface, Etienne Balibar states that we hoped to contribute to the lively debate on the question of the special characteristics of contemporary racism. On rereading these pieces, I wonder how well we have been able to address the question.

To start with, the word 'contemporary' is ambiguous. If 'contemporary' refers to a period no more than a few decades long – say, that since 1945 – I think we have tried to demonstrate that there are no (or very few) special aspects to the current situation; and in saying that, we are disagreeing with many commentators and politicians. But if 'contemporary' is a way of saying 'of the modern world', well then, yes – or at least so we argue – we do distinguish sharply between the 'racism' of the modern world and the various historical xenophobias of earlier times.

Throughout these essays we have emphasized continuously, even repetitively, two themes. First, the multiple communities to which all belong, whose 'values' we hold, towards which we express 'loyalties', which define our 'social identity', are all, one and all, historical constructs. And, even more importantly, they are historical constructs perpetually undergoing reconstruction. That is not to say they are not solid or meaningful or that we think them ephemeral. Far from it! But these values, loyalties, identities are never primordial and, that being the case, any historical description of their structure or their development through the centuries is necessarily primarily a reflection of present-day ideology.

Second, it has been customary to present universalism as a concept or an ideal diametrically opposed to particularist identities, whether these

228

are nationalist, cultural, religious, ethnic or social. This antinomy seems to us an incorrect way of posing the issue, even a deceptive one. The closer one looks, the more one observes that these two ideologies, universalism and particularism, exist and define themselves in function of each other, to the point that they begin to seem like two sides of the same coin.

These two assertions are none the less disturbing. They shock even us, in the sense that the humanist teachings of so-called modern societies have been preaching the exact opposite for a long time now. We have been used to asserting the contrast between the narrow-minded medieval vision of our antiquated traditional roots and the liberal, open spirit of the modern world. And we hang on to these schoolchild myths all the more fiercely as we tremble before the terrible cruel realities of the world in which we live, a world that is still so full of hatred and oppression.

So where are we then? There are really one of two possible conclusions. Either racism, sexism, chauvinism are evils innate to the human species. Or they are evils bred by given historical systems and are thus subject to historical change. If we are of the second persuasion, we nevertheless find no reason whatsoever to be Pollyanna-ish. Quite the contrary! We speak in this book of 'intrinsic' ambiguities in the very concepts of race, nation and class, ambiguities which are hard to discern and harder yet to surmount.

Each of us separately has tried to analyse these ambiguities in these essays and I do not intend to repeat here the various deconstructions we have attempted nor the key elements we have evoked to try to unravel the complex mysteries we discern.

I would rather discuss what seem to be some differences in outlook between Balibar and me. In fact, they turn out to be merely nuances. While saying he does not share various criticisms others have made of my writings, Balibar none the less accuses me of leaning too far in the direction of 'economism'. He says that he himself places greater emphasis on the fact that the confusion between universalism and particularisms in the capitalist world-economy is a product of the dominant ideology, an ideology largely accepted by those who are dominated. This internalization of the ambiguities, this socialization of the mass of the population, is for him a key element in creating the maze in which we find ourselves. Up to a point, he is of course right. Who could in fact deny this? The very terms, 'social formation' or 'society' or 'historical system', necessarily imply a structure held together by the willing adherence of its members and not merely by overt force. Still, even if most of us share the basic perspective of our historical systems, there are always and everywhere cynics, sceptics and rebels. Obviously Balibar would not disagree. I think it therefore useful to distinguish the per-spectives of the small group of 'cadres' and the vast majority of the population. I do not think they relate in the same ways to the ideological constructs of their system.

I argue that universalism is a belief-system primarily intended to reinforce the ties of the cadres to the system. This is not simply a question of technical efficacy. It is also a way to limit the effects of the very racism and sexism the cadres find so useful to the system, since sexism and racism, if carried too far, are potentially dangerous to the system. Thus, universalism is a brake on a nihilism (exhibited for example by Nazism) that can undermine the system from within. To be sure, there always exist other cadres, the second team as it were, who are ready to challenge those in power in the name of diverse particularisms. But, in general, universalism as an ideology serves the long-term inter-ests of the cadres better than its inverse.

I do not argue that the attitudes of the various working strata are simply the obverse of those of the cadres. But they do seem to tend in the opposite direction. By assuming a particularist stance – whether of class, of nation or of race – the working strata are expressing an instinct of self-protection against the ravages of a universalism that must be hypocritical within a system founded both on the permanence of inequality and on the process of material and social polarization.

Which brings me to the second nuance. Balibar says he is reluctant to accept that there exists a world bourgeoisie, except perhaps as a long-term trend. He suggests that I fail to take account of concrete specifi-cities by using a model that is somewhat too abstractly global. I am tempted to respond that a bourgeoisie can exist only at the world level, that being a bourgeois means precisely that one cannot be loyal to any community, that one can worship no god but Mammon.

Of course, I exaggerate, but not all that much. Of course, bourgeois are nationalists, even patriots. Of course, bourgeois all take advantage of their ethnic affiliations. But ... It is mostly when it serves their interests that they are nationalist. Let us never forget those good burghers of Amsterdam who sold arms to the Spanish oppressors in the very midst of their struggle for independence. Let us never forget that the truly big capitalists have never hesitated to export their capital from their own country if their country was declining as a locus of profitable investment. It is perhaps only because ordinary people have less room for manœuvre that they remain more loyal to the others in their group, but the fact remains that this is the case. That is, the nation, the race and even the class serve as refuges for the oppressed in this capitalist world-economy, which explains why they remain such popular ideas. It also explains how it is possible for the working strata to make such rapid swings among these seemingly mutually incompatible particularisms. If one shelter fails momentarily, they quickly seek another.

The third criticism is that I ignore the importance of the 'society factor', allowing myself to be too seduced by the importance of the division of labour. I plead not guilty. My view is essentially this: the division of labour within the capitalist world-economy constitutes a sort of external constraint, defining the limits of survival. What Balibar calls the 'society factor' is the effort of people, especially ordinary people, to break these constraints in order to be allowed to pursue objectives other than the ceaseless accumulation of capital.

The ordinary people are able sometimes, even often, to restrain the excesses inherent in the quest for accumulation. But they have not yet succeeded in breaking the system and thus freeing themselves from subordination to its constraints. This is the whole history, itself an ambiguous one, of the antisystematic movements. Balibar may be right that I am overly optimistic about the possibilities of creating a 'transzonal' alliance of movements. My optimism is a muted one in any case.

In the end, I think, the three objections are but one. I believe I am a bit too 'determinist' for Balibar's taste. I feel, therefore, I should explain myself in this regard. The very long-standing debate among philosophers (at least among Western philosophers) between the proponents of determinism and the proponents of free will seems to me to be a subject that needs to be analysed in the optic of Braudel's multiplicity of social times.

When a historical system is functioning normally – whatever the system, and thus including the capitalist world-economy – it seems to me that, almost by definition, it operates overwhelmingly as something that is determined. What does the word system mean if not that there are constraints on action? If these constraints didn't work, it would not be a system and it would rapidly disintegrate. But every historical system moves eventually towards its end via the working-out of the logic of its contradictions. At that point, the system goes into a 'crisis', enters a period of 'transition', which leads to what Prigogine calls a 'bifurcation', that is to say, to a highly fluctuating situation in which a slight push can lead to a very large deviation. In other words, it is a situation in which free will prevails. It is exactly for that reason that it is almost impossible to foresee the outcome of the transformations.

When therefore we analyse the role of classes, nations, races within a capitalist world-economy, discussing them as both concepts and as realities, we speak quite deliberately about the ambiguities that are intrinsic, which means that they are structures. To be sure, there are all sorts of resistances. But we need to start by emphasizing, rather, the mechanisms, the constraints, the limits. On the other hand, we are approaching the 'end of the system' – that long moment which, I believe, we have in fact already entered, and thus we need to think about the possible leaps we might make, the utopias that are now at least conceivable.

At such a moment it seems to me useful to remember that universalism and racism-sexism are not thesis and antithesis awaiting their synthesis. They are rather an inseparable pair containing reflexes both of domination and of liberation, and history calls upon us to go beyond them as problematic. It is in that spirit, I believe, that we have ever to return to the last and to seek to understand our own ambiguities, since after all we are products ourselves of the historical system of which we are a part.